Zion in the Desert

SUNY series in Israeli Studies
Russell Stone, editor

Zion in the Desert

American Jews in Israel's Reform Kibbutzim

William F. S. Miles

State University of New York Press

Published by
State University of New York Press, Albany

© 2007 State University of New York

For information, contact State University of New York Press, Albany, NY
www.sunypress.edu

Production by Judith Block
Marketing by Michael Campochiaro

Library of Congress Cataloging-in-Publication Data

Miles, William F. S.
    Zion in the desert : American Jews in Israel's reform kibbutzim / William F. S.
Miles.
        p.   cm.—(Suny series in Israeli studies)
    Includes bibliographical references and index.
    ISBN-13: 978-0-7914-7103-6 (hardcover : alk. paper)   1. Jews, American—
Israel.   2. Reform Judaism—Israel.   3. Kibbutzim—Religion.   4. Kibbutzim—
Social aspects.   I. Title.

DS113.8.A4M55 2007
307.77'6—dc22   2006025532

10   9   8   7   6   5   4   3   2   1

To "Alexander" Forbes Lyndon Nutte Jr.

Foin Fellow,
Rigorous Reader,
Beloved Brother.

ALSO BY WILLIAM F. S. MILES

Bridging Mental Boundaries in a Postcolonial Microcosm. Identity and Development in Vanuatu.

Imperial Burdens. Countercolonialism in Former French India

Hausaland Divided. Colonialism and Independence in Nigeria and Niger

Elections in Nigeria. A Grassroots Perspective

Elections and Ethnicity in French Martinique. A Paradox in Paradise

Contents

Illustrations

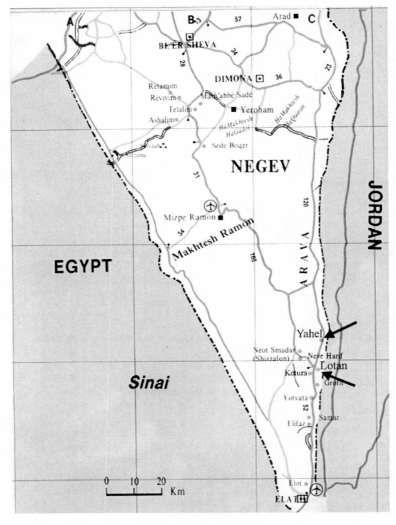

Location of the only two Reform kibbutzim in history.

Prologue To Studying One's Own Tribe

If ever I saw moonlight in *yahel*—
That is, shining as it makes its movement arc—
And I secretly succumbed,
And my hand touched my mouth in a kiss,
That, too, would have been a criminal offense,
For I would have denied God above.

—Job 31:26

"Is this your first trip?"
"No, I was here twenty years ago."
"And you never came back?"
"Israel wasn't at the center of my thoughts, no."
"But you must have gone to other countries that weren't at the center quote unquote. How can a Jew make a single visit to the homeland of his people, and then never, not in twenty *years*—"
I cut him off before he really got going. "It's easy. I'm not the only one."
—Philip Roth, *The Counterlife*

After living among and writing academic books about exotic peoples around the world—the Muslim Hausa of Africa, Francophone Tamils in India, French West Indians in the Caribbean, Melanesians in the South Pacific, Creoles and Hindus in the Indian Ocean—it was time to open my social scientific tool box among my own strange tribe: the Jews. Why not do in Israel what I had done in Nigeria and Niger, in Vanuatu and Mauritius, in Pondicherry and Martinique: observe and write about a small-scale society with its own peculiar brand of religion? Why, from a scholarly standpoint, should the Holy Land be separate from Hausaland, Canaan from the Caribbean? Why should doing fieldwork on an Israeli kibbutz be any different from that in an African village? If I could learn to speak and operate in Bislama and Kreol, in French and in Hausa, why not do the

xi

same in Hebrew, the ancestral tongue to which, thanks to religious school
and ongoing ritual, I had been exposed the earliest and longest?

Why? Because studying the "exotic other" has been for this political
anthropologist—and, I suspect, for many other, less forthcoming scholars of
the "Mosaic persuasion"—simultaneously an escape from, and a foil for, ex-
amining one's own strangeness, as a Jew, in the much wider Gentile world.

This realization has prevented me from writing, as originally in-
tended, a straightforward academic account of the world's first Reform
Jewish kibbutz. It has also made me grapple with the fundamental life and
career questions that I, along with tens of thousands of other Jewishly self-
identified baby boomers who visited Israel in their youth, have at some
point asked themselves: if I *really* am a Zionist, if I truly believe in an independent Jewish nation, shouldn't I have moved to Israel? Who would I be
now if I had indeed made *aliya*, immigration to the Jewish State? And what
would living on a kibbutz—the Western world's best shot at a utopian
community—be like for me and my family?

This last question is of relevance for many Americans, Gentile as well
as Jewish. At the very moment that middle-class Americans are enjoying
an unprecedented high in material comfort, luxury goods, and future
prospects, there is a nagging dissatisfaction with the suburban lifestyle that
still epitomizes the American dream in the early 21st century. For children-
raising baby boomers, the yearning to discover or create a safer and more
meaningful community is particularly poignant. The search has taken
many forms, from the theoretical abstractions of communitarian philosophers to the concrete constructions in Celebration, the Disney-founded
community in Florida. Intentional communities, the New Town Movement, gated communities: all these reflect the yearning simultaneously
to foster neighborly interaction while ensuring—especially in post-
Columbine America—security for one's kids and self. Beyond Zionism, beyond Judaism, anyone searching for a more perfect community must consider the kibbutz, not as it once socialistically was (or pretended to be), but
rather as it is today: a services-oriented, profit-conscious enterprise devoted to the spiritual *and* material satisfaction of its members and families.*

For the kibbutz has grown up. Pioneering members of Kibbutz Yahel, many of them from around America and especially the suburbs of

---

* For anyone interested in a more social scientific treatment of this dimension,
Gretchen Weismann and I have published a quantitative analysis in the *Journal of Modern
Jewish Studies* 3, no. 1 (2004), under the title "Measuring Satisfaction in Jewish 'Utopia': A
Comparative Analysis of The Reform Kibbutzim."

New York, were in their early twenties when in the late 1970s—just as I was graduating from Vassar and flying off to West Africa with the Peace Corps—they cast their lot with a novel experiment in whole-community progressive Judaism. They did so not in the cool highlands of the Galilee nor in the even higher (but politically controversial) Golan Heights. Nor did they settle in the convenient center of the country, within reasonable travel range from Tel Aviv or Jerusalem. As if building the first Reform Jewish kibbutz in history were not radical enough, this handful of young American and *sabra* (Israeli-born) Jews settled in the remote and inhospitable Arava, a burning and windswept corner of the southeast Negev Desert where hardscrabble soil and scarce water made any attempt at human habitation—much less an agriculturally based collective—a defiant challenge to both reason and nature. Yet so great was the religious and Zionist optimism of the times that within five years yet another Reform Jewish kibbutz, Lotan, was established a mere eight miles away.

Two decades have since passed and both the nation and the kibbutzniks have grown up. Israel is no longer the struggling, idealistic, embattled underdog as portrayed in early United Jewish Appeal campaigns. The core founders of Yahel, as I got to know them, are in their mid-forties, wizened by a self-imposed economic restructuring and baited by their younger, more ideologically uncompromising brethren on Kibbutz Lotan. It is a situation with which, after realizing the strange demographics in operation, I easily empathized. In fact, it was both heady and uncanny to live in a society in which my own middle-aged cohorts (I was born in 1955) constitute the "elders," in which "we" are the top dogs, and where there are no living models of our future selves. To paraphrase Rabbi Pogo, "We have met the gerontocracy, and they—already—is us."

Both experiments in socialist Jewish living, so exciting in the 1970s and early 1980s, have been largely forgotten by the outside world. For most Israelis, more concerned with the state of their stock market and their accessibility to Home Depot, the very notion of kibbutz, understood as a socialist egalitarian community, is an anachronism. In the United States few Reform Jews, who otherwise constitute the largest stream in American Judaism, know anything about Lotan and Yahel, "their" flagship communities of Reform Zionism.

But the dilemma of the middle-aged American-born kibbutzniks is more existential than concerns their place in Jewish and Zionist history. Now parents, pondering both the future of their adolescent children and the second half of their own lives, these once young Jewish dreamers and builders are, out in the stark and still isolation of the Negev—far from

New York-style shrinks and call-in psychotherapy talk shows—undergoing midlife crisis. And since it is occurring on-kibbutz, *this* midlife crisis is collective as well as personal.

Given Yahel's relative economic prosperity, midlife crisis here is a "happy" one, borne of normal life cycle questions—such as career choice and professional fulfillment—that nag even at financially secure baby boomers. For American-born Israelis on the half dozen kibbutzim sprinkled throughout the Arava, the crisis joins transcendent issues of spirituality, solidarity, and ideology to worldly qualms about retirement pensions and children's college tuition layaway funds.

Like adolescence, midlife crisis is (all boomers pray!) but a phase. It interrupts the usual stream of things, what in today's computer-laced lingo we might call the "daily default of life." Crisis temporarily overshadows what is otherwise paramount in an individual or society. And what *is* paramount in Yahel and Lotan, in Ketura and Samar, in Grofit and Yotvota— in all successful communes and kibbutzim, in America as well as in Israel—is an abiding sense of community, of interconnectedness, of mutual dependence, and support stemming from having one's fortune, family, and future bound together with those of all other members of the community. *This* is the gem I discovered, during my brief sojourn among former and expatriate American Jews on two kibbutzim in the desert: a place of intense connectedness and daily concern amongst my own kinsmen, the likes of which I had only previously experienced in close-knit villages in West Africa.

This does not mean that all members of the kibbutz love—or even like—each other. Neither Lotan nor Yahel is a utopia, a blissful society in which everyone gets along and all strive for the selfless happiness of the other. Notwithstanding shared kinship and faith, communal meals and equal incomes, as in any small town society or rural village life there is also envy, resentment, gossip, jealousy, backbiting and, on occasion, backstabbing. Far from being saintly, kibbutzniks are quite normal, unremarkably human. What truly distinguishes those who have chosen such a collective lifestyle is how they function in crisis and under the most stressful of circumstances.

In its first twenty years, Yahel experienced more than its fair share of trauma and tragedy: a fatally gruesome work accident; the sudden death of a young child; the widowing of a young mother; testicular cancer and toddler leukemia; marital infidelity; mental breakdown. In most Western societies when individuals are ripped apart like this their ensuing estrangement, loneliness and, not infrequently, bankruptcy can be catastrophic; on-kibbutz, the entire community rallies round. This is why in spite of all the drawbacks of communal life—modest personal prosperity, lack of privacy, insularity—kibbutzniks remain on board. As "Job," the cancer-cursed, cuckolded kibbutznik with custody of the kids, provider of logistical care for the psychiatrically unstable wife who betrayed him and whom he is divorcing—a man who remains willy-nilly corporate partners with his wife's erstwhile illicit lover—puts it: "The strength of a community is really only put to the test under conditions of crisis. I know. I've been there. You can't put a monetary value on what this place gives—lifetime health care, children's education and, especially, communal responsibility in times of need.

"When I got cancer, everyone felt that someone in their family was sick. Even the people I hated came to my help. When Shai (the five-year-old boy of another family) died, everyone felt that they had lost a child. People know that if something drastic happens to them, their children will be looked after by a whole big bunch of people.

"The more social upheavals there are like this," Moshe went on, referring to his wife's affair with a fellow kibbutznik and her subsequent nervous breakdown and institutionalization after being jilted, "the more people can identify with why they're here. They won't say it out loud. Maybe they won't even admit it to themselves. But it's the truth. That's why I've stayed, on account of the togetherness."

Such personal and painful revelations are a far cry from what first drew me to Israel and to this kibbutz in the desert in the summer of 1999. After five years' absence from Israel, I was returning to Yahel on account of an unresolved rendezvous with Zionism, due to a persistent curiosity about whole-life Judaism, and because an old high school buddy was preparing his son's bar mitzvah. I also wanted to confront, head on, the tacit Zionist guilt rap: is he who moves to Israel necessarily a better Jew than he who remains in America? My intention was hardly to infiltrate a Middle Eastern Peyton Place, or to confront the universality of midlife crisis. (Nor did I anticipate hearing the confession of a fellow Jew who before coming to Israel—and unknown to anyone else living on the kibbutz—had killed another man with his bare hands.) Yet both dimensions, the existential and the theological, unexpectedly overlapped.

What you are reading, then, is an exercise in what I call "ethno-autobiography": exploring one's self through the study of one's ethnic peers. Saitoti Tepilit undertook a similar endeavor, using his nomadic hunting kinsmen in *The Worlds of a Maasai Warrior*. The present ethno-autobiography is an attempt to understand, through the lives of my fellow Jewish, formerly American, baby boomer peers my own decision *not* to have moved to Israel, *not* to settle on a kibbutz, *not* to live out the ultimate fantasy of a committed and non-Orthodox Jew. It is the story of a handful of American Jews who have lived out their dream, under extremely harsh environmental conditions in the Arava desert of southern Israel, to create a new kind of progressive religious society. In the process, they have molded an experimental hybrid identity for themselves, their children and, to a lesser extent, for all whom they have touched. Theirs is the ultimate Jewish path that I, along with countless other American Jewish baby boomers, did not follow but about which I cannot help wondering: what if I had?

In terms of life cycle, it was actually the worst time to pick up and commence an empathetic study of a collectivist society in the middle of a Middle East desert. My wife and I had just moved into our new house in New England, with all the baggage that homeownership in America entails: mortgage, yard work, neighbor relations, fence issues. A university professor, for the first time in my life I was now preoccupied—if not obsessed—with lawn mowing, weeding, grubbing, and waging a seemingly futile battle against crab grass. Scotts cycle of lawn maintenance became my new dogma (even if imperfectly followed). We had just planted over a thousand dollars worth of rhododendrons, another one of our very many investments that we were concerned about abandoning for a couple of hot summer months. Each of our two cars was at the 90,000 mile level and automobile maintenance (if not replacement) loomed as another of our all-American preoccupations. We were living out anew, if not being entrapped by, the suburban paradigm.

It was with relief that we had just jettisoned our relationship with the most common American equivalent to kibbutz-style co-ownership: the condominium association. A decade prior we were content to pool our resources with other condo association members for joint upkeep of commonly owned property, happy that there were others to help out in the beautification of our collectively owned yard, enthusiastic about bonding with immediate neighbors over the shared goals of homestead improvement and community spirit.

Several autumns later, the sole remaining owner-occupant of the condominium, literally left holding the bag because no other members showed up for the scheduled leaf raking, I had completely soured on collective property ownership. Relieved of any lingering fuzzy fondness for the virtues of socialistic sharing (deadbeat condo associates had a greater impact than Berlin Wall collapse), I craved a detached house, privacy from neighbors, a separate lawn, and free and clear title (bank commitments excepted, of course) to *all* my real estate. In short, I had become the typical, selfish, middle-class American homeowner.

I was hardly upbeat, then, about jumping into the middle of a collective society—Jewish or not—predicated on joint ownership, communal living, and shared livelihood. Nor was my wife, a heat-and-sun averse French-Spanish-Latin teacher, thrilled about leaving her brand new home in southeast Massachusetts to toil in a desert kibbutz cafeteria for one and a half broiling summer months. This latter point needs to be emphasized for the most important record of all—the record of marital debt.

While six weeks in the desert may have been a long stint for these personal reasons, from a professional standpoint it was much less than the minimum six months I'd spent on any previous overseas fieldwork. My hosts' skepticism that I could "get it right" in such a short time was perfectly justifiable. Even Bruno Bettelheim's otherwise influential study of the kibbutz, *Children of the Dream*, with a much broader scope than this book, had been criticized by fellow scholars for his brief seven weeks in the field. Whether one July and half of an August was sufficient time to capture the essence of the Reform kibbutzim of the Arava can only be answered, ultimately, by the kibbutzniks themselves.

This project would not have been conceived were it not for the foresight of Elad and the friendship of the entire Lending family. Nor could it have been accomplished without the generous hospitality of all Yahel and the particular support of Liora Cohen, Yahel's *mazkira* (general-manager). One member later confided, "At the meeting about your coming here, some people just couldn't understand the purpose. 'What is research? Why would anyone want to come to ask questions, talk to people, study how they are living?'" I am therefore all the more grateful for the permission to let me come. That same confidant also asserted, "If you don't feel that you have total freedom of expression to write your book, as you see and feel it, then there was absolutely no point in your coming here." I trust that, in her eyes at least, I have justified my sojourn.

Without the assistance of Lotan's own mazkira, Eliza Mayo, I wouldn't have been able to spontaneously expand the study as I did. Readers should be cautioned that inasmuch as I lived at Yahel but not Lotan, there is an inevitable imbalance in my personal familiarity between the two kibbutzim. I readily admit that in these pages I do not do sufficient justice to Lotan, a remarkable and vibrant community in its own right that deserves a book onto itself. (May this book be a spur to that future one?) The summer of 1999 happened to correspond with a time of crisis in Lotan's development, one which I am happy to have been reassured has since been overcome. (By the force of time, the "collective midlife crisis" that I describe for Yahel has also been resolved in its fashion.) Indeed, it needs to be emphasized that this book is written in the so-called ethnographic present, describing conditions and perspectives as they existed at the time of my interviews but not currently: "now" is the time of field-work, not the reality prevailing at publication. In the interim, some kibbutzniks depicted in text and photos have departed. As with the seven years that the biblical Jacob had to wait (twice!) before seeing the bride he so wanted, so have the kibbutzniks and friends waited seven years between visitation and book. *Savlanut!* Thank you for your patience.

Michael Langer/Livni, Rabbi Alan Levine, and the late Gideon Elad shared with me the benefit of their intimate and long-standing involvement with Lotan and Yahel. For their own unique insights about the history of the Reform kibbutz movement I thank Rabbis Arik Ascherman, Ehud Bandel, David Forman, and Steven Schaefer. For convincing me to "let go" and write the book I really wanted, I thank my good friend on French Hill, Israel correspondent for the *New Republic* Yossi Klein Halevy. From Rehovot, George and Nina Sobelman provided indispensable succor and trenchant analysis for their hapless diasporic cousin. The "dean of diasporism," Professor Gabriel Sheffer of the Hebrew University in Jerusalem, prompted professional reflections on diaspora and identity; my friend and colleague at Northeastern, Professor David Rochefort, stimulated personal ones.

Temple Emanu-El's "academic *havura*" in Providence, founded by Professor Joshua Stein, provided me my first opportunities to publicly present my findings and receive invaluable feedback and support. More informal but no less important were the several talks I had with Benny Mer, originally from Israel, whose genuine interest in my project provided much encouragement. Seymour Krieger (*z"l*) another Emanu-El co-congregant, never let up on his salutary *noodging* about my writing progress. That I did not manage to get this book into print prior to his death is my greatest regret of the project. Monday lunches (which I sorely miss) with my friend Professor Yoram Meital of Ben-Gurion University of the Negev, a visiting professor at Northeastern during 2003–04, provided a regular and pleasurable opportunity for insightful discussion and feedback, particularly in the build up to the "Diaspora-Homeland Relations" seminar that he convened in March 2004. Institutionally, I undertook this project under the auspices of the Stotsky Professorship of Jewish and Historical and Cultural Studies at Northeastern University in Boston, where graduate students Paul Beran II, Claudia Crossland, and Peter Richardson painstakingly transcribed the many hours of interviews from tape.

For his patience and professionalism in working on the visuals, I again thank Terry Beadle of Northeastern's Digital Media Services. I took all the pictures depicting Yahel and most of those of Lotan; thanks to Eric Block for providing additional views of Lotan's outdoors and architecture. Judith Block is production editor *extraordinaire.*

As always, Loïza Nellec-Miles deserves major credit for bearing the brunt of my overseas research antsyness and my habitual writing-up grumpiness. For *this* project let it not be forgotten that she assumed extraordinary burdens: among her other unsavory tasks as volunteer in the *cheder ochel,* cleaning the sewers of the dining hall. (Still, we thank Mrs. Betty Adler for rescuing Loïza from becoming a chambermaid for the overnight kids' cabins!) Our children Samuel (then 9) and Arielle (11) helped me see kibbutz through new and wonderful eyes ("This is a land flowing with milk in cereal with Hebrew toast and honey.")

From the very outset I need to emphasize—and to Yahel especially apologize for—the major bias in this book. Although my focus is on the Americans who wound up on the only Reform Jewish kibbutzim in the world, it should not be lost that Yahel and Lotan are fundamentally *Israeli* communities. Only about a quarter of the current kibbutzniks hail from the United States. Many of those are married to non-Americans. Overall, sabras easily outnumber the American-born. The daily language at Yahel and Lotan is Hebrew; the temperament, ambience, body language, argument styles, all Israeli. (Indeed, my field notes convey irritation at certain common linguistic tics that my former compatriots, now more used to speaking Hebrew than English, have acquired in their mother tongue.) Although they still may hold U.S. passports, American-born kibbutzniks are living an authentic (if not typical) Israeli life: they *are* Israeli. Readers desirous of a more comprehensive study of the Reform kibbutzim—one that does not emphasize the American dimension—must await a more detached author than I. In the end, though, I have been able to write *Zion in the Desert* only in this way.

Given the intense, close-knit nature of kibbutz society, my hosts were amazingly candid with me. While not confessional in any maudlin way, they were willing to share personal, painful, and even embarrassing information about both themselves and others. Perhaps it is because they felt—correctly—that they have made significant personal sacrifices that are scantly recognized, particularly in the Jewish world at large.

Only one kibbutz resident refused outright to speak with me. But even she, an attractive, sabra of long-standing at Yahel, was revealing in her refusal. "I don't want to talk to you about the kibbutz," she told me. "I don't remember, even if I am a founder. I hate this place, so I shouldn't talk to you." When I protested that I was not out to do a piece of propaganda, she implausibly retorted, "You should."

Not all of the fifty-seven persons whom I did interview on-kibbutz ("Why have you come here? Why have you stayed?") will find their names here. Some will find themselves thinly transformed by pseudonym. For chapter twelve, I interviewed (mostly by telephone) another thirteen ex-kibbutzniks from Yahel and Lotan, now scattered around the United States. (My thanks to Pittsburgh librarian Richard Kaplan, a former Reform kibbutzik himself, for tracking so many of them down for me.) To all of the above I declare: I have done my best to navigate that murky ethical zone between trust and truth. If I have done justice to your life story: *Baruch Ha-Shem*; if not, and for all errors, misinterpretations, and indiscretions—which are mine and mine alone—*s'lach li, b'vakasha, s'lach li* . . .

1

From Long Island to the Negev Desert

WEST HEMPSTEAD AND ISLAND PARK, LONG ISLAND, 1968. In one of the less reported on scenarios of school busing in the United States, the school boards of these two affluent New York suburbs merge their high schools. The decision has nothing to do with race but rather with demography: Island Park, eight miles south of West Hempstead, with attractive beachfront near the Atlantic, just doesn't have enough kids to warrant building its own high school. Island Park's ongoing entente with Ocean-side is breaking down so the town elders approach their cohorts of West Hempstead. West Hempstead Junior High School disappears and a much larger high school, with students bused in from Island Park, takes its place.

In West Hempstead, we are now faced with two new breed of students: "Italians," like our local ones whom we generally avoid and whose male, strapping, football-playing versions we mildly fear; and Jewish kids, somewhat like us. In their own way, the latter are also exotic in that they hail from a little island-enclave of their own: Harbor Isle. By bridge and by landfill, Harbor Isle is physically connected to the rest of Island Park, but it exudes a more orderly and inviting charm. Harbor Isle kids live within a few minutes walk from their swimming and sailing beach club. In West Hempstead, marine life is limited to feeding the ducks at Hall's Pond.

ALONEI YITZHAK, ISRAEL, 1969. From this camp in northern Israel, thirteen-year-old boys from around the United States, part of a bar mitzvah Pilgrimage program, tour Israel. It is a heady experience for a young teenager. We visit the Western Wall—captured just two years prior, during the Six Day War—the winery of Zichron Ya'akov, the lazy town of Rehovot, the dusty frontier of Eilat, the whole Holy Land. In the Arab *souk* (market) of the Old City of Jerusalem, amidst the exotic smells and sights, I learn how to bargain. I feast on exotic foods (falafel), learn to play a then-exotic sport (soccer!), and learn some titilating Hebrew curses (*ben zona*). At the dining hall at Alonei Yitzhak, we delight in asking our fifteen-year-old but already *zaftig* server, Rivka, *Ma ha-sha'a* ("What time is it?"). This requires Rivka to grasp and twist the wristwatch she has efficiently tied to her shoulder strap; in the process she lightly touches her ample but still blooming bosom. We immature boys holler in delight as, meal after meal, innocent Rivka reports the time.

On weekend matchups with an Israeli family, I am paired with Roni, whom everyone calls Gingi on account of his red hair and complexion. Roni's effusive mother so readily regards me as one of the family that she has no compunctions about my joining the other children in her bedroom while she's still in underwear. I like this culture. We communicate in Hebrew, and I am both thrilled and proud to become part of something different, deeper, and greater than my pre-Israel self is. The tastes, the smells, the females—all intoxicate.

Still, there are aspects of this experience that disturb me. While I don't mind our daily morning rally around the Israeli flag, I don't enjoy the gloating tone and triumphant cheers at the announcement that "we" just shot down some Syrian MIG fighters. I'm no early adolescent pacifist but I do regard these recurring dog fights—and related fatalities—as a necessary evil, not as an exciting sports contest.

Entries from my diary from that summer alternately embarrass and illuminate:

> August 16, 1969. Mea Shearim. This is the religious Chassidic part of Jerusalem and walking through we see signs against autopsies. You can't help noticing the way they look.

Surely, I am referring to the ultra-Orthodox, not to cut up cadavers.

> July 31, 1969. A boring whole day trip to Hula Valley. Our destination is found to be off limits because of fighting by the Syrians that morning. It was at the Golan Heights.

Thus, begets my interest in geopolitics.

One entry is relevant in light of my sojourn on Yahel thirty years later:

August 3, 1969. Mahane Shmonim. Army base for new recruits called Nahal where they fight if there's a war and live on and develop kibbutzes during peace."

The proper plural of kibbutz, I didn't know yet, is kibbutzim.

My early adolescent diary is sprinkled with references to Holocaust memorials: at Yad Vashem, on Mount Zion, at the Warsaw Ghetto, and Martyrs' Museum at Kibbutz Mordechai. Through grisly films and nightmarish books, we thirteen-year-olds are already well acquainted with the Holocaust. There is no doubt in our impressionable minds: Israel is necessary on account of the Nazis. Holocaust is subject for conversation, heavy and light. Ever jocular Lazarus tells us about his father: "He's an exterminator. You know, ants, termites, that kind of thing. But when people here ask me what my father does for a living, and I tell them that he exterminates—well, they kind of back away from me."

It is nighttime. A typical Mediterranean evening: hot and sticky. We are in our bunks. Our stay in Israel is soon to end. Too soon. I am arranging camp stuff in front of my cubbyhole. Exceptionally, given the hour, the camp radio is playing. Bulletin: Neil Armstrong has just walked on the moon. On the moon! My God, I think, everything is possible in my lifetime, absolutely everything. It is great to be a Jew, especially when you're in Israel and among friends. It is great to be an American, especially when your country can put a man *on the moon*.

Long Island, 1970–1971. Unlike my friends at West Hempstead High School, after my bar mitzvah, I continue to go to Hebrew School at the Jewish Community Center of West Hempstead. But I hang out mostly with my new friends from Harbor Isle, my Shangri-La of the South Shore: Marc Wolinsky, the irrepressible showman and envied brain whiz; Michael Feldman, political radical and erstwhile girlfriend thief; and the contemplative, mildly hippie-esque Lloyd Lending. Lloyd's father is a leftist war hero, a veteran of the Abraham Lincoln Brigade which fought Franco during the Spanish Civil War. He is also stridently atheistic. Lloyd and I discuss not politics but the transcendental—universes beyond our own, the likelihood of life on other planets, unearthly and counterintuitive laws of space and light and physics. We are not political protesters but metaphysical seekers: our mutual guru is not Abby Hoffman but Isaac Asimov. We meditate on life and girls during endless binges of basement ping pong.

Although two neighboring families, the Hofmans and the Rosenblums, are Orthodox, we as Conservative Jews better typify the religious profile of Jews then living in the West Hempstead-Franklin Square area. We deride Reform Jews for their watered-down services, minimal level of observance, and scant knowledge of the faith. A typical put-down:

A rich but busy Jewish businessman from Westchester buys a Jaguar and tries to get it blessed. He calls up an Orthodox rabbi in Brooklyn, interrupting his Talmud study, and asks, "Rabbi, can you give me a *bracha* [blessing] for my new Jaguar?" The rabbi is annoyed at the disturbance. "No," he replies curtly, "we don't bless pets, no matter how exotic." He immediately hangs up.

So the businessman man phones a Conservative rabbi on Long Island. "Rabbi," he asks, "can *you* say a bracha over my new Jaguar." The conservative rabbi puts the caller on hold, frantically consults his English edition of the Jewish Code, and then gets back on the line. "I'm very sorry," he responds in an apologetic tone, "but Jewish law makes no stipulation for the blessing of automobiles."

Desperate, the businessman places a long distance call to a Reform rabbi in Los Angeles. "Rabbi, please, I've got this new Jaguar, but I can't get a bracha for it. Can't you do it for me?" The Reform rabbi is both impressed and bewildered. "Gee," he says, "I'd love to help you with your car problem, but what the hell's a bracha?"

However funny we think our Reform rabbi jokes are, living next to Orthodox Jews engenders unease about our own religiosity. What are *they*, true "keepers of the Sabbath," thinking when we get into our cars on Saturday? Don't they look down on our nonchalant Judaism and inattention to *halacha*, Jewish law? Do they make jokes about *our* rabbis? I assume that the Orthodox are smug about living Jewishly while the Reform are confused. We Conservatives, upholding the golden middle—knowledgeable about the details of kashrut, for instance, but not actually keeping kosher—are moderately, reasonably, schizophrenic about just how much of Judaism it makes sense to conserve.

Although we do not discuss it, the "new Jews" from Island Park are Reform. Marc and Michael have scintillating South Shore bar mitzvah parties. Lloyd, I assume, does the same. Only three decades later will I learn that Lloyd does not have a bar mitzvah at all.

REHOVOT, APRIL 1971. Having won first place in the National Bible Contest the year before, I am in the august auditorium of the Weizmann Institute, representing the United States in the international competition. No Orthodox yeshiva student, I am tested on Old Testament arcanae not in Hebrew but in English. "Name two instances in the Bible," the quiz master asks me on Israeli television, "when Moses is asked to render a legal decision but, not knowing how to rule, has got to consult God." I answer correctly (see Numbers 27:1–11) and receive the maximum four points. But my heart is broken during this second trip to Israel, not because I do not win the International Bible Contest (I tie in the middle of the pack) but because my first potential real girlfriend in life—Ethne, the South African contestant whose accent seems to drip with precious exoticism— drops me for Amar, one of the Israeli contestants.

With Sefon from Dublin, I am amused to hear Hebrew spoken with an Irish accent. Amnon, my macho Mexican roommate, scandalizes me with his lewd Zionism, explaining—as he insinuates some racy personal experience—that every Jew should move to Israel "because even the prostitutes here are Jewish." Reporting that I left a bag in a taxicab I am told "if the driver is Jewish, he'll return it. If he's an Arab, forget it." We receive a security briefing and are warned that terrorist bombs are disguised in the most innocent looking of objects. I shake hands with Golda Meir. I am fifteen-years-old.

An anti-Vietnam War moratorium has been declared for the very day I return to West Hempstead High School after my Bible Contest absence. Friends inform me that I ought to boycott class along with them (so does Mrs. Smith, my English teacher and sole black high school instructor) but I don't, claiming out-of-the-loop ignorance on account of my recent overseas activity. Henceforth, Southeast Asia competes with the Middle East for my geopolitical attention. Bible Contest exploits are consigned to family folklore.

There is no way for me to know that these two visits, in 1969 and 1971, really belong to an uncharacteristic period, a veritable Golden Age, in young Israel's history. Two years prior in 1967, having been on the edge of extinction, the Jewish State had emerged as the triumphant David amidst Middle Eastern Goliaths. Two years later in 1973 she will be sobered and shaken by the confidence-puncturing Yom Kippur War. The intoxicating spirit of enthusiasm, self-confidence and solidarity which as a teenager I take to be the eternal essence of the Israeli character is really only an aberration, a '67–'73 high.

ISRAEL AND BINGHAMTON, NEW YORK, 1973. A summer program for gifted science students brings Lloyd, my high school friend from Harbor Isle, to the Weizmann Institute in Rehovot. Part of the program includes a stint on a kibbutz. He is turned on by the spirit, the camaraderie, the music, by "really cool young people walking around barefoot, looking really confident." The atmosphere is electrifying. Israel's collective post–'67 feeling of invincibility rubs off on Lloyd. My high school buddy, who definitely inhaled when he smoked and could care less about Judaism, is now turned on by the Jewish State. Until then, says Lloyd twenty-six years later, "I didn't know that anything was missing from my life."

Soon after returning to Binghamton, Lloyd is stunned by Israel's near defeat in the Yom Kippur War. All those new friends he had just made on–kibbutz—are they to be annihilated? Other students fly to Israel to fill in for young workers sent into the army, but Lloyd is unable to just pack up and go. But neither does he adapt to the college groove at State University of New York-Binghamton. Imbibing the disillusionment of the 1960s protest movement, but without a Vietnam to serve as target for the discontent, Lloyd gravitates to Jewish studies as he asks himself: "Who am I? What am I doing here?"

POUGHKEEPSIE, NEW YORK, 1973–1974. Although a good many of my fellow undergraduates are actually Jewish, we willingly lose ourselves in Vassar's traditionally WASP ethos and live, for the first time in our lives, in a predominantly (if nominally) Gentile world. Isn't that, after all, why we chose a Seven Sisters school rather than a local SUNY or a Brandeis? The unrivaled campus hero is the hip southern Baptist chaplain, not the discreet Hillel rabbi. It is not assumed, as it is in high school, that the smartest students are necessarily the Jewish ones. I "pass" (at least I think I do) as just a generic, rather than Jewish, good-grade-getting undergrad. At Vassar, my most relevant minority status is that of male.

In the first month of my freshman year, Israel is nearly defeated in a war that begins on the Day of Repentance. When I am a sophomore, the United Nations resolves that "Zionism is racism."

Freshman roommate Tim Dennison from Baton Rouge introduces me to Southern culture and I befriend (not without a touch of class envy) Dick Cavette look-alike and sophisticate Richard Van Demark. For sure, I do have Jewish friends, male and female. College assimilationist truth be known, however, the most thrilling encounters are with the non-Jewish women whom I meet, date and, when the Master of the Co-ed Universe is merciful, mate.

KIBBUTZ NAN, ISRAEL, 1974. After a summer reading Zionism's best sellers—*Exodus, The Source, O Jerusalem*—Lloyd leaves Binghamton to spend a year studying Hebrew and working on a kibbutz. He drives a tractor—"a revolutionary thing for a kid from the suburbs"—and is asked to become a kibbutz member. But Nan is too big, a place where a young immigrant can get lost. He attends a seminar of Zionist thinkers and philosophers. "Stay connected," his professor, Stanley Merone tells the seminarians at the end of the course. "Stay connected among yourselves. Stay connected with Israel."

Poughkeepsie, 1975–1977. During my junior year, Israel becomes deeply implicated in the Lebanese civil war. In my senior year, a month before graduation, the leftist Labor government is defeated by the revisionist, right-wing Likud led by Menachim Begin. There is nothing cool about being Jewish on a college campus in the 1970s.

She with whom I fall in love during my last year at Vassar is Catholic and Polish-speaking; inevitably, my mother reminds me that the Poles are the worst anti-Semites of all. "Her mother was raped by the Germans during World War II," I feebly offer in her family's defense, trying to evoke a sense of shared victimhood. But in Mother's eyes, Martha remains the consummate *shiksa* danger.

Intellectually, I silently brood at the Jewishless version of Western philosophy and history to which we are exposed in class. Hegel's unfolding of God throughout history is irredeemably Christian. Never do we learn that the major figures of the Frankfurt School whom I study in my Critical Theory concentration—Adorno, Habermas, Marcuse, Lukacs, Horkheimer—are *Jewish* German emigrés. Jews are not yet part of the multicultural curriculum and Holocaust studies are at least a decade away. Jews are still the understated presence in the post-anti-Semitic elite academy: intrinsic, perhaps indispensable, but rarely invoked. As students, professors, and authors, Jews politely blend in. Noisy pro-Soviet Jewry protesters, yelling and wielding "Never Again!" placards on television, greatly embarrass me.

The counterculture years are over but I still retain some antimaterialistic, anticorporate track propensities. Mercifully, each of the top notch law schools to which I apply in my senior year rejects me and so I am free to pursue my true postcollegiate desire: two years of exotic overseas adventure with the Peace Corps. Although I have taken not a single course dealing with the Third World during my four years of high-priced college, Africa is my ultimate assignment. For two years I shall live in a desolate, landlocked desert country that I never even knew existed prior to being offered an English teacher's position there: Niger. Our group of sixty, mostly recent college graduates, fly off to train in Niamey, Niger's dusty capital, in early July 1977.

YAHEL, NEGEV DESERT, FEBRUARY 1977. Near the southern border with Jordan, in another desolate, desert setting, a group of fifty-five young Jewish men and women, about half of them from America, move into their small, spartan homes and launch a new community based on progressive Judaism and communal living. Yahel is the first kibbutz of the Reform Zionist Movement, a brainchild of a few radical rabbis and Israel immigration activists. They have worked almost subversively to buck the prevailing trend which views kibbutz life as passé and actual emigration to Israel as a nonrealistic goal. Dr. Michael Langer, Rabbi Alan Levine, and Rabbi Stephen Schaefer have recruited Israeli kids from a Reform school in Haifa and Americans, especially those who had previously spent a college year abroad in Jerusalem. They tap into a wellspring of idealism among these young sabras and English-speaking immigrants (including a smattering of South Africans). Renouncing America, however, is more complicated than moving from Haifa.

Although officially dedicated three months before, as these Jewish spiritual desert rats unpack their bags Yahel still has no electricity or drinkable water. Given the proximity to the Jordanian border, not having a working telephone poses an especial security danger. Yet the young pioneers decide to make the move, reasoning that "surely others had endured more discomfort and lived in greater danger than we would experience." Michael Madeson, recently graduated from Dartmouth, records Day 1:

> At sunset of our first day we had services. As the first kibbutz associated with the Reform movement, we hope to become a community dedicated both to the traditional values of kibbutz and the search for a meaningful Jewish way of life in the modern world. We prayed and sang: We give thanks to You, O Lord our God, Ruler of the universe, for giving us life, for sustaining us, and for enabling us to reach this day.
>
> We sat down to a supper of hard green tomatoes, cucumbers, warm sour cream, and a drink of concentrate mixed with water. It was good, but what made it special was looking around the dining room and only seeing people dedicated to Yahel. There were no interesting volunteers from overseas with whom you could cuddle up in the pleasures of the flesh and escape from the discussions and pressures involved in making important decisions. There were no host

kibbutznikim to remind us what to do, to ask us to get up because there were not enough seats, or to tell us to be quiet because we made too much noise. It's hard to convey the pleasure we got out of screaming at each other, as loud as we could, to stop laughing, to stop singing, and to stop having a good time. We sat there singing for a long time and then we stumbled back to our dark rooms and lit candles.

The candles did not give off enough light, it was cold and we wanted to be together. Someone lit a bonfire and called us out to make coffee and burn some sad little potatoes. We sang for a couple of hours . . .

Perhaps it was the brashness of youth and the lingering madness which had led us from the comforts of "normal" existence to this stark and lifeless desert. But we laughed at the challenge and called our laughter idealism.

Another Long Islander, Ron Bernstein, recounts the kibbutz's genesis like this: "It was very naïve then. We were all young and idealistic, and I don't think any of us knew what we were doing really. We had no real direction.

"It was exciting, something very new. We were starting from scratch. Most companies, most firms, most governments would never take a group of twenty-year-olds and say: 'Take this multimillion dollar business and make a community that is supposed to be set up as a kibbutz with Reform Judaism as its center.' The Jewish Agency, the kibbutz federation, and the Reform movement were telling these kids to put this conglomerate together, with most of us not having the experience to do something like that. That's basically what it was."

BINGHAMTON, 1977. Lloyd, back in Binghamton, begins tinkering in mechanics, car repairing, manual enterprises of a type alien to our crowd of Long Island Jews. He takes more Judaic studies courses, still trying to build a Jewish identity "from basically an empty slate, because I had no Jewish upbringing. It was a process of discovering roots." But he does not graduate. College is "cold, academic, nonexperiential." *Studying* about Jews is irrelevant for he needs to *live* Jewishly.

We are hardly in contact during these years, Lloyd and I. When we do reconnect in Island Park, Lloyd retroactively admires my having won the National Bible Contest way back in '69 and praises my knowledge (rusty by now) of Hebrew. Without saying it aloud, we agree that the real test of an authentic Jew is one who has mastered our ancestral tongue and can actually converse in it. Orthodox speed-*davening*—the ability to recite, virtually by rote, ancient prayers at breakneck speed—may not, after all, be the defining hallmark of the good Jew, especially when such prayer book Judaism is practiced from the comfortable suburban confines of Long Island. But moving to Israel, regardless of religiosity: *this* is Jewish commitment.

NIGER, 1977–1979. So otherworldly is life in the hinterland of Niger that for the only time in my life I am oblivious to the arrival of Rosh Hashana. So far have I traveled from my previous Jewish life that I do not know when falls (and therefore do not fast on) the Day of Atonement. Living in an Islamic society, however, I become well acquainted with Ramadan, Tabaski, and Id-el-Fitr. Why, not only are some of my best friends now Muslim, but they are virtually the only friends around! A history teacher from Benin—a rare Catholic in these parts—invites me to his class as living specimen for the unit on ancient Semitic civilizations. Feeling rather fossil-like, I address a classroom of young black African Muslims with the heavy burden of knowing that I may very well be the only Hebrew they ever meet in their Sahelian lives.

YAHEL, 1979–1983. A group of prospective immigrants spend a summer at a Reform camp playing kibbutzniks. They pool their money, simulate desert agriculture, wash dishes together. Several of them drop out. But not Lloyd.

In October 1979, Lloyd flies off to Israel and joins the group in the middle of Yahel's third year of existence. He finds "a bunch of twenty to twenty-three-year-olds running things, without any real idea of how to do it, but with a lot of energy and determination, a lot of seriousness, and a lot of shouting and screaming and arguing." It's exciting, intoxicating. A year later he meets a visiting co-ed on winter break from Vassar College. Erica Sussman, originally from Newton, Massachusetts, smites him—and returns to Poughkeepsie. But shortly after Lloyd joins the Israeli army in 1981, Erica, Vassar degree in hand, returns to Yahel. In 1983, after a year and a half of army leave weekend romance, they marry.

MEDFORD, MASSACHUSETTS AND MARTINIQUE, FRENCH WEST INDIES, 1980–1984. Taking a year off from post-Peace Corps graduate school, I spend a year teaching English in the Caribbean and picking up a doctoral dissertation topic. A year later I return and pick up an island lady. I am smitten. A tropical romance ensues. But marriage is impossible, I confess to this French Caribbean mademoiselle, for my future wife must be Jewish. On a former slave plantation at Fonds St. Jacques, on the northern tip of this bewitching island, the petite, café au lait damsel with fine Indian features and slender Chinese fingers, inquires in French, "Cannot I become Jewish?" I am skeptical. She is courageous. She is perhaps the first ever Martinican convert to Judaism.

Niger, West Africa 1984. With an Islamic priest and another Muslim friend, I am seated outdoors on a straw mat on the sandy earth in a remote Hausa village in this former French colony in the Sahel. We are chatting about this and that and I am asked, in a similarly by-the-way tone, "Is Isa"—Arabic for Jesus—"going to come back?"

"How am I supposed to know?" I shrug.

"Oh, you know all right," comes the reply in Hausa. "You just won't tell."

They are a bit miffed, particularly since they think I am deliberately holding back as to *when* this shared Christian-Muslim prophet is scheduled to return. The only way out, I conclude, is to reveal that I am not, as had been assumed all along, a Nasara—a follower of the one from Nazareth—but a Bayahuda.

"Oho," says the Imam, "you don't follow the Prophet Isa [Jesus]. You follow the Prophet Musa [Moses]." To the now confused friend, the priest explains the difference among white folk between the followers of Isa and the Yahudawa, "they who follow the *atora* (Torah)." Then he turns to me to confirm something. "You were under the Faruna, weren't you?"

Faruna, faruna. What is he talking about?

"You don't know the Faruna? Harsh masters, they made your people work hard, so finally you left them." Aha! Faruna is their way of saying Pharoah. When I confirm, the Imam turns back to his friend, points at me as illustration, and recounts how my brothers fled Masar (Egypt), were pursued by the Faruna, and had the Red Split for us. The friend sits up like a bolt.

"That was you?!" he exclaims in utter amazement and admiration. "You are the ones who did all that?"

I shyly admit that it was indeed "us."

With clenched fist, he raises his arm and shakes it, in the traditional Hausa salute extended to kings and rulers. He utters the words of praise reserved for such occasions (*Ranke ya dadi*—May you live long!) and exuberantly continues to recite the story of the Exodus, complete with miracles, with an immediacy, enthusiasm, and faithfulness beyond that I've experienced in the more than twenty Passover seders I can recall. Moses' rod seems to be his favorite feature. "Your brothers did all that? *Ranke ya dadi!*"

"Well," I explain with false modesty, "we had to. After all, we were living under a harsh regime." I use the local term for the colonial period under the French. "We also"—as was the case in Hausaland—"experienced slavery."

"Do you have the atora here with you?" the Imam asks me, expectantly.

"No," interrupts the friend. "He has it at home. How could he bring it here? One needs a camel to carry the Torah." I don't bother to correct him. But in every subsequent Simchat Torah back in America, in my mind's eye I see a Torah-laden dromedary parading around the synagogue sanctuary.

YAHEL, 1987–1988. After years of nationwide inflation, governmental withdrawal of subsidies, and spendthrift policies on the kibbutz, *mashber*—crisis—hits Yahel hard. Financial crisis spurs ideological crisis. Either the kibbutz radically restructures its economic operation, or it threatens to go under. Economic restructuring means privatization and capitalism, hired labor and rent-paying residents, bottom line thinking and preoccupation with profit. Some kibbutzniks are convinced that Yahel cannot survive. Others fear that if the proposed changes are adopted, the kibbutz will surrender its core communal principles and lose its soul in the process.

Matt Sperber of Long Island, John Cohen from England, and sabra Amnon Shimoni go house-to-house trying to convince people to weather the storm and stay the course of the changes. They succeed—partially. One-third of the members throw in the towel and abandon the kibbutz. But Yahel survives.

Lloyd takes the crisis and restructuring in stride. Never the ideologue ("the entire world works on hired labor. What's so criminal about it? What's so immoral?"), he is content to hone new skills and contribute to the community wherever he can. He will become a licensed tour guide, a master electrician, even *mazkir* (general-manager) of the entire kibbutz. Some of the innovations bother him on account of the toll they take on social cohesion but more important is the overall viability of his community. Raising his children takes precedence over struggling for ideological purity.

JERUSALEM, 1994. After ten years as a college professor in Boston, including extended research jaunts to the French-speaking enclave of Pondicherry, India, and to the South Pacific archipelago of Vanuatu, I am entitled to a university sabbatical. Where else to go but the Promised Land, where the very notion of sabbatical year first arose? Affiliated with the Hebrew University on Mount Scopus, we rent an upper story apartment on French Hill in Jerusalem, overlooking a Bedouin encampment below and the Judean desert beyond. I am ecstatic about returning to Israel as a professor and being part of what I imagine to be an intellectual kibbutz in the Holy City. So as to regain my Hebrew, I enroll in an *ulpan*, a language crash course, at the university. An informal, long-term vehicle rental arrangement with my landlady allows us to roam the diminutive country at will. Wheels, pad, freedom, think tank hangout—it's the perfect setup for an American Zionist's university sabbatical.

It is the most disillusioning period of my life.

What was I expecting? The Israel of my youth, perhaps, when American bar mitzvah pilgrims and Bible Contest contestants were the toast of the land. The same Oriental-Mediterranean frontier, perhaps, with the explored exoticism of an Africa, India, or Oceania but in a Jewish key. Instead, I find a rude, often uncouth, fast-moving, stressed-out culture whose Jewish members exhibit little interest in American visitors, marginal patience with Hebrew stumblers, and naked condescension for Arab residents. The cleavage between religious and secular Jews is jarring. Conservative and Reform movements are not only peripheral but positively despised by the Orthodox establishment. There is little theological legitimacy for those of us Ashkenazim who are somewhat observant but do not follow the full panoply of Sabbath strictures. Soon enough I learn to keep silent about my Bible Contest background. For secularists (including virtually all colleagues at the university), it is a suspect sign, the mark, perhaps, of latent religious fanaticism. For the religious, given my apparent secular demeanor of today, it conjures shameful abandonment of previous religious commitment.

In six months in the so-called City of Peace, I witness enough aggressive, argumentative exchanges (usually between Jews) to last any religion's vision of purgatory. Gratuitous nastiness by armed Israeli soldiers towards Arab shopkeepers and taxi passengers sours me on the presumption of Israelis' generic love of peace. I do not find that men wearing yarmulkes are any more genteel, be it in political debate or driving habits, than those who do not. Secularists' stereotypical prejudices against "black hats"—the ultra-Orthodox—begin to make perfect sense. But I am not comfortable among secularists either, for they reject virtually everything that I have grown up to associate with being Jewish. Only after deciding that leaving America to settle in Israel is insane do I realize that, beneath all scholarly pretense, I had also come with a hidden agenda to explore a permanent return to "the Homeland."

On the morning of Purim, when Jews commemorate their deliverance from Persian genocide thousands of years ago, I receive a call from my university office mate Uri, an Israeli graduate student with Hawaiian connections, with whom I'd casually discussed plans for a family outing that would take us through part of the West Bank. "I don't know if you've heard the news," Uri says in a friendly but restrained voice, "but some crazy guy in Hebron has gone on a rampage and killed a lot of Arabs there. I don't really think it's the best day to go for a drive on any West Bank roads."

The "crazy guy" is Baruch Goldstein, an Orthodox Jew, a Brooklynite by birth and upraising, a medical doctor, and now that he has fatally shot twenty-nine Muslim worshippers, a mass murderer. He is emphatically religious but not certified as insane. On television a fellow traveller, when asked to comment on the killings, will only invoke the Talmudic rule about conserving the spirit of a holiday even in the face of personal tragedy; with a malicious grin, he recites the commandment, "You shall be happy and rejoice." Goldstein's shooting down of Palestinians praying in Abraham's tomb sets off waves of violence. Immediately killed by survivors of his massacre, Goldstein's own tomb soon becomes a shrine for other Jewish fanatics.

Respite from the rejection, dejection, and depression that I experience throughout this half year comes from befriending the elderly, Hausa-speaking chief of the Black African quarter in Old Jerusalem and from the few short trips we make to Yahel. Only here, within the safe, enclosed, self-sustaining community gates, where everyone knows everyone else and all dine together in the summer camp-like cafeteria, do I rediscover glimpses of the Israel of my youth. My old friend Lloyd—now going by the Hebraicized name Elad—is a jubilant, extroverted, thirty-eight-year-old head-shaven version of his younger self. Elad shows off his kibbutz with the same pride he displays for his eleven-year-old daughter Chava and his eight-year-old son Gadi. He is an enthusiastic desert tour guide, joyfully chatting with the same American teenagers whose adolescent ilk I am happy to escape while on university leave. (To my long lasting regret, I miss Tisha B'Av in Jerusalem—the commemoration of the destruction of the Temple—to meet up in Be'er Sheva with a Yahel-bound tour group of Reform American adolescents.) Elad waxes rhapsodic about the kibbutz's decision—a hallmark of ingenuous Reform Jewish reasoning—regarding the appropriate use of technology in the dairy during the Sabbath. He is a hands-on electrician and Israeli army reservist, a cow-milking kibbutznik in the Negev Desert, the Hebrew-speaking father of sabra children. The religious school dropout who never had a bar mitzvah trumps me, the Hebrew high school graduate and Bible Contest winner, on every index of

Zionist and Jewish commitment. Which is fine. Only I can't figure out how it happened—from a "Reform" friend, no less.

Boston, 1998. Only in America . . . Only in America could the reasoning and actions of well-intentioned Gentile friends, colleagues, and a dean result in a specialist on former French colonies receiving a professorship in Jewish studies. My appointment is made one year before Gadi Lending is scheduled to celebrate his bar mitzvah and two years before the bat mitzvah of my own daughter. Yahel—in spite of Israel—beckons. Although my sabbatical has painfully convinced me that I do not wish to live in Jerusalem, Tel Aviv, or in any other city or town in the Jewish State, I still do not fathom what keeps Elad and his fellow kibbutzniks on this communal Jewish farm in the desert. I still need to know: had I, when I was twenty-one, gone to Yahel rather than the Sahel, would I have stayed? Would living in this obscure but egalitarian community in the Arava have satisfied both my expatriate urges and my commitment to Judaism?

Under the guise of academic scholarship, I make plans for the family to arrive well in time for the summer *simcha* of '99, that is, for Gadi Lending's joyous rite of passage at the age of thirteen. Deep down, I am also hoping to scratch my last, stubborn, Zionist itch.

Eilat, July 1999. We arrive in the Holy Land, in Jerusalem, in the Negev. To stock the pantry of our kibbutz cottage, we take a kibbutz car to the supermarket in Eilat. Elad ambivalently steers us away from purchasing an otherwise flavorful and well-priced line of wines. "It's produced on a right-wing kibbutz," he explains somewhat sheepishly, not quite sure yet to include us within his circle of fellow boycotters. Perhaps it's a matter of shunning products from a Jewish settlement in the contested Palestinian territories.

In this southern Israeli Supersol liquor aisle, I watch as my old high school buddy from Long Island scans the wine labels in Hebrew lest he inadvertently purchase a politically objectionable bottle from an ideologically rival kibbutz.

Had I been a better Jew and joined him years before, might I be doing the same?

2

A Desert for Reform Zionists

It is at dusk that the changing colors of the Edomite mountains, just a few miles east but in the Hashemite Kingdom of Jordan, work their magic on even the most casual visitor to any of the half dozen kibbutzim in the Arava Desert of Israel. During the short span that the sun sets, with seemingly sudden abandon, the hues on the hills beyond modulate from pale pink and ruby red to deep crimson and, as night falls, into brooding brown. Not even fervent Believers—be they Christian, Muslim, or Jew—who congregate 125 miles northward in the Holy City of Jerusalem lay claim to an equivalent daily miracle that, in the Arava, atheists too behold.

For both artists and linguists it is esthetically appropriate that these mountains are called "Edom," which in Hebrew means red. Yet if the mountains take their names from the people who originally populated them twenty-two centuries ago, their etymology may lie less in colorated imagery than biblical epidermy. Edomites believed themselves descendants of Isaac's son Esau, nicknamed Edom on account of his "ruddy" complexion. In biblical times, the kingdom of Edom covered one hundred square miles, from the southern tip of the Dead Sea to the Gulf of Aqaba, and included mountains and plateaus that lie in present-day Jordan and Israel. The mysterious ruins of Petra, recognized worldwide thanks to Steven Spielberg and *Indiana Jones*, have been inherited by modern-day Jordan. On the Israeli side of ancient Edom, today referred to simply as the Arava, the indigenous population disappeared from the harsh and stony land centuries before.

"It is so quiet that from my house I can literally hear a leaf fall to the ground," gushes Rosealie Sherris, in heavily Brooklyn-accented English. Rosalie is no New Age pushover or matured youth Zionist. In her pre-aliya (immigration) existence, before listening to falling desert leaves on her kibbutz home patio, Rosealie's acoustic background consisted of nightly gunshots in Bedford Stuyvesant. Tough speaking, cigarette smoking, her cynical eyes darting upwards from a narrow, hunkered down face, one more easily pictures Rosalie downing a cannoli in a Lower East Side café than swiping humus in a desert kibbutz cafeteria. Following a spat with her similarly flinty twelve-year-old daughter Ma'ayan, Rosalie will proudly assert, "I could drop her in the Fulton Fish Market and she'd fit right in." Yet the desert peace has tamed the Brooklyn bombshell and won't easily let her go. Rosealie proudly refers to herself as a sociopath—hardly the most social of kibbutzniks—and is not one to mince her words, tinged both in Hebrew and English with her Borough brogue, about fellow kibbutzniks. But the desert—ah, that's something else. "It's priceless, this tranquility," Rosealie, an abstract artist, insists. "Where could you buy such a setting?"

Ask Danny Hayken, maintenance manager, folk dancer, and periodic prayer leader. Athletic, goatee-sporting Danny is an outgoing, articulate, highly intelligent forty-three-year-old, originally from Cleveland Heights, who has chosen kibbutz life over his doctor wife and therefore lives an ocean away from her and their four children. Danny will tick off any number of reasons why he has made his life on Yahel. But mention the desert, and that's when his deep eyes will light up. "[You wind up] falling in love with this place. With the mountains, with the stars, with the Arava itself." Over and over, desert rats of Yahel and Lotan palpably glow when describing their relationship to the land around them. But not all of the kibbutzniks feel this way.

Desert does not permit indifference. Especially in summertime, day after day of over one hundred degree weather bakes brain along with body. As you walk along the gently curving paved paths of Yahel at noon, you inhale wafts of simmering heat and feel them filtering down through your lungs. Your skin cracks, your throat parches. Beware insufficient liquid intake: "Thirst follows dehydration," the doctor warns. "Once you really feel the need to drink, it's already too late."

So quite a few kibbutzniks live in the Arava in spite of the desert. "This is where they chose to put Yahel," says Laura Sperber, originally from Roslyn, Long Island. "I came because it was a new Reform kibbutz *despite* it being in the desert. It does get to me—the heat, the isolation. Would I be happier if the kibbutz were somewhere else, closer to the center of the country? Sure I would." Laura has good reason to bemoan the isolation of Yahel. As a computer programmer in Netanya, in the northwest of the country, she commutes by airplane, spending half the week next to the Mediterranean Sea and the rest of her life deep in the Negev Desert.

Situating Yahel in the Arava was not a haphazard decision. When planners of the Jewish Agency and the Reform movement began scouting for a suitable site in the mid-1970s, they deliberately limited their options to Israel proper. Even as new settlements were sprouting up in the West Bank and Golan Heights, controlled by Israel since the Six Day War of 1967, for political reasons Reform Jews and leftists (practically the same thing) eschewed building in occupied territories. In the north, kibbutzim already pocketed the Galilee. In the south, founding father David Ben-Gurion's vision of "greening the desert" had still gone largely unfulfilled. And so it was decided that a young, largely inexperienced bunch of Jewish kids would not only form the first Reform Jewish kibbutz ever, but also while they were at it, make the desert bloom. Two decades later, as a result of the idealistic and ecological motivations of state planners and progressive rabbis, four hundred people living on two separate communities now cope with extreme temperatures in splendid—and not so splendid—isolation.

Alex Cicelsky of Lotan, whose salt-and-pepper hair adds some color contrast to the desert scenery, views the Reform kibbutzim locale pragmatically. "It's good that the Reform movement decided to put us here," he says. "Had we been placed between Jerusalem and Tel Aviv, we wouldn't be a kibbutz anymore. The outside pressures are too much.

"In order to be a *shtetl*"—for Alex sees the kibbutz as the modern equivalent of yesteryear's close-knit European Jewish community—"you need oppression. Here, the oppression is physical distance." And heat. Geographical reality, according to the Rochester-born Reform kibbutznik, "forces us to be creative, and to be loving and caring for each other. Because we just don't have that otherwise."

Except for two roadside stops and some tiny Bedouin Arab encampments, along the one hundred miles of Route 90 which links the Dead Sea to Kibbutz Yahel—the most northern of the Arava kibbutzim—there is only wilderness. The scenery is as stark as when Moses and the Israelites traversed it during their forty-year trek from Egypt to the Promised Land forty centuries ago. Even today, rumbling along in the bright red conveyance of the Eged Bus Company, there is no denying the eerie feeling that Someone is watching our progress from above—even if only through the lens of the army's hot air surveillance balloon, silently hovering high in the pure, thin, holy, pale blue sky above.

After the torturous twistings of the Dead Sea canyons, the road evens out into a straight, flat line that stretches all the way to Eilat, thirty miles beyond Yahel. Along the way, one zooms past other small kibbutzim: Lotan, even closer to Jordanian territory; Ketura, a little further down the road, on the opposite side; Grofit, on a hill overlooking Route 90; Yotvata, biggest of the bunch, on the western side of the road; Samar, closest to Eilat but furtherest from conformity. Little traffic emanates from these settlements and, for the long distance driver, the monotony of the journey exudes a dangerous illusion of vehicular solitude: Route 90 easily becomes a death trap, so much so that the infirmary at Yahel is especially equipped for emergency roadside trauma response.

Eilat is no longer the dusty, fly-swarming frontier dive remembered by the early Arava kibbutzniks. With its skin-revealing beaches and gaudy outlets, its high-rise hotels and Las Vegas-style gambling, for religious Jews Eilat has merely replaced the original Sodom and Gomorrah de-servedly buried on the other side of the desert; for the secular, Eilat is Is-rael's Miami Beach, a great place to unwind, take the kids to an aquarium, and swim in coral reefs and with dolphins. For the kibbutzniks of the Arava, Eilat is the closest place to go shopping and to revisit the urban, anonymous, "regular" world. On the regional bus, which stops at every kibbutz along the way, it takes well over an hour to get from Yahel to Eilat. Public bus is still the most common means of transportation: on the Re-form Zionist kibbutzim, private ownership of cars is still forbidden.

"Most Israelis have absolutely no idea where we are," says Rosealie, as if she were describing the *New Yorker* cartoon of the world beyond the Hudson. "You say kibbutz and Negev, they think Be'er Sheva." Be'er Sheva is seventy miles away, on another, even less frequented highway, two hours away by public transportation. From his perch in Pittsburgh, more than a decade since leaving, Richard Kaplan still vividly recalls that "the average Israeli family would plan a trip to Eilat six months ahead of time—like we might plan a trip to Hawaii."

You know you have finally reached Yahel when you first glimpse, on an adjacent hilltop, a tiny army outpost. Encircling the kibbutz are one, two, three sets of barbed wire. If you arrive before sundown, you just drive through the open gate; the sentry post is no longer manned. After dark, you call the night watchman from the fixed walkie-talkie mounted at the gate. In the "old" days—that is, up until the 1980s—a rifle toting sentry would come and check you out in person. Nowadays, guard duty is per-formed from the comfort of one's own home, thanks to a closed circuit television system hooked up to each member's TV set. The "sentry" merely switches channels from the late night movie or video she is watching to stay awake, views you on her television screen, and then pushes a button to automatically slide open the gate. Kibbutz is the ultimate gated community where, in turn, every member controls who comes in at night.

Looming garrison, barbed wire, and nocturnal entry procedures inevitably detract from the sense of spiritual transcendence and spatial infinity which desert life otherwise conjures. Kibbutzniks differ regarding the necessity of maintaining such an austere security cocoon, given the quiescence of the Jordanian border that dates from well before the Oslo peace process. But who can forget this cautionary tale? . . .

On her twenty-fifth birthday on August 8, 1989, Lauren Rosen, a volunteer on Lotan from Birmingham, New Jersey, was shot in the neck by a uniformed but supposedly deranged Jordanian conscript who had infiltrated from his border post twelve miles north of Eilat. According to newspaper accounts, Laura was returning with two friends from the kibbutz dining room to the date orchard when private Fareed Ali Mustapha suddenly appeared from behind a tree and yelled out "This is for my brother!" He then opened fire with an M-16, wounding Laura and taking another woman hostage.

A few hours later Mustapha was killed by an Israeli army marksman.

Exactly ten years later, Laura—now married and with twin toddlers—has returned to live on Lotan.

For sure, the isolation of American transplants in the Arava is now greatly offset by e-mail and Internet. In the same way that cybersurfers the world over are connected in a mind-set dismissive of physical distance, so do these kibbutzniks maintain the technological illusion of geographical irrelevance. Walk into Rick Daniels's house on a Shabbat morning—large, lumbering Rick from Flushing, Queens who has lived in the outback of Israel for the last twenty-two-years—and what do you see him watching on the computer screen? The Mets/Yankees Major League Baseball recap on ESPN. It's not as if Rick's sole connection to the outside world is by computer. For two years, in fact, he commuted cross-country to Tel Aviv as regional representative to a date marketing body. But no technology will enable Rick to download Shea Stadium from his boyhood hometown in Queens to his Zionist homeland in the Negev. And unlike Kibbutz Gezer between Tel Aviv and Jerusalem, there is no question of recreating here a recreational league diamond: growing green grass for an entire outfield within central Israel poses less of a problem than maintaining a simple lawn in the Arava. Still, thanks to the irrigational prowess for which Israel is justly known all over the world—including the podunk town in

Niger where I served as Peace Corps Volunteer—Yahel and Lotan are oases of greenery within an otherwise formidable, stony brown desert.

If you drive right onto the outer ring road after passing through the entrance gate to Yahel, you will skirt, to your left, clusters of closely adjacent, modestly sized, single level, detached houses surrounded by small plots of grass and occasional gardens. Housing for nonmember residents and volunteers is clustered closer to the gate side; members' homes are further inside.

A quarter of the way around the perimeter you will pass a locked gate, passage through which leads to the hilltop army outpost. Just before reaching the half-way point, the housing abruptly ends, stark testimony to the inflated optimism of early absorption planners. (Absorption is one of those funny translations decided upon by official Hebrew translators. You don't "join" or "settle" on a kibbutz—you are "absorbed" into one. On our very first day, after filling out some forms and nervously dropping our children off with their respective day camp groups, Elad enthusiastically—but, to my ears, bizarrely—chimed: "Well, that's it. You're all absorbed now!")

Approaching the three-quarters mark, and just as the outer ring road begins its inward curve towards the center of the settlement, far off to the right you will begin to see—or, if your car windows are rolled down, smell—the dairy farm with its six hundred head of cattle. Just to the left, emerging from a converted barn, you may be surprised to see a number of Asian looking fellows. Your curiosity piqued, you will soon learn about the shy, pleasant, hardworking Thai migrant laborers whose very presence speaks, at the very least, to the pragmatic compromises that external forces have imposed upon the original Jewish socialist vision of a purely Zionist, autonomous, agricultural community. To more ideologically pure critics—especially rival kibbutzniks at nearby Lotan—the contract laborers from Southeast Asia represent the ultimate capitalistic sellout. But wait—you've barely arrived.

Just as you reach the main parking area in the middle of the kibbutz, from behind discrete live fencing, you may hear splashing from the Olympic-sized swimming pool. You could drive straight and very slowly now, back towards the entrance gate, and behold on your right hand side a tennis court (floodlit at night), then a soccer field, and finally a complex of warehouse and offices for the fruit and vegetable packing house. It's better to park your vehicle and complete the tour by foot. Kibbutz life is designed to be as carless as possible.

From the parking lot you are steps away from the kibbutz offices and the dining hall, one of two major social centers at the kibbutz. The other meeting point, the sloping domed *sifriya* housing both the library and synagogue, you reach by walking past the charming children's houses and perambulating the campus-like grassy knoll. Truth be told, as a place of prayer the synagogue of the premier kibbutz of Reform Judaism is heavily underutilized. As with the symbolism of the imported workers from Thailand, though, we'll need to approach this topic gingerly.

The library, on the other hand, is both well furnished and heavily frequented. There are books in English and in Hebrew, on Judaica as well as secular topics, and a liberal sprinkling of current magazines on user-friendly racks. Architecturally as well as metaphorically, this sifriya constitutes the hallmark of Yahel. It is certainly more conventional than Lotan's architectural distinctions—geodesic domes and recycled waste constructions—and therefore faithful to the maturer image Yahel likes to project. Lotan's library, its general-secretary unabashedly admits, is "just a few books in a bomb shelter."

The inner ring road is a horseshoe-shaped, pedestrian-only pathway which branches off into even narrower walkways that lead right up to the door posts of the kibbutz homes. Until you note discrete differences— small hanging plants here, a wagon wheel there, upside down bicycles over there—the houses look identical. Not all families have affixed their names to their front door. Since there are no street names, small statuettes—a bunny rabbit, a mouse—have been placed as walkway junction markers. If you don't deviate from the inner ring, you'll wind up at a playground made from a tiny train originally used to transport copper at the old Timna mines several miles away. Such landmarks notwithstanding, you're certain to get lost during the first few days on a kibbutz. In fact, it's expected.

To learn the desert secret of the single, immense, lush green lawn (no family owns the land in front of its house, any more than it owns the actual house), you should stroll the grounds at night. Gentle mists of water making quiet hissing noises spray forth from little black pipes you probably did not notice during the day. If the grounds have been baking all day, if the retreat of the sun has done little to cool your body or the nighttime air, then you may wish to step off the pathway and let a cloud of water mist enshroud you. For the air conditioner in your quarters you are simply grateful. For the greenery cultivated in this open air inferno— especially if you have spent four years in the West African Sahel—you are positively awed.

Beyond the southwest gate, behind the dairy, no longer within smell of cow or man, a stony site serves as seasonal Bedouin encampment for

Abu Jama and his family. A strange shaped crevice recalls a sitting camel
and his hump and is so named. Visiting high school tour groups are
brought here, within walking distance of the kibbutz, to ride camels, sleep
out under the stars, and to experience the long heralded hospitality of the
desert Arabs. This is part of their package "desert experience." Forty-
seven-year-old Abu Jama, serving sugary tea in his flowing white gown
and wrapped turban, looks ever the part of a Lawrence of Arabia extra.
But this is not the outfit Abu wears as he drives his fashionable car to
Yahel from his home outside of Be'er Sheva, his sons hauling in the camels
by truck. Abu is more accustomed to wearing smart Western clothes. In
fact, when he is not dressing up (or is it down?) in his majestic robes, Abu
is unquestionably better appareled than any of the kibbutzniks for whom
he works.

"These people have style," murmurs Rosealie, eyeing Abu Jama and
his Mercedes while still "feeling filthy" from the grungy kibbutz car she's
been assigned to take to Eilat that month as *nehag bayit* (house driver). It
is certainly not condescending, the way in which Rosealie generalizes
about "these people." Nor is it in the naively reverential terms of a Middle Eastern Ashkenazi immigrant to the Land of Israel. Her comment
on Abu Jama and "these people" comes out in an almost begrudging,
I-can't-help-my-snobbish-self tone of the outdone New Yorker making a
fashion statement.

Despite his pure Bedouin pedigree, Abu Jama is a shrewd and unsen-
timental Israeli through and through.

"There's too much stress these days," he tells me in Hebrew, after
changing from his long sleeved shirt and stylish slacks into his Bedouin
tent costume. "Everyone is running around, chasing after money, looking
at their watches. Arabs, Bedouins, Jews, everyone—they're all competing
for this and that."

Abu Jama attended school for eight years before working as a cotton
picker on a moshav, an agricultural collective where homes, land, and
fields are individually owned. He married when he was fifteen and now has
fourteen children. One of his sons is a doctor; another is an officer in the
Israeli army. Before getting into the camel business, he was a fruit and
vegetable trucker.

"What about these American kids?" I ask. "Does the fact that they
can become Israeli citizens just by requesting it bother you?" I had always
been curious about Israeli Arabs' take on the Law of Return, the stipulation that any Jew (barring special circumstances) can automatically become an Israeli citizen upon arrival.

For Abu Jama, Israel is big enough even for Diaspora Jews. "If they want to come and live here, become Israeli—why not?" Nor was he bitter about the 1982 takeover of his birthplace in Ovatim for an Israeli Air Force Base. "There was no problem with that," he declared matter-of-factly. "They compensated us quite well."

Abu Jama is no pushover. He instructs me to place his picture on the front cover of this book. He politely but firmly tells Elad not to let Buffy, his terrier, into the large, open-fronted Bedouin tent. Elad insists that Buffy is well behaved. "It's not that," Abu Jama remonstrates. "It's just not done. Dogs in the tent—it's against our custom." Elad grumbles that he can't tie up his terrier—a canine whom I've seen Elad *carry* down steep sections of wilderness—out in the open desert. "I'll have to take him back to the kibbutz and shut him in the house, then," Elad states in irritation. Abu Jama is unmoved.

Elad does not know, as I do from living in Islamic communities in Africa, that Muslims cannot suffer dogs in their midst. And Abu Jama does not know, as I do from my interviews about Yahel's early days, that even among kibbutzniks Elad is remembered for his peculiar concern for pet canines. I hold my tongue.

One of the reasons that the Bedouin encampment is so close to the kibbutz nowadays evokes the illusion of isolation. If you spread out an official Park Reserve map you see that Yahel is entirely surrounded by red markings: it is technically in the middle of a vast army firing zone. Now you think of all those road signs (updated with army cell phone calling numbers) informing you not to stray off either side of the highway. Kibbutzniks come to view the military restriction of movement around Yahel as a royal pain; after all, shells don't actually land anywhere near the kibbutz, really. The previous years' Bedouin tent site was much nicer, esthetically, but the army arbitrarily decided (for sure, citing safety reasons) that it could no longer stay where it was.

The army, the army. During the year, the army is constantly taking men off Yahel to do their reserve duty. During the day, the army plans its desert night maneuvers and target practice for the morrow. At night, army infrared tracks your every step outside the kibbutz perimeter. You are not as alone in this vast and open desert as you had thought. Still, it is thanks to nocturnal patrolling as a reservist, says my high school buddy, that he gets closest to the surrounding land. "It's at night that you really understand where you are," says Elad. "You come across camels, foxes, scorpions . . ."

Security and desert remind Rosealie, the artist from Brooklyn, of her short-lived training in firearms . . .

"Some time after I came to Yahel it was decided that everybody—women as well as men—would be required to do guard duty. [This was before the closed circuit video system.] Now, not all the female kibbutzniks, especially the immigrants from America, had been in the army and learned to shoot. So they scheduled a day to teach us. I'll never forget it.

"We were brought, under the hot sun, out to this field for target practice, lugging these heavy, *heavy* rifles. And I said to myself, 'What's wrong with this picture?' I mean, after all, we came to Israel, at least in part, because we were part of the peace generation back in the States, and now we babes were here with these guns slung over our backs and wearing mufflers—you know, the kind to deaden the noise?—over our ears. As I said, it was a hot day and I could see myself trudging out there but not really believing it was me.

"As we were getting ready for our turn at target practice I heard a shot. It absolutely shattered something inside of me. 'No way,' I said, 'I'm not going through with this fiasco.' So I stopped right there and"—reenacting the scene with her hands—"I put the rifle on the ground, took those mufflers off my ears and just walked away." Raucous guffaw.

"But Erica," Rosalie went on, referring to Elad's diminutive wife, "Erica did it. She claims she doesn't know how to but she does. The gun probably weighs more than she does but she can shoot." More raucous laughter at Rosalie's only slightly exaggerated image of a bespectacled, waif-like Vassar girl from leafy Newton, Massachusetts wrestling under the burning Negev sun with a rifle heftier than herself, and finally shooting it off, successfully, near her beloved Zion in the desert.

There are today about 270 kibbutzim in Israel, each with its own historical idiosyncrasies, ideological orientation, and religious tendencies. Yahel and Lotan, among the youngest of the group, represent the convergence of three forces in Jewish history: Zionist socialism, Reform Judaism, and American aliya (immigration to Israel).

Groups of secular and socialist Russian and Eastern European Jewish emigrants experimented with collective farming in what was then Ottoman-controlled Palestine as early as the 1880s, before Theodor Herzl's vision of an en masse return to the ancestral land was even mooted to most Jewish communities around the world. The first *kibbutz* (community) to take root and survive was Deganya, located in the Galilee region of what is today northern Israel; it was founded in 1910 before a modified version of Karl Marx's Communist manifesto was foisted upon Russia by the Bolshevik Revolution of 1917. Population upheavals during World War I and the takeover of Palestine by Great Britain both spurred greater numbers of East European and Russian Jews—many of them influenced by the socialist idealism of the times—to join existing or to found additional kibbutzim in northern and central Palestine. So successful was this movement of rural socialism among European Jewish pioneers that parallel federations arose to coordinate the activities of their respective kibbutzim. Thus, arose the United Kibbutz, National Kibbutz, and League of Small Kibbutzim federations, most of whose members were unabashedly secular if not outspokenly atheistic. Only later would kibbutzim of a religious bent develop, leading to the founding of two Orthodox kibbutz federations. Orthodoxy and socialism have always made somewhat strange bedfellows, however, and the religious kibbutzim have always constituted a numerically marginal (albeit internally cohesive) force within the larger kibbutz movement. Still, for most Israelis the Orthodox kibbutzim are the only legitimate (or even recognized) religious ones. Within nonreligiously identified kibbutzim, religiously observant Jews are not only a distinct minority but often an outright aberration.

Internal scissions and partisan realignments (at first largely due to divergences over Marxist doctrine and Soviet allegiance) eventually translated into a fourfold separation of kibbutz federations into 269 kibbutzim and roughly 125,000 members. (Israel's total population is around six million, 80 percent of whom are Jewish; of these, about one-fifth are religiously observant.) The four federations were TAKAM (the Unified Kibbutz Movement), with 167 kibbutzim and 60 percent of all kibbutzniks; Kibbutz Artzi (National Kibbutz), with 117 kibbutzim and 32 percent of kibbutzniks; and the two religious kibbutz federations, Kibbutz Dati (seventeen kibbutzim, 6 percent of kibbutz members) and the ultra-Orthodox Workers of Israel Association (only two kibbutzim). Both Yahel and Lotan belonged to TAKAM. In recent years, the two largest federations have merged, creating a giant Kibbutz Movement conglomerate, Takatz. Yet the persistence of ideological tensions also led to the creation, within Takatz, of Zerem Shitufi (Collective Stream), grouping those kibbutzim that assertively cling to their socialistic identity. (Tellingly, Lotan has joined Zerem Shitufi but not Yahel. With 250 and 185 persons respectively, each is much smaller than the typical kibbutz with a four hundred population threshold.) Although a handful of kibbutzim have been established in the Palestinian territories occupied in 1967, the overwhelming majority lie within Israel proper. Controversy over Jewish settlements in the West Bank and Golan Heights does not directly affect the kibbutz movement.

Two dates—1977 and 1985—represent tough watersheds for the modern kibbutz movement. Menachem Begin's 1977 victorious leadership of the Likud at the polls is usually recalled as the first nationalist, right-wing jolt in Israeli politics, more severe than even Binyamin Netanyahu's polarizing tenure of 1996–99. Less widely acknowledged is that Begin's antipathy for the Labour Party dynasty, from Ben-Gurion to Golda to Rabin and Peres, included disdain for the bastions of leftist socialism concentrated within the kibbutz movement. Likud's preference for nationalistic and religious settlements in the occupied territories came in part at the expense of the kibbutzim. When inflation hit untenable levels in 1985, economic restructuring required the cold shock weaning of heavily subsidized kibbutzim off of the long fraying apron strings of the national budget. Yahel was founded in 1977, remember, just as the revisionist Likud hit the antisocialist fan; and Lotan came into being in 1983, just two years before debt management and financial austerity were to overtake desert greening and communal solidarity as operative kibbutz buzz words.

Despite their relatively small numbers—fewer than 5 percent of Israelis live on them—kibbutzim have traditionally assumed mythic proportions in outsiders' imaginations and in Israelis' own collective sense of self. Less difficult to shake than the antiquated image of male and female pioneers in identical khaki shorts and shirts singing spirited Zionist folksongs and dancing the *hora* by the bonfire after a long day of fruit picking in the hot sun is that of the kibbutznik as selfless, almost superhuman hero, indifferent to personal comfort, and ever ready to risk personal safety to protect the community, people, and nation. ("Some visitors come from the States," says Yahel tour guide Ron Bernstein, latterly of Long Island, "and are surprised to see that we have electricity, that we live in real houses. They came thinking that we must camp out our whole lives.")

It is true that, proportionally, for many years kibbutzniks have led the nation in terms of officer corps *and* war casualties, membership in parliament, and contribution to the gross national product. It is also true that in the early years of Zionist nation-building, in the decades preceding as well as following the official establishment of the state of Israel in 1948, the kibbutzim constituted indispensable components of a land security and border surveillance network. Undeniable, too, is that A. D. Gordon's nineteenth-century prophetic vision of a new Jewish collectivity, empowered by self-labor, agricultural self-sufficiency, and secular but socially just egalitarianism did imbue the early kibbutzniks with an enviable sense of mission. But kibbutzniks were flesh and bone people, too, for whom the rigors of idealism inevitably gave way to practical considerations and ideological compromise. Most emblematic of this shift was the final abandonment, in 1998, of the children's house, the distinct mode of childhood socialization which had kibbutz children sleeping not in their parents' homes but in dormitories with their age cohorts. In principle, kibbutz kids were raised not by their biological parents but by the community as a whole. Even though none of the first founders of Yahel and Lotan were already parents, by the late 1970s it was already a foregone conclusion that Yahel's infants would sleep with and be reared by their parents, not by the collectivity. Whether that other time honored hallmark of kibbutz ideology—equal compensation regardless of work assignment or productivity—will forever hold is less certain at Yahel than on Lotan. Of greater certainty are fissures within the kibbutz movement that recall rivalries among the various *haredi* (ultra-Orthodox) sects: recall Elad's point of not buying an otherwise attractive wine because it was produced by a member of a politically incorrect kibbutz federation.

Whereas Zionist rural socialism had its beginnings with young Russian migrants infused with revolutionary (including antireligious) convictions, Reform Judaism—a full century older—was the product of German rabbis and theologians striving to adapt Jewish faith and practice to modern times and European sensibilities. Ideologically, in fact, Reformism and Zionism were antithetical to one another—until, that is, Adolph Hitler rendered moot all divergence regarding the necessity of a sovereign state for the Jewish people.

If 1910—Deganya's establishment—is a convenient benchmark to mark the establishment of the modern kibbutz movement, 1810 serves as a comparable watershed for the Reform movement. For in that year Israel Jacobson, director of the Jewish School in Seesen, Germany, introduced into his chapel an abbreviated service, choral singing and organ, and German language prayers and sermon. Such "reforms," soon adopted by other German congregations, were adamantly opposed by most Orthodox rabbis who viewed them as little short of heresy. In defense Jacobson and other Reformists argued that, far from contradicting the core of Judaism, such changes were compatible with a prophetic spirit within Judaism which valued relevance and revival over ritual and rote.

Changes in the structure of Sabbath services were only at the surface of the seism then shaking the foundations of Western European Judaism. More than the strangeness of organ music and vernacular prayers, at stake was the very status of halacha, traditional Jewish law as interpreted over the centuries by the rabbis and codified in the Talmud. Judaism had traditionally taught that there were two sets of laws given at Mount Sinai, a written version, the Torah, and an oral version, told to Moses by God. After the Revelation at Sinai this oral version, containing precisions and interpretations of otherwise inscrutable divine will, was thought to have been imparted, by word of mouth, for hundreds of generations. Only after the destruction of the Temple of Jerusalem, in AD70, did the protracted process of transcribing the erstwhile oral version of the Law finally begin. Although deservedly associated with fine point disputation within its coterie, the rabbinic establishment nevertheless constituted the authoritative basis of talmudic interpretation.

Reformists expressed skepticism over the divine nature of the retroactively transcribed "law." While respectful (at least initially) of the traditional rabbis' learning, they claimed authority to re-form Jewish practice and belief in light of evolved standards of reason and the divine imperatives of universal morality and justice. For example, literal belief in a personal messiah whose unschedulable arrival would herald the return of the dead to life and an "ingathering of the (Jewish) exiles" was replaced by a more metaphoric understanding of a messianic era whose promise of social justice and international harmony ought to be initiated by good works and moral behavior—the essence of the Torah—today. Whether uttered out loud or not, Reformists also feared that sclerotic rabbinics were not only intellectually anachronistic, but also positively alienating to the growing numbers of enlightened and emancipated Jews.

Indeed, the emergence of Reform Judaism was part and parcel of the general enlightenment, the nineteenth-century Jewish version of which— *haskala*—entailed the cautious but revolutionary extension of civic rights to the Jews of Western Europe. When Napoleon invited the "Israelites" of France to join in his Empire by renouncing foreign allegiances while retaining their faith, most of *les juifs* were happy to accept the invitation. Official France's enlightened policy towards the Jews caught on, however imperfectly, in neighboring countries. The nineteenth century saw Jews leaving both the physical and intellectual ghettos of Western Europe with an unprecedented choice: voluntarily retain their distinctive Jewishness through self-ghettoization or assimilate into the wider Gentile culture of their host nation. A more difficult middle road—the one advocated by the Reformists—was to retain the integrity of Judaism by adapting it to the modern times and the spirit of scientific rationality. If this entailed jettisoning halacha and the enfeebled grip of outmoded talmudists, so be it.

Such ideas carried important political ramifications, not only for host country-Jewish relations but within the larger Jewish world. If Judaism were no longer a ritualistically infused national destiny of the Jewish people but rather the theological choice of citizens of different countries merely subscribing to a similar Mosaic creed, then there was nothing strange—as would later occur in World War I—for Jews to fight Jews in the name of competing nationalism. (This is not to say that French and German Jews on opposite sides of the Rhine shot at each other because they were Reform, only that the shared values of European emancipation and Reform Judaism carried similarly unforeseen, and arguably perverse, consequences.)

Large scale immigration to the United States shifted the gravity of the Reform movement from Germany to the burgeoning American Jewish community. A theology that melded relaxed religiosity to host nation loyalty dovetailed perfectly with the melting pot creed of America. Since anti-Semitism did persist sub rosa, the challenge for American Jews—the greatest number of whom came to embrace Reformism—was to demonstrate unassailable loyalty to America while retaining some version of Jewish communal solidarity. An early casualty of this tension was Zionism.

Antithetical to the Reform desire to "fit in" as Americans (albeit as Jewish Americans) was any notion to reestablish a Jewish homeland for modern Jews in ancient Israel. Judaism *had* become a religion of the Diaspora; but that condition of universal dispersion, for Reform, was less a hallmark of divine shame than an historical opportunity for worldwide acceptance. A movement preaching the "return" of Jews to a backwater Palestine would raise the canard of double loyalty or suspect allegiance, a stigmatizing perception that even Catholics in America were forced to overcome with respect to the Vatican. It certainly would conflict with the universalistic thrust of the movement. So emphatic was Reform Judaism's rejection of revivalist Zionism (it had more calmly dispensed with messianic visions of the rebuilding of Jerusalem) that in its official plenum, the Pittsburgh Platform, it declared:

> We consider ourselves no longer a nation but a religious community and therefore expect neither a return to Palestine . . . nor the restoration of any of the laws concerning the Jewish State.

In hindsight one can practically imagine the framers of the 1885 Pittsburgh Platform trying to preempt Theodor Herzl, whose clarion for a modern Zionism, *The Jewish State*, was not to be published for another seventeen years. Subsequent events in Europe, of course, would vindicate Herzl's position that the Jewish people required a sovereign state for the sake of self-preservation as well as cultural fulfillment. Hitler's rise to power, even before the Holocaust tinder was ignited, demanded a formal reversal in Reform Judaism's initial anti-Zionism. This came in the Columbus Platform of 1937 which affirmed

> the obligation of all Jewry to aid in [Palestine's] upbuilding as a Jewish homeland by endeavoring to make it not only a haven of refuge for the oppressed, but also a center of Jewish culture and spiritual life.

When the horrors of the Holocaust became common knowledge, only a minority of traditional Jews in America, who still maintained that only the Messiah himself could return the Jewish people to the Holy Land, opposed the immediate establishment of the state of Israel. Even though theology and ritual still divided Orthodox, Reform, and middle ground Conservative movements, post-Shoah consciousness united the overwhelming majority of Americans on the question of supporting the establishment of a modern Jewish State in Israel.

Reform Judaism not only reconciled itself to Zionism, but also has partially fused with it. "Reform Zionism" today stands not merely for supporting the State of Israel from afar but establishing its presence in Israel as an alternative to Orthodox Judaism. International headquarters for the World Union for Progressive Judaism, umbrella organization for the Reform movements of dozens of countries, are based in Jerusalem. So is the main campus of Hebrew Union College. Despite recent Israeli government and court decisions that have accorded the Reform (and Conservative) movements a modicum of legitimacy, they remain relatively marginal phenomena within the wider Jewish state.

Together with the kibbutz and Reform movements, the third convergent phenomenon to birth Yahel and Lotan was American aliya, emigration to Israel. Yet like socialist farming and progressive Judaism, American aliya has fallen far short of original projections.

Despite the enormous political and financial backing of the American Jewish community for Israel, and the millions of American Jews who have traveled there, in the half century of its independence only eighty thousand have actually moved to the so-called Jewish homeland. According to Jay Shofet, New England aliya center emissary: "American Jewry as a whole seems stuck in an ambivalent holding pattern on the question of how involved it wants to be in Israel. The typical American Jewish pattern [is] high emotional attachment *to* Israel but low actual engagement *with* Israel." Annually, only about two thousand Jews uproot themselves from the United States with the express intention of settling in Israel. Out of a total six million persons, this figures represents an infinitesimal three *ten-thousandths*, or 1/20 of 1 percent, of the American Jewish community. Yet despite the tiny numbers of Zionists who actually make the plunge, the idea of moving to Israel—even if it is someone *else* who is doing it—touches some emotional chord in every self-identifying Jew's heart. "Israel is the Broadway of the Jewish world," teaches one Reform rabbi. "Not everybody plays on Broadway but there are those of us who do." To which at least one Yahelnik unabashedly admits, "I enjoy being on Broadway."

For sure, the character of American aliya has changed over the years. Whereas the period following the Six Day War saw a short-lived boomlet* of young secular or Reform Jews galvanized by both the vulnerability and heroism of the imperiled homeland, by the 1990s the more typical profile was that of traditionally religious Jews. A number of these wound up on West Bank settlements, especially religiously nationalist ones. Baruch Goldstein, the mass murderer of Hebron, was not typical of latter-day American *olim* (immigrants) with respect to his hatred of Arabs or his readiness to initiate lethal violence against them. As a Brooklyn-raised Orthodox Jewish doctor, however, he better represents the American *oleh* of the 1980s and 1990s today than do the leftist and progressive Jewish immigrants of the 1960s and early 1970s. Most typical is for American olim to wind up in Jerusalem.

In the 1980s, Professors Kevin Avruch and Chaim Waxman presented, in their respective volumes, thoroughly researched, statistically extensive studies of American migration to Israel. My favorite treatment of fellow Zionists who have made the plunge, though, remains Harold Isaacs' 1967 pioneering book, *American Jews in Israel* . Perhaps I prefer Isaacs because he seamlessly integrates into the book his previous work on American Blacks in West Africa; perhaps it is because he invokes Jean-Paul Sartre, hardly a staple of social scientists today. In any event, Isaacs tackles head on most poignantly the existential dimension:

> A Jew in a world without Gentiles and a Negro in a world without whites can feel relieved of that "uneasiness"—really fear—which the Gentile or white presence creates . . . [A] person was finally able, in all-Jewish Israel, to measure himself and others not as "Jews" but as individual persons. . . . "It was my temperament to idealize," said an older American kibbutznik speaking of his younger years, "and in

---

* Fewer than one thousand Americans migrated to Israel in 1968; the very next year, over six times as many did. The peak year for Jewish emigration to Israel, with 7,364 olim, was 1971.

practice I had to learn that Jews are also human beings, that they act petty, pretty much the same wherever they are" . . . [I]n Israel one could cease at last to be *special* because one was Jewish. But what happened, ironically enough, was that one now became *special* because one was *American*.

Thus, a kibbutz largely composed of Reform American Jews represents a triple whammy: few Israelis care to live socialistically or on a collective farm; Reform Judaism is regarded as practically *treif* (unkosher) throughout most of the Jewish state; and leaving the United States to live in Israel is considered nutty by Americans and Israelis alike. Add to this the less than convenient location, and less than temperate climate, of the remote and steaming Arava, and the recipe for these two communities, Yahel and Lotan, becomes all the more unlikely.

When I think about these larger obstacles alongside Yahel's and Lotan's ill-timed births between Begin's 1977 victory and the 1985 economic crisis, and then roam the quasi-lunar landscape connecting and surrounding them, I can't help thinking of these two communities as a scientific exploration story gone awry. . . . An enthusiastic and resource-rich Earth sends out two crews of astronaut pioneers to settle the first extraterrestrial colonies in outer space. The groups land on a couple of distant moons not far from each other and successfully assemble their rudimentary oxygen-pumped bubble domes.

No sooner have the spaceships been launched, however, then political and economic catastrophe back on Earth forces an immediate reversal of the commitment to space colonization. In fact, the very space agency that sent the groups out in the first place is shut down.

Over the years communication with the lunar stations fades until it practically ceases. After a few decades, the moon settlers are virtually forgotten back on Earth, only their relatives making any attempt to stay in touch.

The moon settlements survive thanks to their own resources, and they are proud of their success at surviving against the odds. But they are also disappointed: frustrated that the noble experiment for which they have offered their lives has been scrapped by their mother planet; resentful of each other for consuming the scarce supplies and manpower upon which they both depend. It would make more sense for the two space colonies to pool their resources and to merge on one of the moons but too many years of living apart and fashioning separate esprits de corps have hardened feelings against the idea.

Over the years a handful of the moon settlers are evacuated Earth-ward but experience a similar psychomedical syndrome. It appears that the oxygen from the lunar bubble domes, combined with the special extraterrestrial atmosphere, had induced a low level but steady state of euphoria that cannot be replicated on Earth. So unsatisfying is earthly air after space colony life that a couple of the evacuees even return to their moon homes. Those that manage to readapt to Earth nevertheless suffer, at some level, the ethereal want for the rest of their lives.

3

Why They Came to Yahel

No single reason explains why American Jews of affluent, solidly middle-class backgrounds would give up a comfortable economic future in the United States for life in a distant desert. Many of them, to be sure, came from families where Zionism meant more than dropping a few coins into the Jewish National Fund *pushka*, or collection box. Attending afternoon Reform religious school programs and participating in Temple-sponsored social events also helped create some future Yahelniks and Lotaniks. An early trip to Israel at an impressionable age disposed many an American to later become Israeli. But the self-selection leading to aliya to Yahel and Lotan often stemmed, just as importantly, from an opportune combination of American malaise and youthful idealism.

The term "malaise" is one that Jimmy Carter used to describe the country's psyche as it emerged from the post-Vietnam, post-Watergate traumas of the early 1970s. Carter was skewered by both pundits and politicians adverse to his gloomy "tell it like it is" characterization of the national mind-set. Ronald Reagan was to capitalize on Carter's frankness by providing an upbeat, if vacuous, alternative to the sobering, spiritual assessment provided by the pastor president from Plains, Georgia. But electoral outcomes apart, Carter had accurately diagnosed the spirit of the times.

For all of its waste and horror, the war in Vietnam had perversely provided a cause uniting hundreds of thousands of college and high school students around the country: opposition to it. With the war's ignominious end (for who could celebrate North Vietnam's takeover of the South in direct contravention of the Paris Peace treaties?), student activism—an activism that had attracted a substantial portion of Reform and unaffiliated campus Jews to its leadership—fragmented. Part of this fragmentation morphed into the identity politics that had already begun to percolate during the Vietnam War—minority empowerment, feminism, gay rights. But most anti-Vietnam War protesters did not find a political home in any of these smaller movements. The overarching cynicism engendered by Watergate (itself a reason for presidential abdication to Communist Vietnam) alienated an even larger proportion of the young from politics in general and from America as a redeemable polity. For a number of self-identified Jews of liberal persuasion—especially those who felt spurned by the fizzling Black-Jewish alliance and were stung when the nations of the world voted to equate Zionism with racism—this spiritual and ideological vacuum could most easily be filled by Israel. But not just Israel as a Jewish State (for any exclusive nationalism was suspect). It had to be Israel at its most ideal, at its most generous, at its most selfless. It had to be Israel of the kibbutz.

For some, there were less ideological, more psychological reasons. Several early Reform kibbutzniks were basically young American adults with postadolescent "issues" still seeking to "find themselves." Here is how one former Reform kibbutznik looks back at it.

> I had a really rough childhood and a really tough time through college. This was an escape for me, to get away from everything and everybody. You take a kid from [California], put him in the middle of a desert in Israel—no one knows anything about you. It's a whole different life. Why else would you go to the middle of nowhere? . . . Some people would take a new name—a Hebrew name—and be reborn. It was a huge attraction for me . . . to recreate myself . . . even though I didn't know so at the time.

Explanations provided both by Theodor Herzl and Sigmund Freud can coexist not only among the same group, but also within some of the very same individuals.

Specialists of migration often frame the decision to move in terms of "push" and "pull" factors. For the young Americans who wound up on Yahel (and also Lotan), the tug of ethnicity and attraction of Reform Judaism "pulled" them to Israel and to kibbutz life. At the same time, disillusionment with America or their particular circumstances in America "pushed" them to leave. The mix between push and pull is different for each individual, and few consciously in retrospect separated the "push" from the "pull" in analyzing their aliya decision. Still, no one immigrates *to* Israel without deciding to emigrate *from* some other country. Whatever emotional attachments they had to America, something about their birth land was insufficient to keep them from leaving.

But there were actually two levels of "push-pull" decision-making process going on for the American-born Yahelniks: first, to make aliya; and second, to do so to kibbutz. They could have settled in Israel without moving to (much less founding) a communal society. The migratory dynamics between Israel and America, kibbutz and "the city," fluctuate over time, if not over lifetimes.

THE EARLY YEARS ON YAHEL

Kibbutz was a heady experience for those who came to visit in the early 1970s. "It was beautiful," says Elad, recalling his days at another kibbutz, Kfar Blum, in the Galilee. "Manicured lawns. Cultural people having tea at 4:00 in the afternoon. Other people playing music—string quartets and such—outside on the patio." But it was a life of leisure earned by hard work, by rising early to weed cotton fields in the heat of July. Not even a severe bout of dehydration, landing Elad in bed for a couple of days, deterred him.

On another kibbutz the young man still named Lloyd found himself driving a tractor through cotton and sugar beet fields—"like a proletarian hero," he says, without obvious irony—and comparing this new persona to the one he had left behind. "I didn't know any Jew on Long Island who could fix their own bicycle or start a car if it wouldn't start. I just figured that was how the world was, that you called in the Gentiles" for practical, technical repairs. "But suddenly, not only were all the Jews around me being garage mechanics, electricians, and plumbers, but *I* was even doing it. What a feeling! It was really intoxicating."

Danny Hayken, from suburban Cleveland, also discovered a new side to himself through old-fashioned labor. "I was a good Jewish boy. I played Monopoly, board games, and sports but I didn't know anything about work, hard work. I wasn't a gardener, I wasn't a Mr. Fixit, I wasn't one of those who took things apart and repaired them. But on-kibbutz I did it and really loved it. Working with my hands, working with the land—grapefruit trees, pruning, harvesting crops—I learned that the hard work gave me something. I didn't know then about committees and all that stuff. I just fell in love with the lifestyle of kibbutz."

Ron Bernstein, from suburban New York, decided to pursue agriculture during his senior year of high school, the second half of which he spent working in a kibbutz cotton field. Ron eventually went on to earn a degree in agricultural engineering at the University of Delaware, after which he moved to Yahel.

Consciously or not, the intoxicating empowerment that American Jewish boys felt when they first began to create and repair things with their delicate suburban hands harked back to the century-old labor-love Zionism of A. D. Gordon. Gordon had exhorted the ghettoized Jewish youth of Eastern Europe to redeem their alienated selves by redeeming the ancestral land. Such ideas were old hat for Israelis of the 1970s, for whom the effetism of Diaspora *Yiddishkeit* had long since given way to the reality of living in a settled and industrialized Jewish State. It was a modern Jewish State (*medinat Yisrael*) that still cultivated, naturally and tangibly, love of the ancient Jewish land (*eretz Yisrael*). But for young, male, middle-class Jews from America, Gordon's old notion of purifying one's soul by doing with one's hands could still spark a revelation.

And the women?

Although the thrill of "building something new" is a common theme among the American-born female kibbutzniks too, that "something new" is usually expressed in more social terms. It was the challenge of building a new community within a whole life Jewish framework. Lori Stark, who was born in 1959 and grew up in Cranston, Rhode Island, well recalls the days of picking peppers, cucumbers, and tomatoes by hand, collecting the produce in heavy orange buckets. But more satisfying was the sense that she had found a "100 percent, twenty-four hour a day" Jewish lifestyle, with a permanent sense of community and ethno-religious identity. "It all meshed together."

Lori contrasts early impressions of kibbutz with her experience working for Israel Bonds in Washington, D.C., an otherwise good job but one that reinforced the compartmentalization of Jewish life in America. It was an experience fraught with social frivolities and petty politics, "lots of social ritual, who sits next to who, who gives more money." Yahel, on the other hand, was the antithesis: a genuine Jewish community, filled with energetic people of high quality, a place where you knew your neighbor and which provided emotional security. The ambience was infectious, with "jokes flying all around, mystery quizzes, mind games." It was heady for the nineteen-year-old New Englander.

Still, Lori was reticent about making a lifelong commitment to something that smacked more of adolescent vacation than permanent lifestyle. "Summer camp is fine—but you don't want to live in summer camp" forever. Back in America, however, even after marrying Drew Stark, a Californian she'd met in Israel, the kibbutz beckoned. "If I wasn't living in Yahel, I thought I would be missing something." In 1981, Lori and Drew returned, for good, to Yahel.

Whole-life Judaism was critical for Lori. In America, there was a split between the religious and the secular spheres. But in Israel, "it all meshes together. My Judaism didn't have to be a section of my life. It could be a natural, 100 percent, twenty-four hour a day experience." Especially on-kibbutz.

MIDDLE-AGED OLD TIMERS

Lori Stark was not the first bride on Yahel, however: that distinction goes to Laura Sperber of Roslyn, Long Island. Laura, who was born in 1954, was already married to a younger man, Matthew of Great Neck, when the two settled on Yahel in 1977. (To be sure, Matthew is only one year younger than Laura but in '72–'73 that meant that the Wesleyan freshman co-ed was going out with a high school senior!) Indeed, Laura and Matt are the "elder" couple of the community—a sobering realization for a visitor in his mid-forties. As living repositories of the original spirit of Kibbutz Yahel, however, they remain in some ways the youngest of the kibbutzniks.

Although I spoke with Laura and Matt separately, the same, curious phrase crept into each of their stories: "professional Jew." It is a role that they both eschew, but that encapsulates what they very well may have become had they remained the good, Reform, American Jews that their family backgrounds had prepared them for. And what exactly, I asked Laura, is a "professional Jew?"

"A professional Jew is someone who makes a living in the Jewish community as a rabbi or a Jewish educator. It is not just your lifestyle but your profession. Part of our fear was that if Reform Judaism has a right to exist it has to be viable as a way of life, not just for people for whom it is a profession."

The decision to marry, and to live together in Israel, concretized during a "test the waters" year in the mid-1970s. Together they enrolled at the Hebrew University in Jerusalem. The student Sperbers were heavily influenced by the progressive Zionist professor-philosopher David Hartman, whose courses and lectures they attended religiously. Hartman, says Laura,

> talked a lot about the Jewish State being the testing ground for whether Judaism really had a reason to exist in the modern age. The only way this could really be tested was in a Jewish State. This was

the time and place, a challenge for the evolution and development of Judaism in a real, full, twenty-four hour a day Jewish context, with Jewish policemen and Jewish hospitals and Jewish laws.

Matthew uses the word "revolution" to describe this new Judaism, seizing on "the opportunity to create the future of the Jewish people."

The young Sperbers could imagine a Judaism that was not only non-Orthodox but close to their own anti-rabbinic (i.e., democratic) tendencies. A "dynamic, vibrant, living Judaism," fantasized Laura, in which the community as whole, not any "professional Jew," would collectively decide questions of Jewish livelihood, agriculture, business, ethics, holidays, and life cycle events. This meant settling a Reform kibbutz: "the first reformed (*sic*) Jewish community," Matt still describes with brio. "A progressive, non-Orthodox, liberal Jewish community. And we were determined to be a part of it!"

Laura stresses the excitement of "starting something new," a "feeling of almost unlimited potential" shared by all of the founders. It was a "tremendous opportunity to have an impact on the direction being taken, the decisions being made, the formation" of the kibbutz and its atmosphere. In hindsight, though, the mother of the oldest child of the kibbutz (nineteen-year-old Shira) admits to "a lot of uncertainty and nonsense and childishness and stupid decisions" of those early times. It was a period of emotional growing pains, "of trying to decide what we're going to do and where we're going ." As one whose married life has coincided almost completely with her kibbutz experience, even when the collective will and direction have teetered, Laura has always (as has husband Matt) been able to fall back on the immediate partnership with her spouse. Some kibbutzniks, in contrast, have had to choose between significant other and the kibbutz collective.

DOCTOR, RABBI, OR KIBBUTZNIK?

Few Reform kibbutzniks have the pedigree of Daniel Hayken (b. 1956) of Cleveland Heights. Danny's great-grandfather, a 1903 graduate from the Hebrew Union College, had been a Reform rabbi in Vicksburg, Mississippi. His grandson, Danny's father, was not only a rabbi but Midwest regional director for the Reform synagogues' youth movement. Even Danny's sister eventually became a Reform rabbi. Yet such rabbinic family ties did not make him a likely candidate for kibbutz life. To the contrary, Reform Judaism is an American life path, not one expected to lead to Israel.

As a boy, Danny—now sporting a goatee but still with a youthful laugh and sparkling eyes—was lukewarm about Israel. "We knew about and studied it but it wasn't ours. It didn't belong to us." At the age of nine, he had the choice of accompanying his family on an archeological dig in Israel, or spending the summer with his grandparents in Florida. Danny opted for Fort Lauderdale.

Eight years later, in the wake of the Yom Kippur War, Danny came under even more intense Zionistic family pressure. "The Jewish people were always very important to my family. When the war broke out my father turned to me and said, 'Maybe you should think about going to Israel to be a volunteer.' There was a crisis within the Jewish people at that time but my parents couldn't [so easily] pick up and go.

"My father suggested this in October. I remember very clearly. I told him to get lost."

On a lark, during his sophomore year at the University of Rochester, Danny attended an out-of-town youth conference convened by an Israeli *shaliach* (immigration emissary) sent to organize young "closet Zionists" dispersed throughout the Reform movement. It was a long, Columbus Day weekend and he had no Monday tests. "You're paying?" he quizzed the inviter. "Sure, I'll come. Why not?"

The importance of the convention was to gather together, perhaps for the first time, like-minded Jewish kids with a penchant for Israel. "There might be this love of Zion but there was absolutely no cognizance, no ability to express it." It was important to realize "that this was something that some of us shared."

Danny was immediately drawn to the other kibbutz-headed college kids—"fantastic people, with dreams"—whom he met that weekend. "It was good Jewish, good Reform stuff about how you want to live your life and how to express a mitzvah," a religious obligation. "It was fun, intellectual, very exciting and the people were great." Danny's ambitions soon veered away from the expectations that family and family friends had for him, the liberal arts scholar.

"In college I was a premed student," Danny explained over dinner in our small kibbutz kitchen, the night before a trip back to the States to see his children. "I was enrolled in religious studies as well. So everybody kept asking me what I was going to do. I didn't know." Conversations with friends and family followed a virtual script.

"What do you study?"

"Biology, chemistry, and religious studies."

"Oh, are you going to be a doctor? You going to be a rabbi?"

Danny was at a loss to answer. He had already joined an aliya group. He was already committed to leaving America. Eventually, he came out with it.

"I'm moving to Israel and helping to start the first Reform kibbutz." That invariably triggered a collective dropping of jaws among friends of his parents. "It was unheard of" in those days. But Danny found that deep down, the more he said it, the more he liked saying it. "It felt great. It *sounded* great.

"It just was right, okay? It wasn't that I needed direction. It just fit the pieces of my history," a history that links the personal with the collective. "As one of my rabbis liked to put it, 'Israel is the Broadway of Jewish life. Not everyone can play on Broadway—but if you can, that's the place to be.'"

Over the next two years, Danny and his Arava group mates prepared themselves by spreading the Zionist word at Reform movement programs and camps. The summer before their actual departure for Israel seven of Danny's group of ten spent a training period together in Wisconsin. When it was over they had a big farewell party at the airport. "Some parents disowned their children. 'How could you do this to us?'" they cried. "But my parents realized that it was just another expression of the faith that they cared about, just a different way to do it.

"The side joke in our family," Danny offered as an afterthought, "is that once my sister decided to become a rabbi, it became off-limits for me. 'She wants to do that, well, I have to do my own thing.'" Only many years later did Danny discover that his sister had been thinking along similar lines, suppressing her own Zionist inclinations for his sake. But brother's moving to Israel prompted sister to tell herself that aliya was no longer for her. "That's Dan's thing."

"It worked out very well," Danny reflected. "She is the better rabbi, and I think I am the better kibbutznik."

In fact, Danny is the ultimate kibbutznik, the individual who has sacrificed the conventional path of love and family for unshakeable commitment to the group.

After eight years or so of living on Yahel, Danny fell in love with an American graduate of Hebrew University, a medical student, who had returned one summer to "reconnect" with Israel. A mutual friend in Jerusalem introduced him to the woman I'll call Miriam. "I decided it was more important for Miriam to finish her education," Danny says. "I then left the kibbutz with the goal of coming back. I just didn't know how long it was going to take."

The original plan was to get married and live in the States only for the necessary time for Miriam to obtain her medical degree. Then the couple would return to Israel, and to kibbutz. But the plan slowly unraveled under vocational pressures.

As it turned out, "it wasn't just medical school. It was doing an internship. Then it was a residency. What was supposed to be one, two, three years turned into seven plus. The relationship became very strained. One of the critical issues was Israel." In the meantime, Danny and Miriam brought four little ones into the world.

Having the children drew Miriam closer to her parents. They, living nearby, naturally developed strong attachments to the grandchildren. "It became harder for Miriam to leave them, to take the grandchildren away from the grandparents," Danny explains matter-of-factly. Just as coolly, he recounts how personal complications intertwined with yuppy materialism.

"Miriam got caught up in the whole doctor business in the United States. Being a professional. The level you can live at," compared to Israel, where the status and income of doctors is so much lower than in America. "But I never gave up my dream and desire to live back here.

"You have never been able to take the kibbutznik out of me," Danny states, in a tone that is simultaneously defensive and assertive. "Even after eleven years in the States, it was still a part of me. In a way, I lived in exile—not just exile from Israel, but exile from who I was." Exile from the kibbutz. "I worked for a company but it wasn't mine. It didn't belong to me. I traveled and saw beautiful sights, but it wasn't my home. They weren't my mountains. It wasn't my people."

Tested again, in a similar way, the tennis playing, sabbath sermonizing, erudite electrician makes the same choice. "As I was going through my divorce, I met a woman in a similar situation, and we became involved. Her husband was Israeli, a lawyer, and they had lived on a kibbutz up north for eight years. They had two kids and she too was concerned about the children being able to see their father from time to time. She was a great woman and we developed a relationship.

"She liked kibbutz life, and said that she definitely could see herself living on one again."

" 'Great,' I said, 'so come down to Yahel and check it out with me.' "

She came down with her kids, and it was a disaster. "You have to remember that although they had all lived on and loved kibbutz, theirs was never that far from a city, from a shopping center, from a mall. And here— well, you know, it's a desert. We're isolated, there's little entertainment.

Her kids complained from the beginning and she herself didn't take to it. So in the end I had to say, 'You're free to leave, but I'm staying.'" Dan, once again, chose his love for Yahel over a woman.

He loves his children and periodically returns to the States to be with them. Yet his true home is with the community in the desert. Tragically, it is a commitment that legal qualms prevent from being requited. Because his divorce with Miriam is still pending, the kibbutz, fearful of exposing its resources to claims for alimony, has not yet accepted Danny back as a full member. Technically, he is an employee (albeit one with a hybrid status especially created for him). It is the ultimate irony—the ultimate kibbutznik whose full-blown membership in the community is stymied on account of his painful sacrifices for it.

FAMILY SEEKER

By her own account, Nancy Reich Immerman grew up in an upper middle-class family in a fairly wealthy town: Larchmont, New York. She, too, was "bitten by the bug" at fifteen, during a summer youth tour sponsored by the Reform movement. Spurred by a miserable first year at New York University, Nancy applied to an academic year program in Israel, sponsored by the Reform movement. That was the year that Yahel was founded. Nancy attended the dedication ceremony, connected with a number of the founding and soon-to-be members, and began to feel that this was a place where she could live.

For sure, Nancy felt the intoxication and excitement of being part of something new, of joining the "religious pioneers." But she coolly admits that, as the child of parents who were divorced when she was three (Nancy was born in 1957), kibbutz appealed to her pragmatic side.

> One thing that I missed growing up, and in my particular constellation, was extended family. I grew up in a dysfunctional family and had been looking for community since the age of fourteen. Community and extended family drew me to the kibbutz.

Although neither of her parents was outright pleased with her decision to become a kibbutznik, each dealt with it differently. "My mother was always more supportive. In the end she even reconciled herself to the idea and was very proud of me." But, she adds ruefully

> my father never really became reconciled to the idea and thought I was wasting my time. He thought kibbutz is a cop-out, and thought

I could be doing better things with my life. I'll give you a guess with whom I had a better rapport. . . .

Relatively soon after joining the Garin Arava, the group of future Yahelniks, Nancy went to work as a representative of the Reform movement to recruit other young Americans temporarily in Israel to come to the kibbutz or to join some other long-term Reform program. "It was a difficult time. I felt that I had too much independence and not enough guidance. I didn't feel that I had much success at what I was doing." So Nancy, still a member of Yahel, returned to New York to work at the Reform movement headquarters, coincidentally within walking distance of Hunter College to which she transferred. But the pressures of working and studying full time were too great: she quit, returned to Israel, and has been living on Yahel since 1980. "Coming to Israel was not just doing something because it was good and positive," she acknowledges, "it was also rejecting something. The United States as a whole, this big, capitalistic, consumer society."

SCARSDALE ZIONIST

With her long legs, beautiful big eyes, short-cut hair and attractive face, the no-nonsense, hard-hitting, cigarette-smoking mazkira (kibbutz manager) from Scarsdale could be a poster girl for the kibbutz movement. As the secretary-general of Yahel, Liora is the first among the community's equals: elected for a three year term, she manages the kibbutz affairs from the central office while having to persuade, cajole, and wheedle fellow members to go along with her managerial inclinations. In many ways, the position of the kibbutz mazkir is similar to that of a department chair in a university: lots of responsibility with limited power. Liora may be in charge of the kibbutz's general administration but that does not exempt her from Shabbat dining hall setup and cleanup rotation.

Liora insists that her background—having grown up as the fourth child in a staunchly Reform Zionist family in New York—is atypical. "My father's parents were the driving force behind our strong Zionistic ties. They spoke Hebrew with us." Although still with a whiff of a New York accent, Liora chooses her words in English deliberately, often resorting to Hebraic vocabulary when her mother tongue fails her. It is common for American immigrants to sprinkle their English with Hebrew terminology. Liora is linguistically Hebraicized more than most American-born Yahelniks.

When she says that she grew up "in a traditional Jewish home," Liora means typical New York suburban. "We were what my mother called 'kosher style.' In the house, we wouldn't mix milk with meat but then again we didn't have only kosher meats. Outside the house we would eat non-kosher." Synagogue attendance (her parents helped found a Reconstructionist *shul*) was limited to high holidays and bar and bat mitzvah celebrations, but it was definitely Israel that constituted the anchor of the family's Jewish identity. Indeed, her mother and father would themselves eventually make aliya, in 1975, before Liora did. And her father's parents—at age eighty-three—permanently moved to Israel two years after that.

At the age of fourteen, having had several seasons in Zionist summer camps in the States, Liora got to spend her first summer in Israel, living with her sister's Israeli in-laws. Each of the next three summers she spent on a kibbutz designed to put Americans in contact with kibbutz kids of the same age.

"It was great. The fifteen, sixteen, and seventeen-year-olds lived on their own. Not at home, and not in the children's houses. They have their own separate campus. Such freedom. Unbelievable. And these kibbutz kids were very open to hosting me. It was a very empowering experience."

But three years later, after graduating from high school in Scarsdale and preparing studies at Tel Aviv University, adolescent Liora was less enchanted with kibbutz life. "I said, 'Nice. Nice experience, nice to be with people so intensely, socially involved but I'd *never* live in a kibbutz.'" The eighteen-year-old's disenchantment solidified in a most down-to-earth detail: footwear. "Seeing all these kibbutznikim walking around in the same—hmm, they call them *na'alei bayit*—these slippers with a zipper on them. All the patterns are the same. A checkered brown, beige, black kind of color" she recalls, still cringing like a fashion critic at the tastelessness of it all. "And I thought, 'This is like a factory—a factory for putting out kibbutznikim.' I'm not going to get involved in this in the future."

Living in Israel, on the other hand, did become all the more natural, now that both her parents and grandparents were living there. Liora had finished her program at Tel Aviv University and was thinking about joining the army.

Joining the army? What could be more incongruous, in an American context, than for a lithe, attractive, left-leaning, Jewish girl from Scarsdale to sign up for a stint in the military? Yet for Israel, where the army serves as a microcosm of society itself, what could be more natural?

"I remember speaking to my grandfather about it. It was important for me to get his opinion because he was such a dynamic force, you know, as far as the Jewish identity goes." Tears come to her eyes as Liora recalls her departed grandfather. But Liora didn't receive the grandfatherly approval she sought. "It was foreign to him, with his own values and how he was brought up, that women serve in the army." Nevertheless, in November 1976, Liora volunteered. As part of her service as a new immigrant, the girl from Westchester was posted to a kibbutz on the Jordanian border in the Arava: Yotvata, near Yahel. Liora smiles at her naïve imaginings of the experience: sleeping in tents, sitting around campfires, living without electricity. Still, the "unique beauty" of the desert spoke to Liora and she was hooked.

After her military service, Liora decided to stay and live in the Arava, in the only real way possible—on-kibbutz. But not Yotvata. Like most kibbutzim, Yotvata was staunchly secular—irreligious, one could say—and reminded Liora of her unpleasant Yom Kippur experiences on her teenage year kibbutz. "They had a sign-up sheet for people who were going to fast. There were only ten of us!" Even for a mildly observant Jew from secular New York, it was hard to swallow that fasting on Yom Kippur would make one a member of a small minority—in an otherwise tight-knit Jewish community, no less! "But on Yahel, Reform Judaism was the basic platform."

So it was on Yahel that Liora became a member and planned to make her life—before quitting. Hers is a common kibbutz tragedy, the recurring tension between the group's inflexible collective need and the individual's frustrated drive for intellectual enhancement. "I wanted to go back to university and study. But the kibbutz refused, and so I left." Fortunately, Liora's brush with dashed dreams drama took a redemptive turn.

"After three years of living in the city" (kibbutzniks tend to divide the social world into *on the kibbutz* and *in the city*), "I began missing the kibbutz. In the city, I was just another number. Here my number counted.

"I missed the social commitment. You just don't find that in the city. That sense of being an active partner in community building, in decision making, in giving of self. Relationships with people here are so much more intense."

It was more than the healthy air, predictable (if extreme) climate, and starkly beautiful physical surroundings that called out to her. Liora just felt that she had to come back. And come back she did, asking for reconsideration as a member. She did need to go through a second period of kibbutz "absorption" but, like the forgiven prodigal daughter, was voted in as a second-time member. "It's like being married, divorced, and remarried to the same guy," Liora observes, with a beseeching smile.

A NOTE ON THE REPULSION
OF KIBBUTZ SECULARISM

Remember Liora's discomfort in realizing that only a handful of others on a kibbutz would fast on Yom Kippur with her? It is noteworthy for two reasons. For one, Liora is hardly one of the "regulars" attending weekly Shabbat services on Yahel; not especially observant, she is nevertheless typical of the many "High Holiday Jews," in America as well as Israel, who are minimalist in overall observance but express disappointment with Jews who disregard Yom Kippur completely. Second, the nonreligious or an-tireligiousness prevalent on other kibbutzim markedly affected other future Yahelniks.

Danny Hayken was similarly disturbed by the casual, almost hostile, attitude to Judaism that he experienced during a previous sojourn at Neve Ur, a small kibbutz he lived on in the Bet Shean Valley before making aliya. For Danny as well as for several other American kibbutzniks, the decision to live on a Reform kibbutz was related to negative antireligious experiences they had had on more typical, secular, kibbutzim. Danny recalls his *hametzdik* (leavened bread) discomfiture.

"On Pesach I don't want to touch bread and I don't want it around, okay? But a lot of people eat bread on a secular kibbutz. [The attitude was] 'You want matzah, eat matzah; you want bread, eat bread.'

"So they put matzah in the [regular] basket and then just put the bread on top of it. I used to have to dig through the bread in the bin to get to the matzah underneath." Danny's disgust is palpable, as he recalls his kibbutz matzah fishing ordeal. *And this,*" went the subtext, "*in Israel, of all places.*"

It is not only potential kibbutzniks from America who preferred Yahel for its "noncoercive" Judaism, as Reform Israelis like to describe their brand of the faith. Haifa-born Idit, now forty-three and a member of Yahel since 1977, tried out her husband Ari's kibbutz near the Lebanese border before choosing between his home and hers. "For the last day of Sukkot [the Festival of Booths], they just told the children to dress up. But they didn't teach them that it was Simchat Torah [celebrating the end-of-cycle reading of the Five Books of Moses]. They didn't know what Simchat Torah is. To be in a place that really ignores everything which is Jewish—I didn't want it." This older kibbutz didn't perpetrate mere ignorance of Judaism. "In the middle of Yom Kippur," Idit relates matter-of-factly, "they had a pork barbeque."

COWBOY RON: LONG ISLAND JEWISH "AGGY"

"How did a nice Jewish boy from Plainview wind up on a kibbutz in the desert?" I jokingly ask the tall, sunburned, lanky ex-Long Islander with the bushy mustache and lined, weathered face. Ron Bernstein (born in 1954) is dressed as always: sneakers, jeans, and signature Australian outback hat. Instead of a six-shooter, in the holster dangling from his waist, he sports a leatherman, a kind of souped-up Swiss army knife. Another small hip pocket contains a knife; still another, the ubiquitous Israeli cell phone.

When Ron smiles, the grin is wide enough to crack the pomelos ("grandfather of the grapefruit") whose cultivation and export is one of his major occupations. It's not only a pleasant, but also a useful exterior demeanor, for Ron is Yahel's public relations guy, the number one kibbutz tour guide, the first (and sometimes only) Yahelnik that one-day visitors to the Reform desert kibbutz get to meet.

But Ron doesn't always smile. Indeed, there is a sad aura that never seems to leave his face entirely. With good reason: Ron and his Israeli-born wife Gila are the only kibbutz couple to have lost a child on Yahel. But that would be many years hence . . .

What was it like in the early days?

I'm not really sure how I can describe it. Kibbutz was very naïve then. We were all young and idealistic. I don't think any of us knew what we were doing, really. We had no real direction. It was exciting because it was something very new. We were starting from scratch.

Most companies, most firms would never take a group of twenty-year-olds and say, "take this multimillion dollar business and make a community." But the Jewish Agency, the kibbutz movement and the Reform movement were telling these kids to put together this conglomerate. That's basically what it was. We didn't have the experience to do anything like that. They just took a bunch of kids to do the work.

(Laura Sperber describes those same early days in the language of the ex-student: "Except for the fact that people were working during the day than studying, it was more similar to a university dormitory than to a community that lived together. Young people partying until late at night and sleeping into late in the morning. Evening entertainment was thirty people crowding into one person's room and hanging out and listening to music. The social life was very groupie in the way that university social life is.")

Until his father took his family along on a sabbatical in 1971, the fifteen-year-old Ron didn't know anything about Israel. That trip was his father's own way of repairing an old regret: on his way back from India during World War II, he decided at the last minute not to jump ship along with some of his buddies when their transport carrier approached Palestine.

Ron admits that, at first, the religious ideal of building a Reform community per se was rather incidental for him. "Starting kibbutz was more exciting for me, more romantic. I was really almost antireligious in many ways. But I guess I mellowed out over the years . . ." Ron now attends kibbutz services every Friday night. "I like the feeling."

BROOKLYN-BRED LEFTIST

Every community requires a dissident, a gadfly to give it spice. Rosealie Sherris is Yahel's pimento, its tabasco. She acknowledges that she has acquired the reputation, in Israeli terms, of being "the local sociomath," she who

> frequently, freely criticizes the society, is the troubleshooting [troublemaking?], finger-pointing, bucking, grinding axes, building little fires, sticking pins into voodoo dolls to sabotage the peace and quiet of the "bucolic and inordinately comfortable" kibbutz scene.

Whereas most members describe their life path to Yahel as consistent with their Zionist and/or Reform Jewish backgrounds, Rosealie describes her own trajectory there in tones bordering on the absurd; most mildly, it was a "chain of coincidental circumstances" that brought her to kibbutz with her husband.

It certainly was not religion. "Disillusionment with the postindustrialist capitalist society," yes. "Getting off the fast track," for sure. And romance. "Romance had a lot to do with it. Romantic, idealistic notions."

Yet even before marrying the man with whom she would settle at Yahel, Rosealie had visited southern Israel.

> In 1975 I was in a group of American university students who were taken to this part of the country from a settlement on the Lebanese border. It was part of the tour of southern Israel which at the time to us seemed pretty desolate and undeveloped. We stopped at Ketura in its founding year. A member got up on a bomb shelter and spoke to us in American-accented Hebrew and English about the cause of settling the southern Arava. It was pretty incomprehensible to us.

All we saw was someone whom we saw as a semi-psychotic, babbling Jewish dreamer, ranting on about flower growing and dairy.... Cows, flowers, and a dining hall, while standing on a hillock on this empty sand hill.

("Today," Rosealie adds, "Ketura is one of the most 'green' kibbutzim in our area—physically, psychologically, politically.")

Because her husband was a skier, they started out on a kibbutz in the far north, in the Golan Heights, which if not quite Alpine, does provide decent downhill thrills under Jewish sovereignty. But Rosealie and Aryeh (a Jew by choice) did not fit the profile of the Golan kibbutz absorbees and, accompanying friends to an interview in Tel Aviv, met a "very clever" recruiter for the Arava kibbutzim. They got "sucked in" and, on an exploratory visit to Yahel, just felt that "the chemistry was right." Six months later, the couple packed up their books, records, and stereo and, in a marathon drive, traversed the virtual entire length of the country. They arrived in July, "the month of five inch cockroaches" and over hundred degree temperature, stunned to encounter an amazingly enthusiastic bunch of Jewish grape pickers.

"They were into the blue collar thing," recalls Rosealie, "you know, 'kibbutz, ra-ra, macho, Zionist.' All very exciting and attractive. It was like love,"

dazzlement with love! So there we were. A year later we became members and two years later our daughter was born. Very much according to the schedule that we had set up.

Unlike most newcomers at Yahel, Rosealie and Aryeh had already lived together for half a decade and arrived prepared to start a family. "We knew that we wanted a place to live and raise our girls. We were very much into all of the interesting academic ideas that come with communal education."

Rosealie was satisfied during her first thirteen years being a "professional kibbutznik," working in service branches. But, as she recalls ruefully: "My work life was not connected to my identity as a painter."

Maintaining individual expression within the collective framework: few Americans in their twenties, excited about founding and settling the first Reform Jewish kibbutz in history, anticipated that this would become an issue. Especially when they would hit their forties.

Yahel Photos

Yahel, as seen from a nearby hill.

Entrance road to Yahel.

On the borderline with Jordan.

Main office of Yahel.

Yahel synagogue-cum-community center.

Some of the 12,000 books in Yahel's library, attached to the synagogue.

Yahel dairy.

Kibbutz store.

"Pedal power" on the kibbutz.

Yahel playground.

Yahel dining hall.

In the kitchen.

Elad Lending, with Buffy.

Liora Cohen, Yahel "mayor" (*mazkira*), who grew up in Scarsdale, New York.

Ron Bernstein, formerly of Plainview, Long Island.

Ex-Brooklynite Rosealie Sherris with her "sabram" daughter Rachel.

Matityahu (Matthew) Sperber, formerly of Great Neck, Long Island.

Teenage kibbutznik, Na'ama Shimoni, soon to the army.

Shari Bernstein, daughter of Ron and Gila.

Yonatan Maximon rests in Yahel cemetery.

Tomb of Shai Bernstein.

Thai workers at Yahel.

Abu Jama, Bedouin host for visitors to Yahel.

The Sperbers: Laura, Mati, Shira.

Erica and Elad Lending perform at services.

Bar mitzvah lesson for Gadi Lending.

4

Why They Came to Lotan

THE VISIONARY

"My father always said I wouldn't have problems writing in Hebrew," wryly recounts left-handed Daniel Burstyn. Yet neither of them imagined, during his childhood in New Jersey, that Hebrew would one day become Daniel's language of daily life.

In this heartland of Philip Rothdom, Jewishly as well as financially, Daniel's South Orange was a competitive environment to grow up in. His peers vied to come up with ever bigger bar mitzvah parties. "I couldn't compete in their league," he still recalls in irony tinged with bitterness.

Pony-tailed, mustached, and bearded, Daniel looks at you with piercing blue Jewish eyes. His parents met each other in synagogue; one of his sisters would become a Reconstructionist rabbi; after his bar mitzvah, he went to Hebrew high school. Feminism and equality, along with Judaism, were family values. Seeds for choosing a progressive whole Jewish lifestyle were planted young, and solidified by a visit to Israel after high school.

Yet in college, at Rutgers University Daniel led a religiously bifurcated life—quite Jewish at moments of ritual, secular the rest of the time. The Hillel youth group scene at Rutgers "disgusted" him: "People were gambling while waiting to go into services." As a theater major, he drifted away from living Jewishly. (Or at least he thought he did—in New Jersey, he jokes in retrospect, even the Gentiles speak Yiddish.)

It was during a junior year in England that Daniel experienced what living in a truly non-Jewish environment was like. To his surprise, he missed being with other Jews, and so joined a Jewish club. Nevertheless, it was in Scotland, among an ecumenical group of spiritually motivated seekers, that Daniel first experienced life in an intentional community. The meditation center "was sixty-ish, like a commune." But sister Gail, then living in Israel, provided Zionist counterbalance.

Back at college, Daniel "no longer had the place in the community" he'd had. He was ripe for a "vision"—that his "path in life was to bring Judaism and New Age spirituality together. It was very clear." The next day he chanced upon a bookstore that was closing down. The only Judaica book left on the shelves was authored by the modern mystic pioneer of the Jewish Renewal Movement, Rabbi Zalman Schachter. It was another sign, he felt. In 1985, after graduation, Daniel left for Israel to study Hebrew on a kibbutz. His search for one "with Jewish content" eventually led him to New Wave, a group of American Jews planning on establishing a progressive community. It is through this group that he met Eliza Mayo, whom he would later marry. After dabbling with a number of experimental communities (including one which "behaved like a cult"), Daniel and Eliza envisioned their ideal kibbutz (kosher kitchen, liberal Jewish expression, economic and social stability); they narrowed down their choices to some of the Arava kibbutzim. Yahel had just gone through "massive changes" and was not socially "stable" (in other words, lots of folks were leaving). Membership at Kibbutz Ketura was a bit too old; but in Lotan, Daniel and Eliza "felt a click." They moved there in 1990.

Daniel Burstyn wants to inhabit a "vibrant, creative Jewish community in a rural area" and is not sure that it exists elsewhere in the world but on Lotan.

The sensitive, spiritual-seeker first worked as a kibbutz cook; then in a date factory; and then, for three years, served in the army. When we spoke, he was working as a landscaper but making plans for rabbinical school. It was, he ruefully admitted, what his father had been telling him to do all along. Daniel and Eliza have a daughter and son.

FROM NEW JERSEY NERD TO KIBBUTZ MANAGER

By her own admission, Eliza Mayo was a New Jersey nerd: "a Goody Two-shoes who loved Hebrew School" and as a result was "not in the cool clique"—not even among the other Reform Jewish teenagers. Ebullient and enthusiastic, this speed-speaking mazkira (director) of Lotan shows not a trace of awkwardness from her childhood days outside of Newark. She is brown-eyed and freckled, almost *gingy* (reddish-complexioned), her long, brunette braid tied into a little rose at the end. Her denims have holes and the T-shirt covering her very full bosom—for she is still nursing her son—is dirty. She loves it. For Eliza, Zionism is more than the abstract belief that Israel is the Jewish homeland. *That* kind of Zionism is no more than "believing in marriage":

> If you don't find the right person, and have a click in your gut, then you're not just going to go out and get married. It can't work. I could give you beautiful, intellectual, ideological reasons why I live in Israel. But the truth is that, in my gut, I knew that where I belonged was in Israel. . . . I am at home here in a way that I am not in America.

Eliza's "click" came when she was only seventeen. It had been nurtured since high school with a network of like-minded Zionists of Young Judea (a group with whom she broke during college for political reasons). At Cornell, she gravitated to the more leftist New Wave Zionists. It was there that Eliza had the next significant "click" in her life—Daniel Burstyn. The two made aliya together in 1989 and, disillusioned with the cult-like direction the New Wave commune was taking, began kibbutz shopping.

Eliza distinguishes between starting up a kibbutz and seeking one out. Preexisting realities in established communities force you to identify your fundamental values and dreams. You can hope to change the direction of the community somewhat. But better to think of it as a wedding.

> You're not going to marry someone thinking, "Well, he's kind of a *shlemazel* at his job right now. But I'll work on him, and he'll end up being manager. Then I'll feel okay about it." That's not a good way to start a marriage.

Yet even "when you're starting your own kibbutz," says Eliza, "you can imagine that it's going to be everything that you could possibly want it to be. And it can't. As a result, some people who were at Lotan from the very beginning fell very hard."

Suckling Eliza offers another analogy, describing herself as a "breast feeding fanatic."

> You have to be 100 percent committed to it and at the same time know that if it's not working for you, you can stop. If you're not 100 percent committed and willing to keep trying, then you'll very easily give up. But if you're fanatical and you *must* do this, if it's "life and death," then you're bound to have a crisis.
>
> Life on kibbutz is like that. Because if you're not committed, then it's really a hard way of life.

Being a kibbutznik, she says, is a "personality trait"—emphasizing the community over self. She admits that she and her husband perhaps go overboard in this respect. "Our house is a mess. *We're* a mess." Eliza and Daniel still hadn't found the time to celebrate their wedding anniversary.

Why does she stay? "It's a combination of ideological commitment and personal connection—family, friends. I'm respected by my peers. . . . At Lotan there is this constant hoping that who we are, and why we are, and who we want to be, and having meaning beyond survival of the community is important. That's part of what keeps me here."

BURGER KING ZIONIST

Some immigrant kibbutzniks pinpoint pivotal moments back home that capture their malaise with living as a Jew in America and prompted them to leave. Alex Cicelsky is one.

Grandson of a kosher dairy examiner and son of a Gentile mother, Alex grew up in upstate and metropolitan New York and in the suburbs of Boston. More than anything—more than the candle lighting and family dinner—Shabbat for Alex meant listening to Israeli music at home. A family trip to Israel, including a stay on a kibbutz, stoked his interest firsthand. A post-high school year (during which time he picked onions at Yahel) intensified it.

Back in the States, Alex did two years of college but didn't stick with it. His work experience in lower-class America (especially at Burger King) convinced him that "a lot of Americans look at Jews as a separate nationality." Yet it was difficult to delve into Judaism in the United States because he didn't want to be Orthodox, and the Reform movement was "white bread"—little Hebrew, not sufficiently Zionist.

But a Reform intentional community was different. "I've never established a kibbutz," he told himself. "Here are a bunch of people going over. Why not? It all made sense. It's still making sense."

Alex's Israeli army experience was also formative. Growing up during the anti-Vietnam movement, he felt that if ever he were to pick up a gun, his soul would spring from his body and declare: "I don't want to have anything to do with you anymore!" In the Israeli army, he realized, bearing arms really wasn't so difficult after all. "Most of my father's side of the family was killed in Europe during the Holocaust," he reasoned. "Being able to protect the family," nullified his American-bred, liberal antigun instincts.

A major reason for staying, for this slightly older Lotanik (born 1960) with frame glasses and fading, salt-and-pepper hair, is his children's education. "I don't want my kids to grow up in America and have to deal with Christmas holidays." In contrast, he notes, "before Passover they bring home little Moses in a reed basket . . ."

Alex's fourth-grader had just completed a year focussing on leadership. Alex is excited to recount his son's curriculum.

> That's really important in Israel for teachers after the assassination of Rabin. What textbook do you use? What resources? They went straight to Moses. There's a lot of material there, both bad and good. His abilities. Overcoming handicaps. Qualities of leadership. Where is authority? How the people respond. Then Aaron. The Book of Judges . . .
>
> So they do Bible studies, but not the religious stuff. And all this is happening at the secular school! You don't get *that* in America.

THIS IS NOT CHICAGO

Her brown hair is turning white, but her brown eyes still sparkle as Gwen Skully arrives for our chat in work boots. She is thirty-five and originally from Chicago. She fell in love with Israel during a high school summer trip with the Reform movement, and made aliya ten years before. For a kibbutznik, Gwen would seem to be over-degreed: a BA from Haverford, an MA degree from Yeshiva.

> It's so different from where I grew up. There's something refreshing about that. There's an attempt at equality.

Gwen praises the "variety of options" to work (although as a date orchard specialist, it is more difficult to be replaced there and rotated elsewhere.) "Especially as a woman." Equality of the sexes at Lotan "is not perfect," but more developed than on other kibbutzim. For instance, there is no expectation that it be the mother who, when the children get out of daycare in the afternoon, leaves the workplace to take care of them. "Here, it's clear that the father is just as likely" to get the children ready in the morning, or pick them up in the afternoon." Female Lotaniks are still commonly assigned jobs requiring physical labor, a fact to which Gwen points with pride (even though for her "the novelty of driving a tractor" has long since worn off.) Gwen, married to a British-born man she met at Lotan, has one-year-old twin boys. She had just finished a year off–kibbutz, in Eilat, working as a social worker on issues of family violence. Still, kibbutz is less radically other than she'd originally assumed: "Although I've come to realize that kibbutz has aspects of an almost suburban lifestyle—very quiet, more contact with people than in a city."

Gwen hangs on at Lotan, even though when she first came she was more of a Zionist than now—"more believing in the possibility of changing things in Israel, more trustworthy of Israeli government policies."

BIBLE EXPERT WITH THE MAIMONIDES SYNDROME

Eight years after I won the National Bible Contest as a high school student and traveled to Israel from New York to participate in the International competition, Daniel Meir did the same from Cincinnati. Daniel believes that he is the very first Reform Jew to have achieved that distinction. Then again, he was always precocious: from the time he was in fourth grade (his Reform college professor father having brought the family on sabbatical), Daniel knew that "Israel was the place for" him. That's not his only distinction: how many Jewish men can claim that, after they achieved adulthood, their mothers became rabbis?

Daniel didn't stay more than one year in college: "The United States was a material-oriented society. Ideals were lacking. Remember, this was the 1980s, the Yuppie generation. My life was not trying to make money. . . . I realized that the only thing I really knew that I wanted to do was to make aliya," he recalls. "I wanted to do the army, and do something meaningful."

A chance meeting landed Daniel a job working with the Israeli Reform movement in Haifa. He was very excited when he discovered plans to build Lotan. "The whole idea of *building* a kibbutz, a Reform Jewish community, was very appealing," he says. It still is, even though "many people think you're crazy to come to a place like this, so far away."

Lotan is a "magnet" for the World Reform movement, Daniel explains. Americans may be lagging, but young Jews from England, South Africa, and Australia make their way in significant numbers. "Holding together and strengthening the Reform movement among Israeli youth is what has kept me here," says the soft-spoken idealist with the broad and easy smile.

"We're no longer as young as we once were," admits the onetime Bible scholar. "Now that we have families, we have to build our ideal within in order to reach out."

As one of his kibbutz occupations, the premed dropout now pursues alternative medicine. "The Maimonides Syndrome," he jokes, staking out a rarefied realm somewhere between medicine and Jewish studies.

Daniel admits to occasional thoughts of leaving, as others have done in recent years. "When you live in a close, tight-knit community, personal tensions sometimes flare up." But for the mild-mannered Meir, departure fantasies stem more from feeling "constrained" geographically. Professional opportunities for his South American-born wife, who studied acting, are much more abundant "up north."

"But," he adds with a shrug, "so far we're here."

IDENTITY SEEKER

For most of the kibbutzniks I interviewed, the path from Reform Zionist upbringing to kibbutz aliya was, if not inevitable, still more or less straightforward. But for others the road to Lotan has been part of a lifelong resolution of an early identity crisis.

Brusque and steely at first encounter, answering the office phone in rapid-fire Hebrew, Ariela Shal, thirty-seven, is the perfect portrait of the no-nonsense sabra. Her swollen breasts, from nursing her seven-month-old son Pele, do little to offset the tough exterior she first projects. Under her jaunty South African-style cap and behind her round metallic glasses and faded "Interns for Peace" T-shirt, Ariela is a pretty woman—another Israeli trademark of the dressed down, unmade up female kibbutznik. That *this* authentic Israeli kibbutz woman originally hails from Los Angeles is incidental. That she was brought up as a Catholic certainly distinguishes her from the run-of-the-mill kibbutznik.

"My mother was originally Christian," Ariela offers, surprisingly early in the interview. "They had a civil wedding, my parents. She converted before I was born so that I would be Jewish." A common American story, particularly in Reform circles? Ariela goes on.

"When I was four they got divorced. My mother went back to being Christian and I lived with her." Before becoming a Reform Jew Ariela's mother had actually been Protestant. But in returning to Christianity she turned Catholic. "When I was between three and eight my mother was in the hospital a lot—a Catholic hospital. That's when she converted to Catholicism. I was baptized and went to Catholic school for a couple of years.

When Ariela was eight her mother died.

"I went to live with my father and his new wife, who was Jewish. They'd had a Jewish wedding when I was six—it was my first real Jewish experience. After that, they gave me the option of going to religious school." Young Ariela opted for it.

"The Jewish atmosphere was warmer and more colorful—more 'user-friendly'—than my experience in Catholic school and church." Israel was an important theme at her religious school. With her classmates Ariela even made a garden for their simulated kibbutz.

"My parents were classic Reform, what here would be considered secular." That amounted to observing the High Holidays, holding a Pesach Seder, and giving money to Jewish causes. They sent Ariela to Jewish camps in the summer. Then they made what Ariela laughingly calls their "fatal mistake"—when she was fifteen, they sent her on a summer trip to Israel. She visited her first kibbutz, and then Yahel. "I thought I'd seen the light—the chance to create, from scratch, something ideologically in tune with what I believe." Four years later, after realizing that even in America she was happiest in Jewish communal settings, Ariela returned to Israel for a full-year leadership program. Lotan was just being established. "It was the ultimate expression of what I was looking for—Israel, kibbutz, and Reform."

I asked Ariela if her parents really viewed sending her on that first summer trip to Israel as a "fatal mistake."

"The 'mistake' started when my father gave me a Hebrew name and named me after Aryeh Ben Canaan of *Exodus*. The seeds were planted way before."

"They're happy, but any time there's a terrorist attack, or a Gulf War, or any time they have a life cycle event there, like a family death, it's always a big thing. Even Father's Day."

However alienated Ariela was as a child—in terms of identity, in terms of religion—there is no ambiguity about her sense of self today. It is bound up with her drive to be politically active on social issues: Jewish renewal, Arab-Israeli coexistence, Palestinian rights, spiritual ecology. "I wasn't happy with the way things were anywhere. I made aliya because I thought I would have more impact on Israel" (it's a smaller country) "and because my leadership tendencies were ultimately more directed to Jewish contexts. More of my national identity was as a Jew than as an American. I felt more responsibility to the Jewish people than to the American people (if you can call that 'a people'). Here, I have a twenty-four hour Jewish community."

Ariela's intense rootedness as a desert kibbutz Jew should not be seen merely in contrast to her late mother's theological wandering, from lapsed Protestantism to Reform Judaism to death bed Catholicism. On her father's side, Ariela also has a couple of Buddhist uncles. One of them is a *roshi*—the Buddhist equivalent to revered rabbi.

FIRST BASE AND FULL COURT ZIONIST

Were the Reform kibbutz movement to choose a poster boy for an ad campaign, they could hardly do better than Michael Nitzan. Tall, athletic, good looking, until his Zionist background directed him to Israel, Michael played ball for the University of California at Los Angeles and Berkeley.

Born in 1959 and raised in southern California, Michael imbibed strong doses of Judaism and Zionism from his mother. So did his sister, who also went on to make aliya on-kibbutz. After college, Michael came to Yahel where he worked, in the early 1980s, in the date grove, in the absorption branch, in tourism, and even as kibbutz manager. Relatively few Reform kibbutzniks have gone on for a masters degree; Michael earned one at Hebrew University, in Jewish history.

Nor do even the most Zionistic of Jews still identify so readily with David Ben-Gurion as their hero, as does the former hoop shooter and first baseman. Yet Michael enthusiastically carries on Ben-Gurion's vision that Israel's future lies in the desert. Pioneering in the Arava is "mind-bending and back-breaking," admits the scholar-athlete. But it is precisely the physical connection to the land into which one sweats that solidifies the person-country link. "Ideology is the icing," for Michael. The essence is "home, identity."

"My father is disappointed because I didn't become a lawyer or a judge," shares the strapping kibbutznik. But it is for the sake of his own children—three of them, ranging from six to fourteen—that he remains where he is. "I don't want to have to deal with Halloween . . . with the Friday night dilemma—'Go out or do Shabbat.'" At Lotan, he continues, "I'm building for myself, my kids, my kibbutz partners." He doesn't do it to mold blindly obedient children, mind you: "I'd like my kids to rebel a bit," he dares.

You know that Michael would have been highly successful in whatever line he pursued back on the West Coast. "Had I stayed," he says with certainty, "I would be a retired baseball player today."

"We all have our baggage," he states, though he himself has few regrets. "You look at their lives," referring to his class peers who came to work for Bill Gates. "They think I'm nuts. But are they happier? It is hard to imagine his college friends saying of Microsoft, as Michael does of Lotan, "I relate to [it] like a family business."

"You can't put a monetary value on our quality of life," says the kibbutz-athlete. Even a "high powered" rabbi friend "doesn't get" why Michael does what he does. And vice versa.

"IS SOMEBODY REALLY GOING TO PUBLISH
  THIS BOOK?"

Happiest as an adolescent while in Jewish environments—summer camp,
College Academic Year in Israel—Wendy Weiss of Bay Ridge, Brooklyn felt
that she would remain happy if living permanently in the Jewish State. But
not just any which way: "I believed in the statement: 'If you are under
twenty-five and not a socialist, just have your heart examined. And if you
are over twenty-five and still a socialist, you have to have your head examined.' Well, I was under twenty-five. I believed very much in kibbutz."

Living in a whole Jewish environment also appealed to Wendy.
While in Israel, she was "enthralled" to see that, "Wow, everybody cele-
brates the same holiday."

Even growing up in New York you still get off on the Jewish holiday.
But still the majority of the population are playing stickball in the
street. They're not sitting in synagogues.

"This," Wendy said to herself about Israel, "is where I belong." As for a
career, she "flip-flopped between law and being a rabbi. I saw myself as
being a Jewish educator." Instead, she became a full-time kibbutznik.

Wendy Simon-Weiss, full in soul and body, has a perfectly sculpted
nose and beautiful blue eyes. When we meet in the Weiss-Simon home
(both she and her husband merged their last names), she is wearing a print
flower dress. For the occasion she is also sporting earrings, an uncommon
esthetic touch among women of Lotan. But Wendy is uncommon in a
much more important way: for the last seven years—almost half of her life
as a kibbutznik at Lotan (beginning during the holiday of Sukkot in
1984)—she has been harboring desires to leave. It has been thirteen years
since she passed her self-declared twenty-five-year-old benchmark of
youthful idealism. So why has she stayed on so long? "I fell in love with
and married a man who would stay here to his dying day."

Perhaps Wendy would have been happier at Yahel, where the domi-
nant culture did not become so "touchy-feely" and "alternative." But
when she came in the early 1980s to visit what was then the only Reform
kibbutz in existence, she had "a miserable experience."

We came down to Yahel for two weeks. For the first week, nobody
talked to us. Until, theoretically, we got "adopted" by families for
Shabbat. But for two weeks we sat in the field and picked peppers

with one kibbutz member. He was the foreman and walked around and told us what to do. Nobody paid any attention to us.

Although Wendy had some confidence in being able to change this cool Yahel atmosphere, plans were afoot to found a second Reform kibbutz. Uncertainty about Lotan's actual viability and future direction made her hesitate (Yahel was, after all, "already established and a little more stable"). Ultimately, hearing that some of her friends were heading to found Lotan tipped the balance.

But Lotan, too, developed in ways that have made Wendy uncomfortable. In some respects (drawing parallels between small Jewish towns that wind up with competing congregations), she finds the changes normal. But the emergence in Lotan of the exclusive, "clique-ish," North End* neighborhood, whose residents were "handpicked" when it opened, turned Wendy off. Above all, she had begun to "feel trapped"—a state of mind as unhealthy in the member-kibbutz relationship as it is in traditional marriage. (Wendy is one of many women, at Lotan *and* Yahel, who compare kibbutz membership with partner commitment.)

And so Wendy has convinced Avi that they should take a sabbatical from the kibbutz. Together, they have convinced Lotan that they be granted an extraordinary three-year leave. "Why three years? I need to feel settled in another type of lifestyle before I can make a decision of whether Lotan is for me or not."

Obtaining kibbutz consent for the leave has been a great relief for Wendy. "Now that I have the option to go and not come back," she says, "I've begun to see again the many things that are very attractive" about Lotan.

"That doesn't mean that I would make some of those decisions that have been made," she goes on. "But that's part of the give-and-take of what you do in marriage, right?"

FINDING YOURSELF IN THE REFORM JEWISH DESERT

For Lotan, the decision to "absorb" young Rebekkah Waples reflects a disposition to do good deeds with a willingness to undertake social work.

---

* This is a deliberate (if ironic) play on the trendy, northern Tel Aviv suburb of Ramat Aviv.

Twenty-one-years-old when she arrived from Iowa—a single mother since the middle of high school—it was more her parents' than Rebbekah's idea to visit Israel and check out Lotan. The elder Wapleses even offered to take care of little Hannah while Rebekkah was looking into the Jewish State as an arena in which to turn her life around.

For things had not been working out back home. Rebekkah had quit community college "and "never really, like, found [her]self." Nor had she totally assumed the onus of motherhood. "I was living with my parents," recounts the freckled, red-haired girl with clips in her hair and a tiny ring in her nose. "So I was never 100 percent completely in charge of my daughter. And she wasn't used to being with me just alone, having only me to depend on." It wasn't until she eventually took Hannah to Lotan that this became an issue. But first her folks sent her to visit Israel by herself.

"I never really dreamt of making aliya, nothing like that. It was just, like, experiencing what life is like for someone my age without the responsibilities of a child and all of that. What I found I really liked."

There are not many Jews in Burlington, Iowa. The local Reform synagogue didn't have enough members to hold weekly services. Going to a Jewish camp for a month one summer exposed Rebbekah to the most Jews her age that she had ever seen. Although her father had converted to Judaism ("I've never seen him, like, as a Christian or anything like that"), December entailed going to his parents' home and—if through "just the present part, the stockings"—celebrating Christmas. With regards to religion, Rebbekah "always felt tension from his family":

> One year I went to a camp for a week and I met this Jewish girl. We really got on well. I think we were probably the only two Jews at the camp.
>
> So I got really excited and mentioned it to my grandmother. She's like, "So what, I meet Christians all the time." It was, like, I didn't understand where all the hostility was coming from.

So Israel was an eye-opener for the Iowan Jew. Yet the first kibbutz she visited was staunchly secular. "I can respect that," she says. But once she decided to return with Hannah, she knew she wanted a community with more Jewish content. When (at her mother's suggestion) she visited Lotan, she found an appropriate fit. "I'd never connected with [Judaism] the way I have here. I'm learning all the time, and I'm living now a Jewish life which, in America, I would not know so much. I wasn't surrounded by other Jews. There was no one to identify with."

Still, the move was traumatic—although whether more for Rebekkah or four-and-a-half-year-old Hannah is hard to say.

She's very, very, very attached to my father. My brother was also in the home—he was, like, a big brother to her.

I don't think we were used to each other being alone together, so it was like this ping-pong thing. For the first year, a never ending battle, like. So then it was making it pretty tough on me, making me uptight.

But after six months Hannah was already speaking Hebrew; after three years, she is, in her mother's words, "fully comfortable. This is her home. I have her and she has me and that's all we have here." It is mom who was "going absolutely nuts."

I felt I was, like, thirty years old, taking care of a child and changing diapers and not going out and partying anymore. So how could I even hang around with people my age? But I think it was pretty normal for me to once in a while be with people my age, and act like my age, and least during the daytime let myself be me. Who I am. Yeah.

I went to, like, music therapy. This therapy and that therapy, trying to get things figured out. I didn't realize how often I wasn't sure what my place was, where I fit. . . . Things are smoother now. I am more settled.

Rebekkah is not, at first blush, the ideal kibbutz candidate. Nor is she typical, even for the most progressive of Jewish communes. That Lotan would try her out at all, nonetheless, speaks as much to the continuing risk-taking spirit of those who originally came as it does to the intentions of the entire Waples clan—whom Rebbekah and Hannah visit every summer—back in Iowa.

Yet kibbutz life is perhaps the answer for someone like Rebbekah, a place where "everyone is basically on the same, fixed level, where you're not looked down upon because you're working with the cows and he's a doctor. . . . People are very willing to help all the time. It's just like a big extended family."

On one issue, Rebekkah Waples is right on target: child freedom and safety.

My child can run free here. She is free. I don't have to worry about her being kidnapped, or about drive-by shootings, or anything like that . . . I never ever realized until I came here how much we in America just drill it into the kids' minds, "You can't go here, you

can't move away from me in the store because someone might kid-
nap you."

The paranoia doesn't need to be shoved into the children's naïve
heads. I think it's very damaging.

"I mean," says the once lost teenage mother, speaking through her
daughter for all the daughters of the world, "she totally has the life that
every child on Earth should be given."

AT HOME ON THE (JEWISH SOCIALIST) RANGE

"In America, you don't know how people feel about you. It's difficult to
know who's going to stab you in the back and who is not. . . . We had a
good relationship with a neighbor in Fresno [California]. After we moved,
we discovered he was a member of the Ku Klux Klan."

So recounts Richard Herman, originally from Cleveland, Ohio
(from a neighborhood that was 90 percent Jewish). With one ear pierced
and wearing an earring, graying long hair, and a funky, full beard and mustache, Richard does not look like a Jewish tribalist. Yet his coming to
Lotan in 1980, one week shy of turning twenty-three, had much to do
with his "need to identify" with Jews, to live amongst his people.

Not that Richard idealizes the other members of his tribe. But at least
they're up front with their feelings and inner thoughts. "Here, if someone
doesn't like you, for whatever reason—race or religion, whatever—they're
gonna tell you." None of the American hypocrisy (and political correct-
ness) of putting on a face, pretending that they agree. Richard Herman
does not beat around the bush. He is a no-nonsense kibbutznik, a concise
interlocutor who embellishes little in his life story. Indeed, my interview
with him was by far the shortest with any kibbutznik.

Richard is also one of the last of the die-hard socialists. "I believe in
socialism and this is the closest thing to a socialist society that there is."
Quite simply, for Richard it's a question of "practice what you preach."

Richard is the first to admit that kibbutz socialism is not what it used
to be. "Society in general—kibbutz included—is more capitalist. It's not
the same way it was when we started. Societies are dynamic."

But much of the blame, according to Richard, goes to the Israeli government. "It has gone overboard in removing farm supports." Nowhere in
the world does agriculture succeed without some kind of governmental
support, claims the Lotanik founder who runs the dairy. It needs crop guar-

antees, price floors. But Israel "has pretty much left most of agriculture to the free market." Politics has also been a factor.

"The government [pours] lots and lots of money down the drain in the West Bank, Gaza, and Golan, areas that are not going to stay part of the country. The rest of the country has paid a large price. Particularly kibbutzim in the outlying areas," those outside the occupied territories.

Although he is not one to patronize prayer services, Richard Herman does identify with the Reform Judaism as embodied at Lotan. "Jewish ideals and values," he says approvingly, "are very rooted in the kibbutz." He includes the no-work, no-trip policy for Shabbat; it creates an atmosphere that he enjoys. Living on a "green kibbutz"—that is, one which actively integrates ecology within its leitmotif—is also a key component for him.

Richard has the air of a kibbutznik who has seen it all. He has lived in Lotan longer than any other single place in his life and "can't see [himself] leaving it. It would be very, very difficult, or painful, to do so . . . This is really home."

Richard is a veritable elder, the only Lotanik in his forties. Husband and father of three, he expresses a sentiment expressed much more emphatically at Yahel than on Lotan. "We have families now, and when you have families you have different priorities. That's a lot of it."

Younger than he, Richard Herman's fellow kibbutzniks cannot share his post-forty view of life. Their reasons for remaining at Lotan jibe fairly closely with the reasons why they originally came. That is much less so at Yahel. For on the "elder sibling" Reform Jewish kibbutz, all the American kids are firmly on the other side of the midlife divide. The reasons Yahelniks stay tend to diverge more from the motives that brought them in the first place.

5

Coping with Crisis

Economic, Marital, and Midlife

THE REFORMS

It took a few years for the national kibbutz crisis of 1985 to catch up with Yahel. But when it did, in 1988, it did so with a vengeance. Yahel was losing money. Debts that up until then were covered by the government became the kibbutz's own problem: the state would no longer bail it out. The kibbutz movement began to dismantle a nearby kibbutz, Shizafon, offering a small financial package and help to resettle on some other kibbutz. "If you don't want to settle on another kibbutz," members were told, "we'll give you severance pay and you're on your own." The very existence of Yahel suddenly seemed at stake.*

Survival required drastic changes in the strictly communal aspects of the kibbutz's life—changes that some regarded as a rupture of the soul. A decade later, members who stuck it out recall those times as traumatic.

Membership was suddenly beginning to dive. "Anytime someone said, 'We want to come to your house to talk,' recounts Erica Lending, "we knew."

"A terrible wave of depression swept all over the place," husband Elad Lending recalls. "Everybody was having these tremendous doubts and going through personal hell—and wondering who was going to be next. Just to make matters worse, people didn't announce they were leav-

---

* Shizafon was to reinvent itself as Naoz Madar.

ing in a week or a month, but only after six months. People who already had one foot out the door" were hanging on for another half a year. "It was just awful." By the time the massive departure was over, membership had practically halved, from eighty-eight to forty-six.

A "change committee" was established. Five or six members went house-to-house asking, "How long are you willing to commit to staying here to see this process through? Six months? One year? Two years?" Two years was the longest they were asking people to hold on. It was a critical phase in Yahel's life, marked by change in its ideology.

"We began to economize, closing down productive branches—like the vineyard for table grapes—they were too labor intensive and not making enough profit. We began to accept non-Jewish volunteers. Hiring people to work for pay." No decision so roiled the community and its outside critics—particularly the "purists" of Lotan—than to employ outsiders to do the manual work of the kibbutz. (The best workers, jokes the economic manager, are the ones who work the hardest but whom you don't have to pay at all: the volunteers from Korea.)

A number of factors went into this controversial decision. For one, labor costs were reduced when unskilled or semiskilled laborers worked at field hand wages. Second, opportunity costs were rationalized: a college graduate member could bring more money to the kibbutz by utilizing her computer skills in an outside firm, for example, than picking onions. Third, kibbutzniks' job satisfaction—an increasing concern among the middle-aging members—was greatly enhanced with the expansion of work choice. For Elad, renouncing self-labor was difficult at the level of ideology but, at the same time, "It's different in reality. For there are jobs that people just don't want to do and we [were forcing] them to do it . . .

> As soon as you reexamine the idea of self-labor you say, "This is not normal. The entire world works on [the basis of] hired labor. What is so criminal about it? What is immoral about it?" . . . It freed members to do what they want.

But, admits this same Yahelnik, "it changed the community. Suddenly you don't have a homogeneous group of people who all went through the same formative experience of creating a kibbutz. [Hired] people are here to make money." Are they part of the community? "They are but they aren't.

> This had major repercussions in the social sphere . . . [But] there is no chance that the kibbutz could have survived in the pure form that it was before this change. I am absolutely convinced of that, down to my toes.

Hired laborers at first included Arab citizens of Israel. But with the outbreak of the first Intifada, not even the liberal-minded kibbutzniks could overcome fears for their children's security. Groups of foreign workers were recruited, the most successful being from Thailand. Yahel, the remote Jewish community in the Negev, very visibly became part of the global economy. Yet social interaction between the kibbutzniks and their "guest workers" was virtually nil.

Snapshot of the Kibbutz Thais

Under the shade outside the dining hall, in a mishmash of English and Hebrew, I speak with the most senior of the Yahel Thais, twenty-five-year-old Niphon Patihipa. Niphon, who back home (where he owns his own land) is a rice and sugar cane farmer, is in his fifth year at Yahel, a veteran of the first group of eight Thais to arrive on the kibbutz. His was part of a 450-strong contingent of Thais then arriving to work in settlements throughout Israel. Niphon had a cousin who was working on a *moshav* (a cooperative but privately owned collection of farms).

Kibbutz work was harder in the first years, says the shy but friendly Niphon, especially when the Thais were under an Arab supervisor. The Thai farmer jokingly recalls enigmatic advice from their early orientation: "Don't touch the backsides of Israelis." Now the work is much more "fun." Being on the kibbutz is "good for work, good for money—but not so good for living." Of the twenty Thais then at Yahel on one-year renewable contracts, ten were working in the melon fields, five in the date fields, and five—including two women—in the packing house.

I leave the *beit knesset*, the prayer hall, where a study session on the Talmud is in session; in the adjoining rec room, Korean volunteers are watching a video. "Cover your ass," intones one of the celluloid actors.

Later, I return to the library next to the beit knesset to retrieve a bag I had left behind. One of the volunteers—a Korean girl—just then enters the beit knesset and, for a lark, picks up a *kippah* (skull cap). She puts it on her head, returns to her friends, and pretends to pray, Jewish-style. Her friends find it very amusing.

Individualizing the Collective

For Lori Stark, "reforms" entailed "shinui with a capital Shin"—change with a capital C: "Once upon a time you would have four movies a year and be entitled to three haircuts and be allowed to take milk from the dining room." If you didn't utilize your allocation for haircuts, or a driver's license, or a wedding, it was lost to you. Somebody would utilize it, somebody would not."

"Who decides what your needs are?" philosophizes Elad. "The kibbutz? The individual? People have different needs. If you didn't get a subscription to a newspaper (because the kibbutz decided that to be a well-educated, politically correct Zionist, one should read a newspaper), the money simply went away at the end of the year. The same with haircuts, furniture, travel. Even love. Got yourself a girlfriend up north? You get money to go visit her. No girlfriend up north? You don't get the money."

Elad's wife Erica elaborates. "It was called the 'love budget,' for single people. To send them to singles events run by the kibbutz movement."

Members decided to take all the money they'd spent on personal items and divide it across the board. No longer would people be bringing in their little receipts for a hundred different items for the accounting office to reimburse. Cost accounting became much more professional. It increased the size of personal budgets and gave members more control over their spending lives. Whatever you did with that money became your business. "I could decide I didn't want the little blue work clothes anymore," says Lori Stark. "I could buy new CDs, save for a trip with my family."

Communal services, from bathing young children to laundering, were given up: kids could be showered at home rather than by caretakers in the children's house, and families allotted extra money to purchase washing machines and pay for the electricity.

People used to get new work clothes—blue shirts, Mao-style—every season. (But there were special categories. For instance, "if you became treasurer of the kibbutz and therefore had to go to Tel Aviv and meet bankers, you suddenly got two nice shirts a year in addition.")

> We had one person whose entire job was to take care of the work clothing supply. She would go up to Tel Aviv twice a year, look at stocks on sales, order the clothes, and have them shipped down. In terms of cost, it was like you were wearing silk shirts to work in the field.

"People were tired of eating a tomato, a cucumber, and white cheese on bread for dinner every night. So we decided to divvy up the food money as well." Except for Friday nights and holiday meals, the dining hall was closed for dinners. (For a while, it was even closed for breakfasts.)

Initially, the kibbutz made monthly calculations concerning the number of "private" meals families had eaten at home. It was constantly changing: some months had five Saturday lunches as opposed to four, sometimes a bar mitzvah meal would change the calculation. "We spent so much energy on this stuff!" one member says, in incredulous hindsight. Eventually the community agreed that "There's no point. You win a little, you lose a little. Just take an average!"

"Once a week you used to come to the dining room to get flour, sugar, eggs; and margarine for baking your Shabbat cake, and fruits for snacking in the afternoon," recalls Erica. People took whatever they felt they wanted to have. But once they actually had to put down money for it" consumption plummeted. By 30 percent. Similar savings were made after meters were placed on individual homes, and family units began to pay for their own electricity.

"There is no doubt about it," says the kibbutznik who installed the electricity meters. "Socialism encourages waste. Waste and slothfulness. If you're offered something for free, you take it. Only afterwards do you ask whether you need it."

"We got a lot of criticism at the time for making these changes. In the kibbutz movement, Yahel was considered to be almost *apikoras* [heretical]. People would glare at us and say, 'You're not a kibbutz anymore. Call yourself something else, not *Kibbutz* Yahel.'"

And the Yahelniks' response?

"We were defensive about it. But some people would say with foresight, 'Wait, you'll come to this, too.' Now"—with respect to the extent of change—"we're considered to be conservative! Many kibbutzim have not only done what we have, they have taken it several steps further!"

Thinking Like a Corporation

Seven years later, in 1995, the ideological reforms having been accepted, a new phase arose: long-term strategic planning. The spur was a course the kibbutz treasurer had taken in small enterprise planning. It could be adapted to "a small set of companies trying to hold it all together, to be one big community."

"If something doesn't grow it dies, right?" asks economic manager Matt Sperber. "We knew by that point that in order for the kibbutz to survive both financially and socially, we needed to grow. But we needed to decide as a community how much we wanted to grow, how big we wanted to be. To remain a small community of members but to increase the size of nonmember residents? This is what we've been doing with strategic planning."

With strategic planning comes a mission statement. This is Yahel's: "A new cooperative settlement striving to grow, integrating the maximum quality of rural lifestyle with the high standard of living based on mutual support and the values of Reform Judaism." Seven critical success factors were then specified: profit, education, growth, human resources, social justice, maintenance services, partnership.

Yet even the most strategic of planning cannot trump human nature. One persistent source of tension is inequity in work commitment: even on-kibbutz, some people just don't work as hard as others. From one perspective, some members are thought not to work hard enough, and are resented as slackers. But from another perspective some kibbutzniks work *too* hard, and unjustly criticize those who can't keep up. This, too, undermines morale. The old Marxist saw "from each according to his contribution, to each according to his needs" oversimplifies the notion of knowing what precisely constitutes a "fair contribution" from each member of the society.

CRISIS OF THE TUBE

Nowadays, there is nary a kibbutz home without a television set. It is such a common accouterment that few kibbutzniks give it a second thought when they turn it on. Perhaps that is why the "TV crisis" is so little recalled by the kibbutz home viewers of today. Yet several ex-kibbutzniks well remember the controversy the proposal for individual sets engendered. For some, the onset of TV marked the end of kibbutz as they had known it.

"We couldn't afford to give everybody TV," recalls Richard Kaplan. "For me, it was going to tear the sociological fabric." But the issue went beyond equity. "After dinner, people just went home to their living rooms" to watch. For the still unmarried Kaplan, the introduction of individual TV watching contributed to "a decline in a way of life."

Similar to Kaplan's recollections are those of Mike Madeson: "At the time, I thought, 'Oh, we can't allow TV into the people's homes. They should all come and watch together. Television will bring people *out* of their homes for the news.' Two months after we left the kibbutz, everyone got a color TV and two phones in their homes."

In the early days kibbutzniks would fight about somebody having a *kum-kum*—an electric coffee pot. People would say, "No, if everybody has their own electric coffee pot people won't drink coffee together in the dining room. It will ruin the kibbutz." But that's really what it was like. We really felt that if people started getting TVs in their own homes, they wouldn't come to the Wednesday night movie. They wouldn't come to hang out in the *mo'adon*, the lounge. And that's what happened. It became less and less communal.

—Lisa Schwartz

"Everyone used to hang out, and have coffee and tea in front of other people's houses and play guitar." Ex-member Neil Frankle recalls kibbutz as a "a youthful, fun experience." But "when they introduced the television—where everyone had their own [set]—it became less social." The introduction of personal television (along with the baby boom with which it coincided) "destroyed" the ambiance that had typified the Reform kibbutz scene up until then.

CRISIS ON THE REFORM KIBBUTZ

Crisis—who needs it? Perhaps the kibbutz does. For crises solidify a sense of community, galvanize communal commitment, and contribute to a member's decision to stick it out. But for a member who is tasked by the community to deal with the personal crises of others, the task is not easy:

"At any hour of the day or night someone can phone up the head of the members committee and tell them, 'There's been a death in the family. I need a plane ticket, I need a car, I need money, I need support.'"

Or, "My child is dead. I need you to get over to this house and help me get through this."

Or, "My husband just left me. I need you to get over here *right now* and help me to deal with this."

Or, "I'm leaving my spouse—I'm in love with someone else. I need a place to stay as of *now!*" The same members committee head has had all these calls.

MARITAL AND MENTAL CRISIS

Is marital disintegration more common "in the city" or on-kibbutz? In secular kibbutzim or in religious ones? Among the Orthodox or the Reform? For the individuals involved, such questions of frequency are besides the point. Suffice it to say that, as in any society, Yahel has had its share of spousal suffering. Separation on-kibbutz, however, is not as it is in the noncommunal world. Here is how a members committee head recounts one such crisis, involving married members with children.

"I heard it from the woman herself. She met me at the grocery store and told me she needed to walk with me. (But I'd had warning signs. She was in therapy, seeking help to solve marital problems.)

"She blurted out that she was in love with another member, and immediately said that this fact would have absolutely nothing to do with what would happen to her and her husband—that being in love with another man had no bearing on the decision to leave her husband! Loving this other man would have no bearing on what *he* decided to do with *his* wife. After hearing all this," she recounts, still incredulous, "I really needed to get home. I was very angry.

"But I immediately checked the anger and said, 'Well, I'll just have to forget about what *I* think and just work with this as a case.'

"A month later the man [involved] appeared at my door and told me he also needed to leave his house. It was because he was not able to state to his wife that he was not in love with the other woman. So I again had to go through the entire tactical and physical problem of finding the next person a temporary place to live.

"So we had a situation where the two alleged lovers were living on the other side of the kibbutz in separate houses but would frequently receive their children in the temporary housing. They went on working and living, getting together only in the evenings, in what they felt was a 'discreet' way. The entire situation was quite absurd. In the life we live out here, it was considered to be a huge scandal with a capital S, occupying every waking hour of talk time, dinner time, breakfast time, pool time.

"*They* felt they didn't need to offer explanations but frequently insisted on their rights. To privacy, to be discreet, to be left alone, to enjoy life. Days off, time, money, to housing, to visitation. Tables and chairs and beds. Hot plates."

As with divorce in "normal" society, there is a "great deal of stress, hurt, revenge, and need to express negative feelings." But on-kibbutz, so many more people are involved than just the principal parties: those on the work committee, the housing committee, the members committee. Eventually, "the kibbutz society burned themselves out on the case. After all the talk and the gossip nobody really wanted to get too involved in it anymore," to help resolve the deeper issues at stake.

The case had become "very complex, with lots of intermediaries and negotiations. Like a cease-fire agreement." But the double marital "cease-fire" was also full of "violations, inconsistencies." By the time of my arrival, one of the married couples (both high-profile members) had already reconciled. But the straying partner from the other couple had suffered what some would characterize as a nervous breakdown and others a "manifestation of a more serious mental illness." Regardless of diagnosis or precipitating factor, this member's condition required institutionalization—an expensive proposition born entirely by the kibbutz. "Technically," my interlocutor went on, "it means the person is going to need a special relationship with the kibbutz," one that in the insurance realm would be defined as precipitated by a preexisting condition. (At Sabbath services, the prayer leader would offer a *mishaberach*, a prayer of recovery, for the institutionalized adulterer.)

Neither medical nor liturgical intercession can save troubled kibbutz couples from the logistical discomfort wrought by life in a closed society.

There they are, the recently adulterous philanderers, on opposite sides of the sole checkout line at the single (and) tiny store on the kibbutz. The body language is transparent—neither looks at the other, at least not when the other might be glancing back. The woman's body visibly tightens in the presence of her former lover. Mercifully, the line moves quickly and the tension disappears. But just a few minutes later, they both wind up at the swimming pool. Where else can one go on a hot summer's day in the middle of the scorching desert?

"They are both incredibly proud people," explains a less than sympathetic fellow member, referring to the illicit pair. "It is a matter of great importance for each of them to maintain their membership and standing in the community. It was extremely important to [the adulteress] that she be given a house in the members' quarter, that she not be relegated to where volunteers or other nonmembers live." For her state of mind and pride, she thought that being relocated to the wrong side of the kibbutz would be very disturbing and stressful to her children. As a result, she was assigned a new residence within eyeshot of the fellow member she had betrayed by sleeping with her husband.

As for the complicit man, "he said to me, 'I have to be able to walk through here with my head high.' What arrogance! What he really means is to still walk through the kibbutz with his male organ standing high!"

Strange poolside scene: Naturally, the former lovers do not interact but have nevertheless staked out territory not far from each other. And I have business to conduct with both! With the man, I have questions about kibbutz land issues and the peace agreement with Jordan; the woman is interested in the book I am reading about kibbutzim. Stupidly, I begin to share with her the bibliography. It is a thoughtless act, for the only reference I have marked with my highlighter is an article entitled "Gossip and Scandal." For sure, it is an old, 1963 piece in the

academic journal Current Anthropology, *written by veteran anthropologist*
Max Gluckman; yet it is undiplomatically evocative of her present situation. I try
to distract her attention from the bibliography.

One critic claims that social sanction for the marital crisis is unfair,
and relative to the prior prestige of the parties. "The fact that the [unfaith-
ful husband] is a high status member has helped him regain his family, his
privacy, and continue to move on in the day-to-day world. Judgment on
him is less harsh."

Is there a lesson? "They're members, so no one has freedom of privacy. It's a deadlock. One does not sign on to a place like this if one is enamored of privacy. This place is about sharing—including your whole
fucking setup." And moral repugnance creates no escape:

It was a horrible, horrible day—I am currently on driver's duty. I
hate it, absolutely hate it. It's being everyone's Mommy. "Mommy,
get me this. Mommy, get me that." Now, I had already told everybody to lay off the personal requests, because I had a very bad day.
But I have no choice. I have to do it.

Well, what really pissed me off is that this guy [the adulterer] told
me that I had to pick up some fresh fish for him in Eilat, for his "romantic dinner" with his wife. You know the scene: Guy cheats on his
wife, the kids are now away, so he tries to make it up with a nice meal
on the grill. Some wine, maybe even some candles.

You have to know that I hate the smell of fish. During the summer, it's not only the smell—it's the heat, the flies. And the fish eyes,
just staring at you, as these brawny Eilat beach fish fryers stand
ahead of you on line—these guys with humongous thighs and ham-
mocks, ordering fifty kilos of fish at a time.

They're scaling the fish, the heads are flying, the guts are vacu-
umed in front of you. Horrible! But I get ____ his fucking fish. And
there is *the* kibbutznik question: "Did he thank me?" No!

How much of an aberration was this ongoing drama? I am told of
a twenty-year-old case of a married member sleeping with a volunteer: the
kibbutz put an end to it. But I am also informed of more recent cases of
"suspected adultery."

As head of the members committee, "You are meant to be a super-
ego. But you are also involved in the lowest forms of sludge, bottom-
feeding, bloodsucking, parasitical, gossipmongering. You're kind of like
the Pope who lives in the bordello. (I don't mean that in a sexual connotation but in a political way.)"

MIDLIFE CRISIS*

> There is a group of us here who, past forty and now hitting [our] mid-forties, have a common psycho-social arrangement about the second half of our lives. A lot of it has to with living here [on-kibbutz]: Why are we here? What are we looking for? What we are going to live for? What will our [future] goals be?
>
> —Rosealie Sherris

Two age-related impressions struck me when I began my sojourn at Yahel. First, almost by magic, I felt that I was the same age as all the adults in the society. This was reassuring, and helped me feel demographically at home. Only after my stay did I do the math that confirmed how eerily accurate my intuition was: the average age of my American-born counterparts on Yahel was 43.2; I was 43.5. None was under forty; the oldest were forty-five.

Yet soon thereafter the disconcerting flip side to this reality set in: this was a society in which there were no older people. Suddenly, I had entered an age-cohort of "elders." For someone in his early forties, who had been successfully clinging to a relatively youthful outlook, it was a sobering world to be suddenly inhabiting.

It didn't take long to realize that the reality of "middle-age seniorhood" explained many of the changes that Yahelniks were going through as individuals. Yet since all the adults were going through the same age transition at the same time, there was also a shared change going on. As the year 2000 approached, Yahel was experiencing a collective midlife crisis. Several of the crises the kibbutz was weathering, I have come to conclude, were tied to this critical time of life.

Midlife is the period in which middle-aged individuals take existential stock of their current condition and intensively assess their present with respect to past goals and probable future. In "ordinary" society, this crisis is mitigated by the sandwiching of midlifers between other adult age groups. But at Yahel, the middle-aged are on their own, bereft both of the experience and wisdom of seniors before them, and the support and cushion of juniors behind them.

A foretaste of the significance of middle age had already occurred, in fact, a decade earlier. The "change" and "reforms" of the late 1980s were

---

* A broader treatment of this theme can be found in my article in *Shofar* 21, no. 2 (2003), "Mid-Life Crisis, Kibbutz Style."

not a result of the aging of the kibbutzniks per se. However, the fact that they were entering their third decade of life certainly softened the way for it. Elad Lending reflects with anguish:

> That was a terrible time. The kibbutz was not making a living. It was even losing money. There was no light at the end of the tunnel. Members were reaching the age of thirty and many simply came to the conclusion that the party was over. It had been fun, but now it was time to start looking to guarantee the security of their families.
>
> Many of them thought to themselves, "I'm still young enough to start again. But who will hire me when I am forty?" So, after many years of having virtually nobody leave, suddenly there was a wave of [departures]. A terrible wave of depression swept all over the place.

Yahel survived—at the price of ideological integrity, according to its critics and ex-members, but with its financial prospects more secure. Those who remained consider themselves survivors of a terrible storm, the likes of which they hope never again to weather. Now in their forties, however, their near-collective death remains part of the group psyche, a reminder of the fragility of group existence.

Laura Sperber contrasts youthful idealism with tolls taken by reality.

> [In the beginning] there was a very exciting feeling of starting something new . . . a feeling of almost unlimited potential, of tremendous opportunity [and] satisfaction of creating all these things. [Now], sometimes you just feel like you need a rest. You get burned out.

Elad Lending recalls the difficult reassessment of "self-labor," the notion that the Jewish collectivity should undertake all of its work without relying on Gentile outsiders.

> Kibbutz believed in the Jewish "farmer-soldier." . . . After our regular jobs all of us would work extra hours picking tomatoes or packing melons. We grew as much as we could back then—if it is ripe you have to pick it, whatever it [took]. You can do that when you are twenty. Maybe even when you are thirty. But when you are forty?

Yet it was not physical aging that prompted the move on Yahel to hired labor so much as the psychological shift in source of self-worth. The ideology of self-labor was fine in the abstract; but at some point as the baby boomers fully entered adulthood, career satisfaction became increasingly paramount.

"In the early days, when people would come to you and say, 'We really need you to work in education. Would you help take care of our children?' it was exciting. You get satisfaction from providing a need of the community." That's what Danny Hayken did, being a (rare male) caretaker for toddlers. But after a while, Danny acknowledges, "It gets to be old hat. If you don't enjoy taking care of four-year-olds, it doesn't speak to you. You do it for a year but not with your heart in it." The same with working in the fields. "It's hot and it's weary. Okay, so I do it for a year. I do it for two years. But eventually, you want a job, an occupation that you enjoy somehow to spend the time of your day. . . . You have to let people develop careers, and become specialized, in order to have that job satisfaction."

Allowing members to work off the kibbutz solved some of these problems. It brought more revenue to the community. It provided greater work satisfaction. It created perks. But in turn, such changes planted seeds of petty jealousy. More fundamentally, it heightened implicit inequalities in status.

"If you work in a regional factory, and have to be there at five in the morning to unplug the forklifts from the electricity, you need a car. Of course, once you have it, you use it when you want—you take the kids to the pool in it, for instance." In a society that does not permit private car ownership, such things matter. And they are scrutinized.

"You work in an office, they buy you baguettes in the morning."

Off-kibbutz opportunities used to be restricted to the regional school and industry. Compensation, paid not to the member but to the kibbutz, used to be fairly uniform. But as off-kibbutz work opportunity expands, so does the variation in what members bring in to the kibbutz. With it comes invidious comparisons, based not on personal wealth but on prestige: some members are "worth" much more to the kibbutz than others. Compensatory egalitarianism is offset by psychosocial inequity. Perversely, such inequity is based on one's communal contribution.

Even on-kibbutz, observes one Yahelnik, "it's normal for some people to feel marginal. They prefer to remain marginal." Is it any wonder that they are treated marginally?

"Something happened when I turned forty," says one ex-New Yorker. "Up until then, I never questioned anything the kibbutz decided about me, for me, on my behalf. Then I hit forty and, boom, I started acting up, questioning things."

At least in the realm of politics, Rosealie Sherris is not shy to stake out a marginal position, criticizing the "lack of democracy at Yahel." It's a reflection of her feelings about Israel as a whole, itself linked to an unusually leftward progression as she approached middle life.

> My sense of the country is more and more critical about the real, long-term meaning of the so-called Jewish State. Yahel is a very middle-of-the-road kibbutz, right-leaning Labor. Over the years, I've had an uncomfortable feeling about it as a mother. As an American citizen as well. It's very difficult to live here and teach my daughters about equal rights under the law, and equality of all kinds of people in society. It's very difficult to show them.
>
> [In America] I grew up in the society of the '60s and '70s [with] serious political divisions. Race, gender, ethnic. I am very much a child of the Vietnam War. And I cannot see justice here. I do not share my politics with members of the community.

If her fellow members heard these views, she says with a laugh, "I'd be lynched!" Elad of Yahel formulates a classic ode to the middle-aged institution:

> Maybe some of the fire and brimstone has gone out of it, and it is a little bit more staid and less passionate than it was. But it is a lot more comfortable. The feeling is optimistic towards the economic future and people are encouraged to develop careers in things that interest them.

Nowadays, the post-forty Yaheniks dream less and plan more.

Parental priorities shift the consciousness of parents, on-kibbutz and off-kibbutz, as the children themselves grow older. They shape the prioritization of resources and perspective on the future: as children grow, long-term planning for their welfare impinges on the consciousness of the parent. On Yahel, with fully half of the children of the American-born already teenagers, and another quarter within a year or two of entering adolescence, issues such as bar/bat mitzvah preparation, secondary education, looming military service, and college financing mitigate against a consciousness of just "going with the flow."

"Elder" Yahelniks Laura and Matthew Sperber (aged forty-five and forty-four, respectively) were seeing their daughter—the eldest child of the entire kibbutz—through her first year in the army. That fact alone focused their attention on Shira's day-to-day welfare within an expanded range of politico-strategic concerns (even before Intifada II) and her future life choices.

"The army is a grind," states Matthew Sperber, economic genius of Yahel, matter-of-factly. "Thinking about it in terms of Zionism—that's really esoteric, at this point," he says, decades after doing his first stint in the Israel Defence Forces. Now military service for the Sperbers means more than Matt having to leave home annually to perform his reserve duty: his Shira is the first child of the kibbutz to have been inducted. "Look, my daughter is working in *modi'in* [intelligence], in the middle of the country, doing interesting things, and enjoying her work. If I had a son posted in Lebanon, that would be a different matter, and I'm sure I'd feel much differently about it."

One sobering realization on Yahel is that their community is not necessarily being built for the second generation.

> I don't think anyone would say they are building Kibbutz Yahel in order to have an inheritance to pass on to our children. That is not the goal. . . . We would love our children to stay but we want them to have higher education, go on and study at college, and find their course, their path. [The goal] is to realize our dreams. To create whatever it is that we thought we could, and to make it work.
> —Danny Hayken

Envisioning the next generation of the kibbutz is a significant consideration. The realization for parents on Yahel that their children will not necessarily build their own lives in a remote Arava desert community inevitably evokes existential comparison with their own youthful settlement decision. Assessing the life choices of their offspring forces parents to confront their own. Questions answered long ago resurface: *Why have I built this community? For whom?* New questions arise: *If my own children don't settle here, who will rejuvenate the community? What are the true motives for newcomers who wish to live here now?*

On-kibbutz, where otherwise private dramas become matters of public interest, the intersection of midlife and marital crisis highlights the vulnerability of a society whose entire cohort of "seniors" has recently turned forty.

> Well, I think that for myself, for a long time, I was very unhappy, feeling not fulfilled personally. Feeling that I was always doing what the kibbutz asked me to do. I think that I had a forties crisis that set in somewhere around the age of 37–38 where I was terribly, terribly unfulfilled. I had worked here and worked there and been secretary

of this committee and chairman of that committee and still didn't know what I wanted to do when I was going to grow up.

Marital infidelity, of course, occurs throughout both American and Israeli societies: the point here is *not* that it is especially endemic to kibbutz life. However, its resonance *is* all the greater in a community in which the entire cohort of "elders" share a similar age profile to the unfaithful couple and are therefore prone to the same age-based life questions. In demographically heterogeneous societies, depending on prevailing morals and individual sentiment, midlife affairs may be dismissed, hushed up, rationalized, or condemned by the community at large. When virtually all of the adults are themselves undergoing midlife transition, however, any instance of marital breakdown among them becomes cause of both private *and* collective soul-searching.

Gerontological homogeneity—the fact that kibbutz members are of the same age—creates special challenges for the entire community. On the one hand, it reflects the most exciting aspect for the founders—that, as youthful peers, they were truly "creating something new," a novel community with unlimited potential, unimpinged by past practices or history. From that time forth, their developmental and demographic path has been one of lifelong pioneering. It also carried an unintentional economic benefit: with no residents older than themselves, there would be no need to provide for nonworking seniors down the road.

On the other hand, gerontological homogeneity means that when developmental life transition doubts set in, there are no resident "sages," or models of the future, to guide, counsel, and assuage sufferers through their midlife angst. Midlife crisis is collective, a malaise of not just a demographic segment of the community but of all its leaders. With all the "elders" of a community in their mid-forties there is an intensified generational compression of responsibility. The future is a blank slate that the kibbutzniks, as always, are creating anew. Only this time, it is a future that includes preoccupation with the welfare of their own growing children. It is also a future that, unlike in their formative years as young adults, requires the kibbutzniks to seriously consider living not only as pioneers in religion, but also as pensioners in retirement.

"Coming here was a way to live out a dream that I had begun to nurture since I had my first experience in Israel," says Nancy Immerman. "As I grow older—and I'll be forty-two this year—I find that it is more and more difficult to maintain that integrity, that authenticity in expressing one's personal ideology that I felt when I first came here. I suppose this is part of growing up, growing older. Maybe part of a forties crisis."

"After the fifth year, and during the years of the change in kibbutz policy and structure at Yahel, I felt very uncomfortable," recalls Rosealie Sherris. "In particular, I felt that I was at a dead end as far as my work was concerned, time was breathing down my neck. I was working in jobs that had absolutely no meaning to me. I felt isolated from the rest of the world (very specifically the world of art-making). I didn't come to kibbutz to seek friends. Yet after a certain junction my personal interests and expression and need for a human contact—people who shared my interests—was not fulfilled here. My husband"—from whom Rosealie has since divorced—"kept me here.

"One of the things about reaching the mid-point in life was the need to push the envelope to find out how truly independent and free we could be. How far could we push ourselves, towards professional and personal goals? How much we needed to break out of various little demagogueries and bureaucracies that rule our lives at a very intimate level."

It is remarkable what a difference just a few years make between a post-forty collective mind-set and a pre-forty one. They explain a good deal for kibbutzniks who have made the midlife transition on Yahel. They also explain much of the distinguishing mind-set between the Reform kibbutzniks of Yahel and those of Lotan.

6

Aging, Envy, and Death

THE REALITY OF MORTALITY:
DEATH ON THE KIBBUTZ

According to Jewish tradition, no new community is complete until it contains a cemetery. Only with the passing of a member and his proper burial on consecrated land can the community claim to provide for the full gamut of the life cycle.

Implicit in this religio-holistic vision of communal life is the hope, if not expectation, that death will occur in the natural course of events; that old age will fell the individual after he or she has grown to maturity, raised a family, and contributed to the society at large.

Tragically, this has not been the case at Yahel. Death has prematurely descended on the kibbutz three times in its short life span. While meting out intense sorrow to survivors' close friends and immediate family, the dark angel has also forged empathetic unity through collective grief. Each of the three mourned died during a holiday: a religious sabra on Shavuot, an American-born founder on Sukkot, and a four-year-old child on Hanukkah.

Gruesome End to a Saintly Kibbutznik

In the early days of the kibbutz, before the dairy was as mechanized as it is now, feeding the cows was much more labor-intensive. Dangerously so.

Out of respect for the coming Sabbath, dairy workers used to provide a double order of food for the cows on Fridays. In 1982, Saturday was followed by one of the holy days of Shavuot. Therefore, a triple dose was

89

required. The person in charge therefore "had to work like a maniac to get it all done on time." And that was Shmiel.

"Shmiel Amatz was a remarkable person," recalls Elad. "A *tzaddik*, really," a truly pious person. A quiet kibbutznik, observant, peaceful, and unassuming. He was never spiteful or vindictive, "no matter how much he was provoked." Nor would Shmiel gossip. "Never! He would just turn around, leave the room, and go someplace else."

On that holiday eve they were using a mixing wagon that, attached to a tractor, is powered by a spinning axle, known as a power take-off. The mixing wagon works like a giant blender: concentrated foods are poured in but the bulk of the food comes from hay. The hay is in bales, tied together by string. "Two loops of really cheap nylon cord," recalls Richard Kaplan, formerly of Yahel.

"Most people would just rip off the cords and throw them on the ground," remembers Elad. That wasn't good practice, though, for some of the strings would eventually clog up the blades and get into the food, causing blockages in the digestive tracts of the cows. Much additional time would also have to be spent on cleaning the mixer. Shmiel was conscientious, though. He collected all the cords and draped them over his shoulders, like a giant necklace.

It happened, recalls Drew Stark, who was driving the front loader, when Shmiel reached up to retrieve a piece of hay that had fallen outside the mixing bin. He lost his footing on a slippery piece of the food wagon, and fell towards the tractor. The cords strung around his neck caught in the power take-off, and Shmiel was at the mercy of the spinning axle. It pulled him in.

"It was horrible. He died on the spot," from deep lacerations on the neck and a broken spinal cord. As word spread that one of their fellow kibbutzniks was now dead, Gila Bernstein immediately fainted. Who would have imagined that, fifteen years later, Gila herself would suffer the death of a son, not yet even conceived at the time of Shmiel's death? And how might the kibbutz have been different, wonder some, had Shmiel—one of those rare individuals who is influential on account of their modesty—not died prematurely? The same question is asked about another kibbutznik who, albeit with a much more outgoing personality, also died prematurely, leaving a gaping hole in the soul of the community.

"Giving Life to the Wilderness of the Land of Israel"

These are the words inscribed on the tomb of Yonatan Maximon, a passionate believer in the mission of Yahel, a proud American-born Zionist soldier-farmer, who, in his mid-twenties, succumbed to a rare form of cancer. In 1984, "Yoni" left behind a sabra wife, Aliza, and a one-year-old daughter, Moriah.

Yonatan (Jonathan) grew up in Brooklyn, the son of a Reform movement librarian who taught his son to speak Hebrew at an unusually young age. His grandfather was the Hebraicist Shalom bar Maximom, next to whom the poet H. N. Bialik requested he be buried.

Yonatan wound up in Cincinnati, where he went to college and worked as a journalist before making aliya. (His parents followed two years later). Settling on Yahel, this "firebrand," as Elad Lending describes him, made an early and lasting impression on the new Reform Jewish kibbutz in the Arava desert. An officer in the reserves, Yoni was manager of the kibbutz vineyard. He provided security for the community, served as its fireman, and chanted the *haftarah* (passage from Prophets) at its services. Drew Stark recalls Yonatan's "clear and logical voice . . . an example to those around."

Former Yahelnik Jay Mandelsberg (nicknamed Dennis the Menace for the comic relief he unintentionally brought to the kibbutz in the early 1980s), recalls Yonatan's influence—and his uncanny ability to confer *menschkeit* (dignity) upon others.

> I had always been afraid of him. He was imposing and had a temper. Then, one summer when I was visiting, we worked together—and I became Yoni's right hand guy! Because I had worked in the fields and in the packing house he looked up to me and it was, like, "Wow, I'm in with Yoni!" He treated me with a lot of respect—which is more than I can say for some people. . . . He appreciated my serious and dedicated side. There was deep connection from that, and we both thrived on [being] Labor Zionist.

Yonatan's death was "a big blow" to Jay, who had begun to wavering about his commitment to kibbutz, and [it] drew him "back to the fold."

Aliza had been manager of the kibbutz for half a year when her husband first manifested symptoms. She "didn't even think about quitting" her job, so unforeseeable was the outcome of Yoni's illness. But Yonatan's condition deteriorated rapidly, and he had to be hospitalized—three times—in Tel Aviv.

"People would travel everyday" from the kibbutz to visit him in hospital, Yonatan's widow recalls, a distance of four hours each way. "Even after he could no longer see." Food was always provided, nursemaids assigned to look after the toddler daughter. "In this kind of time, the community is very supportive," Aliza acknowledges in gratitude.

Although Yonatan was undeniably very sick, nobody from Yahel—including his wife—expected him to die. Only twenty-four hours before-hand, four months after he first fell ill, did the inevitability of this key member's death sink in.

"The kibbutz went into high gear to deal with this horrendous, unpre-cedented event," recalls Elad, concerning the imminent demise of a recently healthy, fellow twentysomething, kibbutznik. Earth-moving equipment had to be requisitioned to landscape a rudimentary cemetery, around which the requisite fence was hastily erected. The same rabbi who had married Yonatan to Aliza was brought in from Eilat to consecrate the new cemetery.

Dazed by the turn of events, except for walking behind the vehicle that bore the casket to the cemetery Aliza recalls few of the details leading up to and the burial itself—only the "great number of people and their pa-tience waiting to help cover the grave." But Elad vividly remembers the cemetery consecration.

"We were all out there. The rabbi was at the head of the procession. We walked around for what seemed like hours, singing psalms. At first I thought we'd make one circumference, and then maybe three. But it just went on—walking around, walking around, singing, walking around. It was pretty surreal."

When the funeral march was over, "we gathered around, and the rabbi spoke. What I most remember him saying is 'the creation of this cemetery is what transforms Yahel from a temporary Jewish settlement into a permanent Jewish settlement.'"

Yonatan died on the eve of Sukkot, normally a joyous holiday that commemorates post-Exodus life in the desert. "So we buried him in the morning," wistfully recounts Aliza "and there was a holiday in the evening." Jewish law truncates mourning periods during religious holidays: on account of Sukkot, Aliza sat *shiva* for only one day instead of the usual seven. That year, of course, there was none of the music that the kibbutz sound system customarily blasts out during the holiday. For many years, Sukkot was no longer a happy time—neither for Aliza nor the precomprehending Moriah.

Two decades later, the evening that marks the annual onset of Sukkot begins with a memorial service at the cemetery. An even more tan-gible commemoration is *Laughing Wheels & Crying Wheels*, the kibbutz-produced volume of poems and reminiscences that is dedicated to the memory of Yonatan Maximom.

Although she realizes that "it was easier going through this here than in the city," like everyone else on-kibbutz from time to time Aliza has considered leaving Yahel. She especially recalls lonely nights and the difficulty of caring for little Moriah by herself. She also remembers the pain of watching, from her new assignment in the kitchen, the kibbutz tractors returning from those same fields in which her late husband had worked. But then she thinks of the gravesite, and the image reconnects her, inexorably, to the very earth of Yahel and its scruffy, wind-whipped cemetery.

"Good Night, Shai"

It was Hanukkah, the Festival of Lights, a favorite of the children. But even in the desert Hanukkah occurs in winter, a time of year that even in the Arava can be cold and damp. A number of children at Yahel were ill from the weather, several down with the flu. That's what Shai Bernstein, four-year-old son of Long Island-born Ron and sabra Gila Bernstein, was being treated for by the kibbutz nurse.

Four days into sickness, at nighttime, Shai's condition seemed to deteriorate. "The medic on call went to their house and recommended the hospital," recalls a close friend. "For whatever reason, Shai started to feel better. Kid feels better, everybody's happy. Ron himself was sick with the flu. So they didn't go" to the hospital in Eilat.

But it was a bad night after all, and at four in the morning the parents were still up with little Shai. At that point, they figured they ought to wait a little longer. When you live on Yahel it is not a question of just jumping into your car at will and heading off. Members do not possess their own vehicles: the kibbutz has its own fleet (including an ambulance) and, for emergency nighttime use, there is a rotating list of on-call drivers. One does not choose to drive to Eilat down the unlit, desolate Arava highway in the middle of the night on a lark; it is not a trifle to ask someone else to do it. ("I know I myself as a parent have [thought like] that numerous times," comments Elad. "You figure, 'Middle of the night, who wants to bother somebody? Wait till morning. It can certainly wait till morning . . .'")

In the morning, calls went out from the household for a driver, though they were not heard to carry a sense of urgency. Whose task it was to leave the kibbutz and make the spontaneous trip to Eilat also had to be sorted out. Finally, the nurse tasked a member to drop everything immediately and to commandeer the ambulance.

"I knew I had to drive fast," says the kibbutznik, "but it never dawned on me that we wouldn't make it. It didn't dawn on anybody, really, because Shai was talking. He looked terrible but he was talking."

"About half a kilometer before the bus stop at Yotvata, where the doctor was to meet us"—the plan was to have medical supervision all the way to the hospital—"I slowed down from the 140 kilometers an hour. Just then, apparently, Shai lost consciousness. Because when I opened the ambulance door, the doctor said 'respiratory emergency. Go to the infirmary at Yotvata.'" The doctor slammed the door, hopped into his own car, made a U-turn, and drove off . . .

"So I turned on the siren, made a U-turn on the Arava road, drove into Kibbutz Yotvata, sirens blazing, over the lawn. Sammy [the doctor] parked and ran to the infirmary. I drove up to the door, and got Shai inside. It couldn't have taken two minutes, from the time the doctor said 'respiratory emergency.' Together, with two nurses, we did CPR. Strapped him on to the monitor. Nothing worked. He died there on the table." Yahel's third death, as unexpected as the first two, had struck its first child.

"The doctor said nobody could have saved him, unless he had gone to the hospital much, much earlier. Shai had double pneumonia. Both of his lungs were full of fluid. You can't bypass the lungs. If it's one lung, maybe, but two?"

Eighteen months later, the memory is still painfully fresh.

"It wasn't the first time that I'd seen someone die," the driver of that fateful morning goes on, "or even that someone had died with me doing CPR on him. But it was the first time it was the child of a friend of mine. Words can't describe how it affected everybody here. Most of all, of course, the parents . . .

"The whole region came to the funeral. The rabbi said, 'As hard as it is to accept, some people are ordained by God to live out a full life in a short amount of time. Time is flexible. Time is not constant. A person can live a full life in four years as if he'd lived eighty.'"

The ceremony was partly traditional, partly not. Rick Daniel—an old college friend of the bereaved father—read the deceased child's favorite bedtime story, *Good Night, Moon*. In place of the last line, that in the text echoes the book's title, Rick read, "Good Night, Shai."

Aliza remembers the burial for the little boy much more vividly than she does that of her husband. "It was five o'clock in the afternoon, in January. Very windy, cold. People were freezing. There were many people at the funeral, from up north and around the kibbutzim. It was very difficult walking behind the small casket. Everybody felt for Gila." They also feared she might faint any minute.

Little Shai Bernstein had been very close to Aliza's own children. With her son, "he used to play with guns and fighting all the time." With her daughter Tamar, "he always got married."

It was striking, for Aliza, to see all the older kids of the kibbutz at the funeral. "Usually, you look at them as a group that doesn't care about anything—only about themselves, about how they look. Their hair and their clothes. But they were standing here"—she was telling me this inside the cemetery—"and they were crying."

Shai's tiny gravesite is a heartbreaking display of parental memento and children's toys: a Superman puppet, an image of Spiderman.

Ron, the lanky, leathery, cowboyesque kibbutznik from Long Island, struggles to come to terms with the loss of his son, and its significance for his attachment to Yahel.

"I couldn't leave because Shai is buried here. It would be very difficult to leave. It's also hard to be here because everywhere we go—by the playground, by the kindergarten, the pomelo grove—we see him. It was part of him. Wherever we go, Shai is around. It's not easy.

"That's the worst tragedy of all. I don't get any feelings when I hear about a father who passed away, or a grandfather. I feel bad for him, but that's the way it's supposed to go. But this is totally wrong. It's supposed to be the father who goes first, and then the child. I also lost a brother, in 1992.

"Kibbutz helped a lot. It was very involved and didn't leave us alone at all. They did everything they could to support us, and still do. That's the idea of kibbutz—gathering in time of happiness, and also in times of tragedy."

Ron doesn't say so, but the circumstances of Shai's death did stir feelings of guilt, anger, and even hate among some of the parties involved. Was everything done to save Ron and Gila's young son? Did Shai receive all the care he ought to have? And then there is the suppressed question: Does living in a remote kibbutz in the desert endanger one's children? Some time after my stay, Ron and Gila left the kibbutz for a year, to work for the Reform movement in the United States. They have subsequently returned to the kibbutz, and have adopted a baby girl whom they have named, appropriately, Yahel.

IDEOLOGICAL TABOO: MONEY AND JEALOUSY

Kibbutz is the one society in which money is not supposed to matter, not with respect to interpersonal relations, at any rate. But as consciousness has grown that the kibbutz is a collective *financial* enterprise, so has the realization that money does count. But never was filthy lucre supposed to contaminate relations between fellow members in the Israeli bastion of egalitarianism.

Yet from the very outset, the issue of personal money has percolated under the surface of life at Yahel, undermining the kibbutz myth of material equality. In particular, it created an early wedge between sabras and American-born founding members. It remains an issue today.

In the eyes of the Israeli-born, Yahelniks from America hail from wealthy families back in the States. They continue to receive the benefits of their pre-Yahel background: supplementary bank accounts, off-kibbutz apartments, annual overseas vacations. It is, says one Haifa-born woman, a "very heavy subject. . . . Twenty years ago we tried to talk about these things, but we failed. We never touched seriously upon what to do when your parents die and you [inherit] money. Then the changes [i.e., economic reforms] came and everybody became free to do what he wants with his money. We're not looking for equality anymore."

Recent home improvement and expansion by the kibbutz for the larger families provided conspicuous evidence of extra-kibbutz wealth differentials. "You could see the houses with thirty thousand shekels [privately] invested in the new part of the house, in the furniture. And there were people like us—the only thing we bought was a new lamp."

This particular informant is philosophical about the egalitarian contradiction. "I always said, 'It's not my business.' There is an expression in Hebrew that goes, 'Don't have an eye on the others.' I am at peace with myself."

But with the passage of time and the birth of a new kibbutz generation, discrepancies have intensified, as doting retirees from abroad lavish their grandchildren with gifts that Israeli grandparents can rarely afford. "There is a girl who has five pairs of jeans, and another who has only two because she doesn't have a grandmother who lives in the States. My husband and I decided to do less for ourselves. It was [more] important to buy our daughter another pair of Levi's."

But the sabras cannot always keep up with the Cohens. "Every family has to deal with this in their own way. Sometimes we tell our daughter we don't have the money and we must manage on what we have."

W. hopes that if her children see that she and her husband are neither angry nor jealous with the wealthier kibbutzniks, then "they'll grow up with the mentality that 'others have money and we don't, but maybe we have happiness that others don't.'"

An otherwise banal statement becomes poignant when heard on-kibbutz: "We always try to explain to the children that money is not everything." That it stems from the moneyed privilege of fellow kibbutzniks infuses the poignancy with irony.

To the extent that the American-born Yahelniks are conscious of this latent jealousy, they are defensive. "Most of us Americans grew up in a family with more wealth than what we have here, that's for sure," admits one. *Ergo*, "it wasn't money motivating people to come and be pioneers in the desert, in progressive Judaism, in the kibbutz movement." People should appreciate the overall material sacrifice these Jewish "Anglo-Saxons" made for their Zionist ideals, not the relative financial advantage that some of them may still possess even as kibbutzniks.

Diana, the seventeen-year-old who spent the first ten years of her life in Armenia, is emphatic that there is a difference between those on Yahel who have money and those who don't, between children of "rich" and non-rich families. "They say we live in an equal environment and have the same things." But it isn't so. Where do you see differences? "In Nikes, toys, bigger TVs."

One might think that such discrepancies are minimal in absolute terms. But that would be to miss the point: kibbutz life was not supposed to give way to *any* material jealousy. When it comes to the children, it is more difficult to tolerate invidious comparisons. Even if it's a matter of the number of blue jeans and size of your television screen.

BURNOUT

Most of the people who have been living here for a long time are pretty burned out. There aren't enough new people here to allow a real turnover and so people keep doing things simply because they realize that there isn't someone else to do it. And if you don't do it, it's not going to happen. You don't want the community to die. But at this time, I just find it more burdensome than fulfilling.

—Laura Sperber

So significant has the problem of burnout—in Hebrew, *shechika*—become at Yahel that the kibbutz has set up a committee to deal with it. Laura Sperber attributes much of the burnout problem to the small size of the population and its inability to grow. Founders and early kibbutzniks had a vision that they assumed would attract others, that of a dynamic, expanding, egalitarian, Reform Jewish intentional community. Others would come and help it expand, thereby assuming some of the responsibilities. Instead, a perpetual cycle of self-selection seems to have set in: the same people. Volunteer to serve on the same committees, in part because no one else will step in otherwise.

The smallness of the community, according to Roselaie Sherris, heightens the intensity of self-reflection within the group. "Some people might call our perceptions of ourselves 'egocentric' or 'provincial.'" Constant self-analysis compounds the work exhaustion. Sometimes you just want to be by yourself and you can't get away. In the pool, for instance, I witnessed this exchange between Rosealie (swimming on her back) and another female kibbutznik, who wanted to talk with her:

> Rosealie: "Leave me alone. I'm busy."
> (Ofrah follows, by swimming alongside Rosealie.)
> Rosealie: "Get away from me!"
> Ofrah: "You're a member of the kibbutz. If it's decided that we swim together, then you have to!"

Back in the States, Laura says, it is good that citizens committed to their community serve as head of the PTA, or volunteer at some level in their children's school, or join a committee of their church or synagogue. "But most people do that kind of thing for a year or two," and then take a break for several more. "They don't spend their whole lives holding five ongoing positions like that all the time." But on Yahel, "people here sit on one, two, three permanent committees, and another one or two ad hoc ones." They get involved in informal forums, and other organizational obligations. "It's too much. You get burned out."

Even Liora Cohen, otherwise a most enthusiastic cheerleader of kibbutz life, admits "Sometimes I would just like to close the door of my house and never leave, and just forget about everyone else. All their demanding, demanding, demanding my attention—I don't have anymore to give to them!" But then she laughs, as if to say, *But I'll go on anyway. Because I have to.*

GENDER EQUALITY?

What is gender equality supposed to mean on a Reform Jewish kibbutz? In the realm of religion, there is no question: women at Yahel are accorded full rights and participatory honors in ritual life: counting as part of the *minyan*, leading services, reading from Torah, and so forth. While this is unremarkably consistent with Reform Judaism, it remains an anomaly within Israel. Israeli congregations where similar gender equality is practiced are few and embattled. They are often the targets of Orthodox wrath. In the remote Arava, the practitioners of egalitarian Judaism are left alone—except for the occasional intrusion of less tolerant relatives from "the city."

Women kibbutzniks have also regularly served in the highest elected and administrative capacity on Yahel, that of mazkira. They take leadership roles in committees, in decision-making writ large. Yet despite their apparent equality in liturgical and managerial spheres, in terms of occupational pathways a rather conservative, stereotypical pattern has set in: most female members have gravitated towards desk jobs on- and off-kibbutz, whereas manual and agricultural positions are occupied almost exclusively by men. This is not the way it was supposed to be, nor the way it started out.

In the early days of the kibbutz, women did work the fields alongside men. They drove the tractors, too, fulfilling the pioneering Zionist goal of an egalitarian and ungendered work life. Conversely, in the past the men of Yahel also undertook child care. With specialization, however, this responsibility has increasingly been farmed out to full-time, professionals—nonmembers, both hired workers and army service cadets. Invariably, they are female. As with Israeli society in general, more traditional sexual divisions in occupation have gradually set in. Yahel women are unapologetic about the role of motherhood in returning them to more "traditional" work expectations.

Here are some typical work assignment pairings: husband, fruit orchards—wife, librarian; husband, electrician—wife, accountant; wife, nurse—husband, irrigation worker; wife, teacher—husband, dairy worker. Yes, there is a female gardener, and one woman working in the packing house. But in general, the outdoor and manual jobs are allocated to men.

American-born women on Yahel left the States at a time when feminism was still more an ideological struggle than a workday reality. Had they arrived a few years later, perhaps they would have more stringently resisted relapse into stereotypical gender-based occupations.

AGING PARENTS

"We've basically written off our families [in America]. We knew it when we made the decision to come here."

Few kibbutzniks will express this sentiment with the same bluntness as Rosealie Sherris. It is not even sure that, back in the late seventies and early eighties, the twenty-something Americans fully appreciated the familial implications of leaving behind the States for Israel. Now that their parents are themselves in their seventies and eighties, carefree, youthful choice is now fraught with related emotional conflict. Relationships with blood relatives back in the States are also affected as the onus of responsibility for aging parents rebounds to the less Zionistic of siblings, who remained in America.*

During the summer of 1999, no fewer than three sets of grandparents visited the kibbutz: the Lendings, the Sperbers, and the Sussmans. Theirs were joyous reunions, and in the Sperber case included a three-generational vacation to Turkey. But the most recent visit of Rosealie's father was more prophetic. During his last trip, he announced that he would no longer come visit. Physically, the voyage had become "just too much."

Heat and distance: rare is the aging Jewish American senior who, regardless of boundless love for a grandchild on Yahel, does not perceive these two immutable facts as increasingly dissuasive factors in the decision to return to the Arava. Not that they were ecstatic about their own children's decision to emigrate in the first place. Abstract love of Israel for cultural, historical, ethnic, political, sentimental, or religious feelings is one thing; seeing one's progeny voluntarily relocate to another continent is another.

Parents of Pioneers

Milton and Ruth Sperber, for example, lived for decades in Jamaica Estates, Long Island. Before retiring Milton was a caterer; he counts among his clients such prominent artists and actors as Alan King, Harry Belafonte, and Anthony Quinn. Members of Temple Israel, Ruth and Milton sent all three of their children to Hebrew school and supported son Matthew in his decision to spend a college year at Hebrew University in Jerusalem. For sure, they raised their children "to understand their heritage." But, insists Ruth, "I did not raise my children to come live in Israel."

Their son Matthew and daughter-in-law Laura "never asked or consulted with" Milton and Ruth about moving permanently to the Jewish homeland. The elder Sperbers were simultaneously "sad and happy" at the decision: "Sad to lose them. Happy for their love, and satisfaction of their dreams, of coming to Israel and making a life here. They endured a lot of hardships on this kibbutz."

But no hardship was greater for the grandparents than enduring the first Gulf War from afar. Grandson Ari was still a toddler when Saddam's Scud missiles began to drop haphazardly on Israel. "When they put gas masks on him, he would cry." Ruth pleaded with her son and Laura to come back to America.

---

* Given Yahel's relative remoteness within Israel itself, this problem also affects Israeli-born kibbutzniks whose aging parents live in "the center."

"We promised them our four bedroom house in Great Neck with a full-time maid. I promised that each child would have their own room." Securing employment would be easy, Ruth insisted. But the inducements didn't work. "They vehemently said they would never leave Israel. They would remain forever. They would stay and endure and be happy, and we were not to worry. Of course, that never placated us."

Looking back, that their son made aliya "wasn't something that made us happy," reflects Matt's Mom, "but that's the way it is. One has to live one's own life. But it has turned out beautifully." After all, the youthful-looking eighty-one-year-old mother admits in all honesty, "I did not ask my parents what I wanted to do. I did what I cared to."

Ruth and Milton celebrated their sixtieth wedding anniversary on Yahel. But with Milton already eighty-five-years-old, it seemed unlikely that they would travel back to the Arava Desert to celebrate their seventieth.

Escape from the Shoah

More than other parents of American-born Yahelniks, the father of Erica Lending appreciates full well what changing one's country and acquiring a new citizenship entails. Unlike for his daughter, though, Jewish migration for Stephen Sussman, was not voluntary: born and raised in Forzheim, Germany, Stephen and his family fled the Nazis when he was already a teenager. He thus has vivid memories of Brown Shirts forcing their way into his home during Kristallnacht and searching for his father.

> My father was fortunately out of town. But the Brown Shirts broke in the apartment door to search for him and did a lot of damage. We contacted father, and told him to lie low. Being a super-conscientious Jewish person, he reported himself to the local police.

They had no interest in him and let him go.

The young Stefan also endured the indignity of being forced out of public school on account of his "race." A worse fate awaited the relatives who ended up in death camps.

Mr. Sussman's background as a fugitive from Hitler does not entirely explain the commitment to Jewish history and nationhood in his progeny: despite the Reform Hebrew school education that he and his wife Dorothy ensured that their two daughters and one son received, only Erica took Judaica seriously and became a committed Zionist. Indeed, not all of the Sussman children married within the faith, and one line of grandchildren is being raised as Lutherans. Yet the elder Sussman is quite philosophical about the life choices of his offspring. "There you have it—three different children, three different directions."

Dorothy Sussman also wished to impart the values of Judaism. "My mother was a religious Zionist," she says, "and as a child I was always in Jewish groups." In her household, "there was always a feeling between Israel and the United States. Maybe for some families it's very strange that a child would take off." But not in hers.

Still, Dorothy admits to "mixed feelings" about Erica's choice to leave America permanently. "It's quite a distance away"—and especially felt so when the grandchildren were born. For sure, "it's her life," says Dorothy, speaking of her elder daughter. "She has always done her own thing and done it well. At least communications are better now, with telephone and computers."

Stephen Sussman admits disappointment that the only part of their family living "a truly Jewish life" is so far away from their home in Littleton, Massachusetts.

Dorothy Sussman: "We love her, and she's family. But we miss her." Mrs. Sussman mentions the many trips made in both directions. "That's what you do when you have family in Israel."

But a bronchial condition in the elderly Sussman is making it increasingly difficult to endure the trek to, through, and in the Negev.

My Friend's Folks

"I had imagined some kind of professional job," recalls Florence Lending, speaking of her son Lloyd, my high school friend. "I never envisioned life for him on a kibbutz. This—*this*—never occurred to me in a million years!"

For sure, there was nothing in the way the Lendings raised their child to suggest an anti-Israel outcome. Elad/Lloyd's father Ed himself grew up, in his own words, "in a profoundly Zionist home." For sure, he goes on, "in my twenties, I became an atheist" (a belief outspoken Ed volunteered to me at his grandson's bar mitzvah). "Despite that, I've been a passionate Jew all along."

Ed Lending was also a passionate political idealist. In his own youth, during the Spanish Civil War he fought in the Abraham Lincoln Brigade. Yet the idealistic commitment his son made still confounds him. When he flies to Israel to visit the younger Lendings, "sometimes, at airport security, they ask me, 'Why did your son come?' 'Beats me,'" Ed replies.

Florence is less flippant. "I didn't stop crying for a month," she recalls about the time young Lloyd announced his decision to emigrate to Israel. "It was too hard. I think you can be a good Jew in the United States."

Of course, as most American parents of Yahelniks, Florence says, "I'm glad he's happy and has such a wonderful family. . . . I've made my piece with his lifestyle. Before, it was primitive. Now, this is like luxury." But there are limits to resignation.

"Parents always say all they want is for their children to be happy. But that is such a crock! I want to be happy, too. I'm not unhappy. But I would be much happier if he were closer. If I could pick up the phone without figuring out how many hours difference there is, and if they're sleeping, or if they're working. I'd like to have them up for dinner every now and then. I would like to be involved in my grandchildren's lives on a more continuing basis. It's not the same thing seeing them once or twice a year."

His own folks don't quite seem to appreciate that Yahel is Elad's own Spain—a field upon which he has to prove his own ideological commitment. To each his own sacrifices. The onetime anti-Vietnam war protester not only still serves in the IDF Reserves, but he and wife Erica also have subsequently sent their own daughter to the Israel Defence Forces.

Yet the immediate battle the Lending family confronts is not the one with Arabs. It is with Alzheimer's. Ed has succumbed rapidly to the disease, and even in Florida it is increasingly difficult for Florence to cope by herself with the myriad complications wrought by her husband's illness. So more frequently than he would prefer, middle-aged Elad waits at the desolate Eilat-Jerusalem bus stop to begin the first leg of a long journey that brings him from the Arava to Boca Raton. It is not a vacation trip.

7

Why They Stayed

It's all about choice, personal choice. Life is a series of choices.
—N. R. Immerman

What sacrifice are you willing to make for your ideals? For Zionism, Danny Hayken risked—and lost—his marriage. It all started in 1986 . . .

"She had studied at the Hebrew University, had a masters in public health, and was in the process of studying for her medical degree in the United States. Then she came back over a summer to re-connect with Israel. I met her through a mutual friend in Jerusalem and we fell in love. I decided at that point it was more important for her to finish her education. So I took a six month leave of absence [from Yahel] to go to the States to live with her, to see if it really was meant to be. We decided it was. We wanted to get married and so, technically, I left the kibbutz. But it was with the goal of coming back. I just didn't know how long it was going to take.

"Then, in marriage, the plan got dragged out. It wasn't just medical school—it was doing an internship. Then it was doing a residency. What was supposed to be one, two, three years turned into seven plus. Meanwhile we had four children and the relationship became very strained. One of the critical issues was Israel.

"She wanted to live in Israel. She was willing to live on-kibbutz. But in having children she became closer to her parents, who lived very close, and they had a relationship with our children, their grandchildren. It became harder for my wife to leave them, to take the grandchildren away from the grandparents.

"She also got caught up in the whole doctor business in the United States. Being a professional, living at a certain level, on that kind of income. But I never gave up my dream and my desire to live back here . . .

"People here always knew that I would come back. You have never been able to take the kibbutznik out of me. Wherever I have been, I have been a kibbutznik. Even when I went back and I lived eleven years in the States, it was still a part of me. There was that piece that was always missing. In a way I lived in exile. Not just exile from Israel but exile from who I was, from the kibbutz. In America I worked for a company, but it wasn't mine. It didn't belong to me. I traveled and I saw beautiful sights but it wasn't my home. They weren't my mountains. It wasn't my people, okay?"

Few of the kibbutzniks on Yahel, American-born or otherwise, have made as wrenching a personal choice as Danny to live out their lives on Yahel. Yet *particularly* for the kibbutzniks who hail from America, there is an acute awareness that, had they established their lives in the land of their birth, their standard of living would be considerably higher than what it is now, on a remote kibbutz in the Negev desert. Although my visit coincided with a time of unprecedented prosperity on Yahel, there is also an underlying concern with respect to their long-term financial security. So why, so long after they have already proven to themselves and the world that they *are* social idealists and committed Zionists, do they remain?

Reasons for staying at Yahel vary from person to person. They range from attachment to the land to loyalty to old friends, from the variety of work to the normalcy of leisure, from model child raising to mixed gender praying. For sure, all kibbutzniks readily *kvetch* about conditions in the community and about their fellow kibbutzniks. Even the most outwardly committed admit that their decision to remain has not been made once and for all but rather is renewed each and every day. Only one generalization is safe to make: the original reasons why they came, as idealistic youngsters in their twenties, no longer suffice to explain why they remain, as sober adults in their forties.

DESERT LIFE

"Before coming, I learned to listen for the difference between gunshots and backfire," recounts Rosealie, describing her past life in the jungles of Brooklyn. "Here, I can literally hear a leaf as it drops to the ground. A leaf!"

The decision to establish the Reform kibbutz in the remote Arava desert near Jordan, remember, was not made by the founders themselves. It was rather made by the architects of the movement, with input from

Israeli defense strategists. Reform Jewish kids from Cleveland, California, and Connecticut signed up for Yahel for what it stood, not for where it stood. Over time, however, the reality of living in this stark, arid environment has come to divide the lifetime kibbutzniks into two psycho-ecological camps: the Desert Rats—those who have come to love the immediate environs of their home—and the Elsewhere Drutherers—those who remain in spite of the harsh environment. Elsewhere Drutherers would have preferred just as readily a Yahel in the cooler Galilee, or on the more convenient coastal plain.

Rosealie Sherris has two pre-Yahel life reference points, her native Brooklyn (in whose background noise she came to distinguish between malfunctioning automobiles and Saturday Night Specials) and her in-laws' Buffalo (where winter survival depends on snow shoveling). In the superbly quiet desert, the painter has found a natural bliss that compensates for the social frictions that otherwise irritate her. Roselaie's brash Brooklyn accent waxes uncharacteristically poetic as she describes another daily miracle offered in the fiery furnace a few paces beyond her humble homestead: a drop of dew dropping off a desert plant. But how can Rosealie's proud and tough kibbutz-reared daughters, for whom the Arava is as commonplace as Bedford-Stuyvesant was for Mom, appreciate desert solitude in the same way?

Ask Danny Hayken, originally from the Midwest, why he remains—the same Danny who has twice chosen desert kibbutz over family life—and he, too, will begin by lyrically invoking the lure of the land. It has to do with

> falling in love with this place. With the mountains, with the air, with the Arava itself. Walking around here you can look up and see the stars shooting and know that there's a big world out there . . .
>
> Everyday I wake up to the mountains in my backyard and know why there are people in this world. Because otherwise, there wouldn't be anyone to appreciate all this great beauty around us.

Desert Rats insist that you watch the Edom mountains at dusk, their hues spanning in sheer minutes the color gamut from lavender to crimson to scarlet. If you are not deeply moved by that daily spectacle, you are assuredly unsuited to life in the Arava.

Ron Bernstein, from the flatlands of Plainview, speaks matter-of-factly about the agricultural prowess of a community thriving "in one of the harshest environments in the world." He'll regale you less with artistic analogies than statistical wonders: summer temperatures ranging up to

120 degrees, relative humidity as low as 10 percent. But behind the farmer's phlegmatic exterior is an undisguised pride, if not awe, in the grafting of suburban Jew to hardscrabble desert.

Not that Ron, or any other Yahelnik, has made a fetish of the land. He readily admits that, in these lightly patrolled and little contested borderlands, his kibbutz got away for decades with cultivating land that technically belonged to the enemy. (Early settlers had few compunctions about moving the demarcation fence into Jordan itself, beyond the gully that topographically served as official boundary.) But in the wake of the Oslo Accords, Ron was quite willing to cede those valuable plots for "the most important gift we can leave to our children, and to all the generations after them—peace with our Arab neighbors." It is a position shared by his fellow kibbutzniks. Unlike the case with settlers in the West Bank, on Yahel there would be "no protests, no hunger strikes, no burning of tires."

Matt Sperber points to the tangibility of achievement that creating life in the desert fosters. "What we do here is very clear, very sharp.

> In the first year we planted the first grass. It was one meter by two meters—and it was very significant. It was very clear that we now had grass on the kibbutz! You could go somewhere and say to another member, "You know that tree next to Hadassa's house?" They would immediately know which tree I was talking about, because it was unusually large for our kibbutz, where the trees were smaller than the people. If you had a couple of trees that were larger, it made a big difference. You felt that.

Nature's growth is intrinsically tied to that of kibbutz life: "You felt that the kids grew while the trees did." Mati sees a strong parallel between the physical development of the community and its economic, cultural, and spiritual growth.

(Alex Cicelsky expresses Lotan's collective ecological view of its locality: "The desert is a place to clean yourself. You get rid of the stuff you don't need. You got to be in awe, and you have to respect it. Because if you don't respect the desert, you're dead. So we have to respect our environment.")

Although few of the actual first founders still live on Yahel, those who have remained from the early years take great pride in having seen the community grow virtually from scratch. Even if they were not present at the inaugural ceremony, theirs remains a Genesis generation: "One of the reasons I'm still here," goes a typical response from an American-born Yahel veteran, "is because I've invested twenty something years in building it, in its success." Some of the pride comes from tangible achievement;

some is purely relational: Danny Hayken speaks of the powerful bond with the "friends that you pioneer with, that you build something with."

Liora Cohen, long ago of Scarsdale, does not hesitate to use spiritual language to describe her spatial attachment:

> The desert holds its own unique beauty. I'm a part of this nature, and the nature is a part of me. There's a real connection there.

In the off-season—that is, when the sun does not broil the skin—Liora likes to take her family hiking in the desert. "What a luxury, to be able to walk out of my back door and just walk for miles and miles! Not to come across another person, not to worry that the kids are going to get run over by a car. Not to hear the noise of the traffic in the city." Sometimes, as she's driving along the Arava highway, Liora will imagine that she's a tourist, viewing the landscape for the very first time, taking in

> the dust of the desert. Yellow, yellow. Brown, brown. Mountains, flat plain, and mountains again. Barren.

Then she'll glimpse "a little dot of green"—fields on the eastern side of the road, trees, and houses on the western side. She's home, but still puts herself in the eyes and mind of the casual passerby, undoubtedly thinking, "You'd have to be nuts to live here."

And she sees the imaginary tourist's point. But then she recalls her intimate connection with that very oasis: "I planted those date trees on the other side of the road. I planted the grass in front of my house. I made a settlement blossom—literally. This is my community, and I built it with my own two hands!" Then, rhetorically, she asks, "How many people have that kind of opportunity in their lives?"

Roslyn, Long Island is not all that different from Scarsdale, New York. But Laura Sperber, originally from Roslyn, typifies that other, much less romantic view of desert life, that of the Elsewhere Drutherers. For Laura, the geographical bottom line is this: Yahel is "in the middle of absolute nowhere." It's not a recent revelation, either: "I didn't come here because it was in the desert. I came here because it was a new Reform kibbutz *despite* the fact that it was in the desert."

The remoteness, Laura claims, is largely responsible for the community's depressed and static size: relatively few people even consider inhabiting such an environment. This, to her, creates the kibbutz's major problem: "It's too small to be a viable, social entity." Laura feels the consequences not only as a community leader—burning out from unrelieved committee work—but as an athlete—having only a single tennis partner. (For the same reason, the bridge games have all but disappeared.)

Then again, Laura has particular reason to be sensitive to the geography of her home: every week she commutes, by airplane from the regional airstrip a good twenty miles away, all the way to her computer programming job at a company in Netanya, along the Mediterranean Coast.

So why *does* she stay?

THE TUG OF COMMUNITY

"People have need for community," Laura maintains, even as she expresses skepticism over the long-term prospects of kibbutz-style economic interdependency. Mutual cooperation is precious. Particularly for people who value Judaism—its holidays, cultural celebrations, and life cycle events—living among like-minded people in similar stages of family life, with whom one can consistently share these experiences, is priceless.

And why, in the Jewish State of Israel of all places, need this translate into living out in the remote desert?

One need only see and hear Laura lead Sabbath services to know the answer. Even among nonreligious Israeli Jews, the notion of women donning prayer shawls, physically embracing the sacred scrolls, and praying on behalf of a mixed-sex congregation is still somewhere between alien and anathema. In terms of religious ritual, Yahel (as well as Lotan) is absolutely egalitarian. While nascent Reform congregations are forming in urban Israel, they remain marginal phenomena that do not come close to approximating the kind of whole-life, gender-equal Judaism prevailing on the Arava kibbutzim.

For most kibbutzniks, however, the tug of community encompasses much more than religious equality between the sexes. Kibbutz manager Liora Cohen, who as wife and mother of three, would seem to have enough to occupy her life, is perhaps most articulate on this score.

Why am I still here? A lot of it has to do with my personality.

I just find myself being committed to relationships and taking them seriously, not willing to let go of them easily. It's true with every kind of relationship I have to this day—personal and social and family. It's my fault. It's not necessarily because of the kibbutz, it's because of me. I'm the kind of person that I am and I find myself very involved—in spite of everything else—in my commitments and loyalties and social issues around me.

Yet after explaining her staying at Yahel, almost apologetically, in terms of her own mental makeup, Liora waxes outright altruistic about the essence of communal life:

> You can give of yourself for somebody else without any ulterior motives. That's because this is one big family and that's what we do: we take care of each other. You're giving not because of what you're getting in return, and knowing that you've done something for somebody else—for other people, for the community. It's an opportunity that you wouldn't [easily] have outside this kind of framework.

After a moment, and in a tone of undisguised revelation, Liora adds: "You know what? I suppose you do get something out of it in return. You feel a great deal of satisfaction."

Ironically, Laura finds the community in Yahel to be more heterogeneous than the life of her most Jewishly committed friends back in America. "Who am I to talk, right? Maybe I just see the closure of their society more than I see it in my own. But things outside of their work pretty much revolve around Jewish involvement. They live in a very closed society—as if they are still living in Camp Ramah," the summer camp of the Conservative movement. This Laura contrasts with an even higher comfort level she has with friends who are not as totally wrapped up, socially and professionally, in Jewish circles, who send their children to public school and who display greater balance between synagogue and non-synagogue activities. On-kibbutz, it seems, the many nonreligious preoccupations tend to make even a progressive synagogue life in the Diaspora feel stultifying in comparison.

Lori Stark, the former Rhode Islander, puts it this way:

> Whatever tomorrow brings, be it for me or my neighbor, there is an extended family here. That kind of support is unique—and what keeps many people here.

Whether on holidays, in tragedies, or for life cycle celebrations, "the community comes through. Knowing neighbors. Security, emotional security. (And, more recently, financial security.)" For sure, "it's not a utopian community." ("We're not angels," adds Matitayahu Sperber.) "But anywhere where I'm living, I'd put on a scale. If the positive is over 50 percent, I stay." For Lori Stark, Judaism at Yahel is part of the positive.

Nancy Reich Immerman, originally from suburban New York, still feels the tug of community that Yahel represents for her: "It's like a miniature welfare state wherein we take care of each other. We are all responsible for everything that goes on here. All the property belongs to every-one." She illustrates:

> When I go down to swim at the pool, I'm going to *my* pool, okay?
> When I go down to eat at the dining hall, I'm eating at *my* dining
> hall. When I walk around unkempt areas of [kibbutz] gardening, I
> take a look and say, "Gosh, my garden is really growing out of con-trol." In other words, we are all involved, and we are all responsible.

Nancy well understands why others left when structural reform threatened long-held tenets of socialistic ideology. "When you begin to feel you are compromising your integrity, maybe it is time to get up and go somewhere else. On the other hand,

> this is my home now. It's the only home that I have and it's more
> important to be [here]. Commitment means riding it out, in the bad
> times as well as the good.

Some speak about the kibbutz as a living being with which the mem-ber has an active, ongoing, personal relationship. As Danny Hayken says, "The kibbutz cares about me and I care about it.

"In some ways," he goes on, describing the other members, "they're my best friends. They are not necessarily my best friends emotionally, but they know me better than anybody else could. Because they see me in any and all situations. I have no need to hide anything from the people here."

Another male member (the men wax less gloriously about "relation-ships" on-kibbutz) puts it this way. "As a group of people, we're pretty good together. We're friends. Not *great* friends. Not everyone is a great buddy with everybody else. But because we're also involved business-wise, we're more than acquaintances."

Ron Bernstein illustrates. "On one side, I have a business relation-ship with Matt because he's the business manager and I'm the head of the pomelo branch. On the other side, we sit together at services on Friday night and pray together. Our kids are friends."

"Each of us is a little unusual in our own way," observes Danny Hayken wryly. "And that is what makes it fun living here."

LIVING LIFE JEWISHLY

"The Jewish elements of life at Yahel are so ingrained in our lives. We have put a priority here on community and [Jewish] learning." Adult education is as important as children's: "You don't have to be a rabbi to become an educated Jewish person."

Lori Stark points out that, compared with other kibbutzim, Yahel's community dining room is rather plain, if not outright drab. She is proud of that fact: it reflects an early decision of the kibbutz to put its resources into building an impressive synagogue and library complex as opposed to beautifying the dining hall.

As we'll see in chapter eight, the kibbutz also provides an opportunity to perform tangible acts of *tikkun olam*, social justice. This, too, retains the loyalty of members like Lori Stark.

Lori believes that Reform Judaism's theological encouragement of religious adaptation has enabled the community to survive in hard times, and later to thrive. "We're not afraid of change, as long as it is positive and natural. That comes from our Reform background." Such open-mindedness liberates the community from remaining in a "this is what a kibbutz ought to be" mind-set.

"I'm happy that I live here," affirms Matt Sperber, "in Jewish time in a Jewish holiday framework in a Jewish week, reading a Jewish newspaper. I find it very satisfying that the culture is an integrated Jewish one for me. I guess my kids will have to find that out for themselves."

VARIETY OF WORK LIFE

"I've done all sorts of jobs here without having the right qualifications," says the Scarsdale beauty, self-depreciatingly. "Moving from one profession to another. Dealing with absorption [of potential members], then people's workplaces." The enormous range of professional experiences on-kibbutz has exposed more than this one Yahelnik to a multitude of issues, ideas, perspectives.

Economic specialist M. Sperber also acknowledges with satisfaction the variety of work he's been able to do. "As opposed to certain types of businesses where you get into sort of a straight line, moving up the ladder, just staying on the ladder, not having opportunities to do a lot of different things."

Danny Hayken absolutely "loves" the variety of work that life on kibbutz affords. "I am not just an electrician. I love being a tour guide. I like being able to drive people to the airport if they need it, to fill in anywhere and everywhere. I would gladly milk cows and drive tractors in the fields" again. Danny jokes about his job search in the States after eight years living and working on-kibbutz. His resumé reflected all this job experience, including kitchen supervisor and workforce manager. The re-action of prospective American employers, unfamiliar with kibbutz life, was similar: "You did all of that in eight years? Couldn't you keep a job?"

The rabbi's grandson recalls how he first developed his reputation as a maintenance maven: A soldier was serving part of his stint at Yahel, where he was assigned maintenance detail. Suddenly, he was called back to his unit to serve. The kibbutz had no one to take his place.

"I didn't know anything about maintenance," Danny confesses, but they asked him if he would take over, anyway. Danny revealed his techni-cal ignorance, but added: "You don't have anybody better, so, okay, I'll do the best job I can." What was the secret to his success? The utter sameness of kibbutz construction.

"If something breaks in your apartment, I can go to the one next door and have an exact example to see how the thing really works. I take it apart and figure out what doesn't match. That is how I learned to fix things on kibbutz."

From the time I knew him in high school until I began writing this book—three decades during which books (reading, writing, and teaching about them) have constituted my entire professional life—Elad né Lloyd has been a tractor driver, desert tour guide, army medic, kibbutz manager, electrician, vocational instructor, and kibbutz manager. His wife Erica has also had several vocations, ranging from pepper picker to bookkeeper.

My old friend, the optimistic pragmatist, sums up his work life like this: "I like my job most of the time, though, I could be challenged more, professionally. Maybe 10 percent of the work that I do is challenging.

"I'd like it to be more, but how many people actually get that?"

HAPPINESS?

> What does a kibbutz really offer? What kind of security? Financial security? Long term security? It can offer a minimum amount of money, good standards for the children, an adequate pension fund. But it certainly can't offer what a lot of people make in their own private occupations. The only thing the kibbutz really has to offer people is their happiness.

These sentiments, expressed by Danny Hayken and shared by an-other Yahelnik I'll call Job, sums up well the existential tug that keeps long-term members, from wherever they originally hailed, living in the desert community. Job knows better than most: When I spoke with him, he was coping simultaneously with two unrelated traumas—spousal infidelity and testicular cancer.

"I owe this community a lot," he says. "It's difficult to understand what it's like being with the same people all the time—eating, working, socializing. It's not a place where everyone likes everyone. A few years ago, there was even a lot of human hate going around. Backstabbing, and so on. But when I got cancer, everyone felt that someone in their family was sick. Even the people I hated came to my help.

"Everyone here is a believer in lifetime insurance. I'm not talking about personal insurance or pensions, and you can't put a monetary value to it. It's about knowing that if something drastic should happen, you'll be looked after by a whole big bunch of people. If my cancer had spread, and I was to die, I knew this was the place I'd want my family to be."

After her affair with another member became public knowledge, Job's wife had a mental breakdown. She no longer could work and required hospitalization. Job appreciates the community efforts expended on behalf of the woman who caused him such pain and embarrassment. "There was a whole group people, five or six people, running around to arrange support for her. These people were not even especially her friends. If I had to handle this on my own, living in the city, it would have made me bankrupt." Even while remaining separated, that's why Job and his wife each decided to stay on the kibbutz. Both of them believed that, "down the road," the community would help them out.

"The more social upheavals there are like this, the more people can identify with why they're here," reflects Job. "I've been there. I've tested that the community does look after its own. I've cashed in," he reiterates metaphorically, "on part of my insurance policy."

My high school friend Elad/Lloyd ties it all together:

I'm a happy person right now, I really am. There were times I was much less happy, even though I thought I was living in a more ideologically pure way. I have a wonderful marriage, a wonderful family, a job that I like. There's community. Materially, I feel comfortably off. My house was recently expanded. My kids get excellent education in one of the finest high schools in the country. . . . I work hard, I play hard, I do things outside of work. We have a country club here, tennis courts, swimming pool. I play music in a regional ensemble, tennis in a regional league. I am always doing something or studying something.

"FOR THE CHILDREN"

As Yahel's older adolescents begin to imagine their future, they unwittingly describe kibbutz by inverting the old joke about the big city: *It's a nice place to raise children, but I wouldn't want to live there.*

Outsiders invariably take this as a sign of failure: if the kibbutzniks' own offspring do not wish to remain there, then how can the community replenish and survive? What does this say about the viability of the Reform communal experiment in the desert?

While naturally concerned about the community's future, Yahel's parents do not share this negative assessment. To the contrary, the privilege of raising their children on-kibbutz has become the strongest justification for their own decision to stay on, overcoming countervailing pressures of geographic isolation, group insularity, social intrusion, ideological compromise, and financial dependence. They take enormous satisfaction in seeing their scions grow up in a safe, secure environment, nurtured and protected by the entire community. They take pride and pleasure not only in the development of their own offspring but the entire community's. Even more than Israeli youth in general, kibbutz kids exude personal autonomy, self-confidence, mutual obligation, a sense of responsibility, and a work ethic. Seeing the values of Reform Judaism take root anew—as when the elder Stark boy participates in an Arab-Israeli coexistence program, for instance—provides great satisfaction for the more religiously motivated parents.

Liora Cohen, mazkira of the kibbutz, contemplates the changes wrought by privatization. She can tolerate most of it, including that for culture (cost membership to partake in organized cultural events). But not when it comes to her children's education. The kibbutz needs to retain "a commitment to educate my child in the best framework that it can afford," she says. "I need to be involved in that process."

Successful parenting was far from the minds of the mostly single American twenty-something-olds who, in the late 1970s and early 1980s, decided to join this experiment in communal living and Reform Judaism in the Israeli desert. But as they have grown and matured, it *has* become a major motivation to stick it out—particularly after ideological zeal and idealism have yielded to capitalistic pressures and middle-age sedentarism. Those who made dramatic decisions to leave behind comfortable, suburban, middle-class, American upbringings to fulfill their own dreams and ambitions are not about to begrudge their own children similar freedom to make choices about their own lives.

"I would like my children to have many experiences like I had growing up, postadolescence," says Nancy of Larchmont, speaking of Michael, Gai, and Inbal. "To travel, learn other languages, immerse yourself in other cultures." Eventually, "if I'm living here, yes, I would like my children to join me. This is a very hard place to live. I don't fancy growing old down here by myself." But Nancy knows this is more of a wish than a likelihood.

I confess to Ron Bernstein my sentiments that it would be strange to raise children who don't share my own American culture. It doesn't bother him for his own kids.

"Well, they understand the culture. They know what's going on there. If I wanted them to feel part of the States, we'd be living there. But they're Israelis.

"They may eventually decide to move" to America, Ron offers spontaneously, speaking of the country of his birth, "and I have no right to tell them not to." He is referring to his Shani and Chagai, his two surviving children. "People must live where they're most comfortable, and most happy." As the official tour guide of the kibbutz, this is what he tells countless groups of young American Jewish teenagers.

"I never, ever tell them, 'You all must to live in Israel. It's the only Jewish country.' What right do I have to tell them that? I have nothing against Israelis who leave. It's up to you. It's your decision."

"Are they going to come live here?" Laura Sperber wonders aloud about Shira, Noam, and Ari. "I doubt it. I really do not think that they will. At one point that was *the* test of the success of a kibbutz—what percentage of the children came back to live on it. That was in a very different society, where the choices available were far more limited.

"But in today's world, I have no such expectations—in the same way that, if I lived in Ramat Gan [a suburb of Tel Aviv], I wouldn't expect my kids to be my neighbors. Israeli society as a whole has undergone tremendous changes," including the family. More nuclear. More job-oriented. "I don't see it as a failure of the community if the kids don't come back to live here." But husband Matt places a firm limit on how far from the Zionist nest their Jewish children should fly.

"For all of my attempts to let them live a guilt-free life up until now," admits Matt Sperber, "I'm willing to lay a guilt trip on them if they leave me here and go live in the States, in the Diaspora. I'm not willing to pretend that that won't make me disappointed and unhappy."

Is it too soon to anticipate the hope that, after their children have finished the army, traveled the world, completed their education, gained some work experience and gotten married, they will eventually return to

Yahel to raise their own children? Just as they themselves at twenty could hardly imagine being the parents of grown children, is it premature for them now, even before their kids have yet to do their military service, to envision themselves becoming grandparents? And will it matter all that much if the Yahel to which their grown children come back is no longer the kibbutz that their parents founded? What if, in the decades to come, it simply evolves, in the words of one of the veterans, into "a successful community of people who are happy and enjoy their life, and their lifestyle, and the people that they live with; a community built on non-Orthodox, religious, Jewish, Reform, progressive, liberal democratic principles" without any lingering pretense of socialism or egalitarianism? Should the experiment of Kibbutz Yahel then be adjudged a failure?

"My parents put aside money for my education so that I could study, get the right job, and grow up in suburbia," recalls Liora. "And then I chose to go in a totally different direction. So why shouldn't my children have the opportunity to go in their own direction? . . . It's important that my children understand my dream. Why we came here, what I did. My identification, the ideology. As far as their aspirations go, they've got to do what they want. Just like I did." Since Yoav, Adi, and Carmel are also of British parentage, they have even greater overseas opportunities.

Yahelniks who have spent most of their adult lives building up their community, and have weathered the storm of structural adjustment, have proven their willingness to accept change. Not only do they acknowledge that the kibbutz as an institution has changed, and will likely continue to do so; but they also understand that, as they transition through different phases of adulthood, their dreams, goals, and aspirations are also subtly shifting. Until their children are on their own, Yahelniks' reasons for remaining will continue to revolve around them.

And if their children do ultimately decide to live "in the city," that is no tragedy. Even if, for Israel, Yahel is "at the end of the world," in fact it is no more than four hours away from most urban centers. Younger couples who grew up "in the city" throughout Israel do apply for membership, and it is they, not the founders' own children, who very well may constitute the next kibbutz generation; immigrants from Russia and elsewhere may, too, replenish the working ranks. Whether they are joined by "returnees"— children of the first generation—probably depends on whether the kibbutz will have succeeded, in the words of its economic manager, of

enhancing and creating greater economic opportunities that would attract and satisfy a wider range of types of people. Not just agriculture and industry but teachers and educators and psychologists and hardware and software computer people and communications and marketing and lawyers and journalists and doctors.

In the meantime, the idealists-turned-parents stay on.

A PERMANENT DECISION?

"I'd be very surprised to hear there's somebody who wakes up in the morning and says, 'This is where I want to be. I'm 100 percent here. I've got no questions about what I'm doing and where I'm going.' Life is so dynamic and things change. In another ten, twenty years we might not be a kibbutz anymore. Who knows? I choose every day not to leave," reflects Liora Cohen.

Another stalwart of the community, the economic manager, concurs. "Everybody thinks of leaving at various times. Sometimes it's the husband and sometimes it's the wife. It usually goes back and forth at different times for different people for reasons." So why does the veteran stay? "Ultimately, I still enjoy and get excited by the challenges of what we're trying to build here."

Perhaps the greatest of all the original challenges—and the one most difficult to judge—is the creation of a community entirely devoted to the principles of Reform Judaism.

8

Praying—and Not—in the Wilderness

I'm very proud of what we have built as Reform Jews—the attempts to be creative, to live life in a Jewish way, not just a kibbutz way. The way we relate to the *mitzvot* [the commandments], the covenant.

—American-born Yahelnik

Prospective members merely have to agree not to be opposed to Reform—that's what it has come down to.

—South African-born Yahelnik

It is Friday night and the desert rays are finally relenting. As the sunlight recedes, hints of Sabbath stillness already permeate the kibbutz. Those on duty in the dining hall finish setting the tables—the only time in the week this is done—now that they have spread the tablecloths and posed the flower vases. Challah bread and wine are placed at every one of the long tables, as well as at the small head table one from which he (or she, in this egalitarian community) assigned to make *kiddush* this week will say the blessings. (You check the list on the dining room bulletin board to know whose turn it is.)

A few minutes walk away, three rows of sleek, upholstered wooden chairs line the airy, air-conditioned prayer sanctuary. Behind the chairs is a wall of windows, emphasizing the openness and transparency of the synagogue. Straight ahead, built into the northern wall—from here, the direction towards Jerusalem—is the ark holding the Torah scroll. Between the chairs and the ark is the lectern from which the prayer leader of the week will conduct services.

Compared to the grandiose, elaborate, ornate Reform temples in America, this simple kibbutz chapel is downright homey. It is inviting in its casualness: come to shul in shorts, if you will, or wearing sandals, if this be your pleasure. Come on in and pick up one of those melody inspiring prayer books, designed especially for joyous, Reform-style group singing. Just come on in!

Here's the problem: on a typical Friday night, it is touch and go if more than a few Yahelniks will actually show up. Even counting the women (which Reform Judaism emphatically does, to the consternation of the Orthodox), it is not sure that the requisite minyan of ten adults will be present to officially initiate prayer. Those who do arrive are the regulars, the die-hard *daveners* who are increasingly discouraged by their marginality in what was supposed to be the flagship community of Reform Judaism.

How does one measure the success of any religion? By attendance at services, or by the behavior of its followers? By the number of rites performed, prayers recited, and injunctions observed? Or by the degree of ethical humanity fostered by the religion's principles?

These questions, thorny for any denomination, are particularly acute in Yahel, the kibbutz whose very genesis is anchored in creating a whole life, noncoercive version of community-centered Judaism. Doing so in a Zionist state whose constitution mandates freedom of religion but whose religious establishment delegitimates non-Orthodox branches of Judaism has both facilitated and complicated Yahel's role as an embodiment of progressive and communal Judaism.

The spiritual leader of the Reform kibbutzim, ever since their founding, is Rabbi Alan Levine. Toronto-born and bred, son of the first Jewish Canadian major league football player, Levine shocked his Reform parents when, after graduating from McGill University, and knowing little Hebrew, he announced he wanted to become a rabbi. From a traditionalist perspective Levine was so lacking in Yiddishkeit, so culturally "un-Jewish," that one of his Hebrew Union College professors advised him to take a half a year's leave in Williamsburg, the ultra-Orthodox section of Brooklyn.

But Levine's Judaism was indistinguishable from his Zionism. It also was tightly wound up in the prophetic tradition of social justice. In the 1950s, still in his twenties, Levine gravitated between Israel and Mississippi, between Ben-Gurion and Martin Luther King. He worked with the latter—knew Malcolm X, too—and was arrested during one of the early Freedom Rides.

"The thrust of my life, from my youth and childhood," explains the blue-eyed rabbi between puffs on his pipe, "was the social message of Judaism. Judaism is not just ritual. It's our daily life in terms of ethical behavior, which involves a lot of social action. There is a relationship between Judaism and the everyday social problems of Israel.

"Certainly Ben-Gurion's message was one of prophetic Judaism. The idea that the State would be based on the principles of Judaism, meaning justice, equality, concern for the disadvantaged. Not a state for the privileged. That's Isaiah, that's Amos, that's Jeremiah."

Some time after making aliya, Levine was asked to head the Israeli Reform Youth Movement, a position from which he closely collaborated with Henry Skirball, another rabbi oriented to social action. The two discussed the possibility of incorporating the prophetic ideas of Judaism into a new community, one composed of youthful, idealistic American and Israeli Jews.

"The problem with the existing kibbutzim," according to Rabbi Levine, "was they had prophetic Judaism but left it out as a concept. In other words, they lived prophetic Judaism but didn't necessarily connect it with Judaism. They connected it with socialism. And they connected it with secular ideas." So Levine and Skirball, with the assistance of another rabbi, Stephen Schaefer, plotted a scheme that never really was embraced by the Reform establishment, either in the United States or Israel.

"If we had a kibbutz, if we had our own community, we could establish rules of society consistent with what we believed to be the thrust of Judaism. Why don't we form a Reform community and make real changes, not only for ourselves, but also as an example for the community at large? Our own Reform community, with values that have to do with Arab-Jewish relationships, with war, social justice. This would be a first." Levine launched the idea at a Reform youth conclave in Israel, over Hanukkah in 1973. It did not seem like an auspicious time to mount new, idealistic community planning schemes—the Yom Kippur War, a military rebuff and psychological disaster, had ended but two months prior.

"Suddenly there was an awareness that we were really very vulnerable. The country was depressed. But that is what youth conclaves should be all about—introducing lofty ideas to kids, especially at a time of terrible national problems. How do you give hope when people are not sure whether they should be hopeful or not?"

It was at the conclave that the prophets of Reform kibbutz Zionism were able to touch some sensitive chords, finding future recruits among youthful, questing Jews.

"Professional Jew": the term makes you cringe at first blush, conjuring up seedy images of greedy yids plying their religion for money. But in the

mouths of the kibbutzniks the notion of professional Jew, while not exactly complimentary, merely describes a state of affairs in which a Jewish
community—in particular, one in Diaspora—requires paid career specialists to perform the tasks necessary to preserve the tradition, the faith, and
the people. A rabbi is obviously a professional Jew, as is the cantor who
regularly leads prayer in the synagogue. But so is the community leader,
and the youth organizer, and the hired expert (and his underlings) who
directs any of the myriad organizations from the AJC (American Jewish
Committee) to the ZOA (Zionist Organization of America).

Whole-life Judaism, as realized on the religious kibbutz, obviates the
need for professional Jews. All members are committed to maintaining a
fully Jewish component to their lives and do not need professionals to help
them along this path. Ritualistic Judaism, in any event, requires no inter-
mediary or expert to lead prayers: any adult (for the Orthodox, any man)
is empowered to be a *shaliach tsibur*, a prayer leader. On Yahel, there are
several former Americans who know that, had they not become kibbutzniks in Israel, they would have become professional Jews back home.
One of these is Matityahu (né Matthew) Sperber, a strapping man with
curly hair and rambunctious laugh. Matt who grew up on Long Island
(Queens and Great Neck) majored in religion at Emory University. He
met his future wife, Laura, during a junior year abroad at Hebrew University. They arrived at Yahel as the only married couple on the kibbutz and
remain, at forty-six and forty-four, kibbutz "elders." Matt and Laura also
parented the oldest Yahel child—eighteen-year-old daughter Shira. Matt
was on reserve duty with the army for the first weeks after I arrived at
Yahel, but we eventually spent a relaxed couple of hours by the poolside.

"Both of us were going to study, to be Jewish educators [but] decided
not to go into the rabbinate," Matt recalls. We were anti-rabbinate, in fa-
vor of democracy." Matt in particular disliked the non-egalitarian reality
of Reform Judaism in America.

"All the things that a synagogue has to decide—what the religious
rules are going to be, the content of the services and how much English,
whether they're going to read Torah on Friday night or Shabbat morning—
are, if not decided by the rabbi, influenced very greatly" by him. "If the
rabbi even lets the ritual committee participate in those decisions, then
he's a democrat. The level of participation in the community in those decisions is usually very minimal."

So when they heard of plans to establish "the first Reform Jewish
community—progressive, non-Orthodox, liberal," Matt and Laura were
turned on. "Our goal was to have a community based on a much greater

level of participation," where religious decisions—"how to study, how to celebrate Shabbat"—would be taken in tandem with work decisions—"whether to grow lemons next year, or peppers, or whether we're going to pay to send the children to summer camp." Connecting religion with community and business, in an egalitarian Jewish mode—this is how Matt, Laura, and the other visionaries saw the distinctive future of Yahel. Call it pragmatic spirituality.

From the lips of such hip Jews, it is bemusing to hear of the talmudic-like debates common in the kibbutz's early years. Is it proper to milk cows on the Sabbath? What about crops whose timely harvesting is critical? Can a modern agro-business survive if it follows the Deuteronomic injunction of the jubilee, leaving all fields fallow for one year? Do we still need to sell all our *hametz* (leavened foods) to a Gentile before Passover?

Interpretation of the mitzvot, the commandments, had constituted the hallmark of traditional Jewish scholarship; these young, Reform Jews, while coming up with different answers for a "noncoercive Judaism," still wrestled with the same, ancient questions. While spiritually uplifting, the process was ultimately exhausting. Theology-by-committee has also bequeathed some inconsistent results. Take the Messiah, for instance . . .

Meetings were held in the early days of Yahel to formulate an appropriate *birkat hamazon*, the grace after meals. Now the traditional, unabbreviated grace, from which Yahel was modeling its own, contains several references to *ha-Moshiah, ben David*. Reform Judaism, however, had long before replaced belief in an actual earthly appearance of a Messiah-Man of Davidic lineage with a more metaphorical anticipation of a peaceful, messianic age. Thus, in the first meetings dealing with the beginning portions of the birkat grace, the old-time references to "the Messiah, son of David" were deleted. But in subsequent meetings, dealing with the latter portions of the grace, reference to the literal Messiah reference survived. This was not a result of deliberate messianic compromise: quite simply, a different mix of members had shown up at the various meetings! At Yahel, there is thus a Reform grace after meals which both includes and, on principle, excludes, references to the Messiah.

"Today," Matt admits, "we are less of a full participatory, democratic-oriented" society. "It's too tiresome. It [takes] too much energy. It's appropriate for people in their twenties who want to sit and talk and think and struggle in meetings that go on until two o'clock in the morning. They were fun and we enjoyed it and it was exciting. That intensity is an important part of any young, dynamic group. It's less appropriate for people as they get older." As a result, relatively few religious questions are decided anymore in the *asefa*, the general assembly. Indeed, secular as well as religious matters (although the line is not so clear-cut on the Reform kibbutz as in the wider Israeli society) are decided more and more in smaller committee meetings. The asefa no longer pretends to the radically transformative and collectively democratic role that it once did.

And so the religious contours of the Yahel community were defined in the early years, contours within which individuals are free to observe—or not—within their private space. Take the case of *kashrut*, the observance of dietary laws. Early on the kibbutz decided that its communal eating facility would indeed follow the traditional strictures of separating dairy from meat foods and likewise maintain separate sets of dishes and utensils. This, even though the Reform movement as a whole long ago decided to jettison "keeping kosher" from the core principles of modern Judaism.

Yet while Yahel's public kitchen and dining facilities are kosher, there is no parallel expectation that families will necessarily observe kashrut in their own kitchens at home. Most, indeed, do not. (At least not by halachic standards; there is no alternative Reform type of kashrut.) Similarly, while the use of motorized vehicles for official kibbutz purposes is prohibited on the Sabbath (except for previously decided exceptions, such as necessary harvesting), individuals are free to drive or travel on what is, essentially, their only free day of the week. Since kibbutz rules do not (at least yet) allow private ownership of vehicles, this often means requisitioning kibbutz cars for Sabbath day outings.

Since Yahel's pupils attend a regional school frequented by schoolchildren from other, mostly secular, kibbutzim, the question of Shabbat driving becomes problematic as a matter of parenthood as well as piety. Take the case of the Sperber family. Laura and Matt—among the most religiously active of Yahelniks—would not drive during the Sabbath. But friends of daughter Shira, from other kibbutzim, would regularly throw parties on Friday nights. At first, she simply couldn't go. Then the family decided that she could attend these parties, but only by staying away the whole weekend: traveling before the Sabbath began, returning after it had ended. "Later on," recounts Shira, "when I was in the seventh grade, we reached a family decision that it was more important to be together as a family for Shabbat than not to drive. So we would have Friday night dinner together and then one of my parents would take me [to the party]." Similarly, when Matthew would have a weekend leave from his army Reserve duty, "we would rather have him come home than not drive."

Nowadays, when most issues of ritual have long been resolved, it is the social application of Judaism that reflects Yahel's spirit of Reform. Mati gives an example from a recent meeting he had attended.

After a year's residence, a family was requesting that its "guest" status be upgraded to that of "candidate." (After another year as candidates, they could then be considered for full membership.) There was a problem, however. "There were rumors" about the family. "Nasty social rumors." It would have been inconsistent with Mati's moral message to divulge the rumors and so for once I did not pry.

So the discussion turned to the soul of the kibbutz: "who we are as a liberal, progressive, Reform Jewish community." In the end, the assembled members decided that "this type of behavior is unacceptable."

What was unacceptable? The moral lapses of which the family was suspected? No—it was the *richilut*: malicious gossip, formally chastised within Jewish tradition. It was the unsubstantiated, unproven, merely rumored nature of the charges that came under scrutiny. For Matityahu, it was solid vindication that the Jewish spirit of Yahel is relevant and dynamic, even if debates over ritual and liturgy no longer muster the excitement that they once did.

Matityahu, with his infectious laugh and optimistic personality, nevertheless admits to Yahel's "greatest failure":

> We have not succeeded in attracting a large or larger number of committed, Reform, progressive, non-Orthodox Jews, people who came here because that was what they were looking for. When you do it percentage wise, we have 25 percent serious, committed, Reform Jews—active, participating, after 20–25 years in the community.
>
> That certainly holds up well against any Reform Jewish synagogue in the world, in terms of involved members in Jewish communal life. But we're only fifty people. So the fact that there are just fifteen of us—barely more than a minyan—is frustrating, tiring, and difficult.

But Matityahu doesn't draw any categorical lines.

> There are another ten, fifteen, twenty people who are passively committed. It's difficult to live in a relatively serious Reform Jewish community [for] fifteen, twenty years and not absorb that reality and identify with it.

These are kibbutzniks who never had much of a religious background, Reform or otherwise, to begin with. If only by default, though, "they participate in the cultural events and the way we celebrate the Shabbat and holidays." For Sperber, study and "contact with educators" who pass through heighten that exposure to Judaism for the theologically lukewarm kibbutz members.

And the rest? Incredibly (or maybe not so incredibly, when you realize that not long ago a neighboring kibbutz officially voted to be secular),
in the past there were potential members who opposed Yahel's Reform vision outright. "People arrived here [just] because they had a friend, or for
some other reason. They were serious secular. Antireligion. Quite some
time ago we were successful in making it politically incorrect to be opposed" to Yahel's religious side. Still, there are Yahelniks—Matt estimates
between one-fifth and one-quarter—for whom religion "is not really important. But even they occasionally participate" in the religious life of the community. Matt readily places this denominational crisis in broader context.

"Our failure was no different from the rest of the Reform Jewish
movement in Israel. Over the twenty-something years that we've been
here, in Israel itself the real number of people who identify as Reform or
progressive Jews has not grown." Matityahu is fully aware that in recent
years there has been a boom in Israelis seeking life-cycle ceremonies—
weddings, bar mitzvahs, funerals—conducted by non-Orthodox officiates.
But these are not people who will go to Friday night services. "The fact
that they get married by a Reform rabbi doesn't necessarily mean that they
identify as Reform Jews." For some, a Reform service is an anti-Orthodox
statement. For others, Reform requirements appear less rigorous, and so
they are attracted by the convenience.

Put in global perspective, Yahel's Reform vision was downright anti-
historical. "Reform Jews from around the world didn't make aliya in any
significant numbers," notes the ex-Long Islander. "Those who did [so]
didn't identify strongly enough with the challenges and opportunities of
being part of an intensive Jewish community. A kibbutz out in the desert
thins out the potential pool."

Laura, Matt's wife, is more categorical. "As a Jewish community, it's
not big enough to be viable. Three or four people lead services here on an
informal basis because we don't have a full-time professional Jew doing
that for us. It's nice to have that informality but sometimes if I don't do it,
there's nobody else to." Laura wistfully imagines "just a pool of people
large enough" so that the religious onus were not always on the same few
folk. "It's draining not to have a minyan."

A more upbeat understanding of Yahel's Reform Jewish profile comes from
Lori Stark, coordinator for several of the tikkun olam, or social action,
programs of the kibbutz. Tikkun olam literally means "repairing the
world" and is embedded within a venerable religious literature. For Lori,
doing just acts for the needy is an essential part of Judaism. She also sees it

as one of the major successes of the kibbutz: "Yahel has always had the outlook that, as Reform Jews, tikkun olam is a responsibility."

On the grounds that Judaism does not separate the spiritual from the quotidian, Yahel's founders decided *not* to establish a separate committee for religious affairs. Members of all other committees were thus empowered to consider the religious dimension to their activities. This extended to tikkun olam, which became an imperative for all constituent groups on the kibbutz.

Another early decision was how to deal with the biblical injunction to not harvest the "four corners" of one's fields, leaving them for the poor. "A secular kibbutz wouldn't even have thought of it," observes Lori. But from the very first year of Yahel's existence "we studied and decided to take the proceeds from those four corners and start some sort of tikkun olam program.

> In the beginning it was a Big Brother program with underprivileged children in Eilat. Once a week kids would come up here and have nutritional meals, do arts and crafts, get help with their homework, and be on the farm with a little space to breathe. [They saw that] life exists outside of the apartments where there isn't enough food, employment.
> That lasted for a number of years. Then things just developed.

Tikkun olam on Yahel has expanded to hosting children with cerebral palsy, mild retardation, and leukemia; taking diabetic children (otherwise excluded from school trips) on hiking trips; and putting up adults with Down's syndrome. The culture committee raised money to donate to a nonprofit working on behalf of the nation's elderly. Younger kibbutzniks have traveled to Be'er Sheva with gifts for children in the hospital there, and for the holidays of Purim and Rosh Hashanah annually distribute packets of food to needy families in Eilat. Enthusiasm for such activities was stimulated by the strategic planning process that Yahel went through in the mid-1990s, and out of which tikkun olam emerged, according to Lori Stark, as a "top priority value."

That same strategic plan, it might be said, articulated profitability as the kibbutz's very first "critical success factor." Highlighting profit (along with other capitalistic indicators) as a measure of kibbutz success may well have generated unease for some Yahelniks. It certainly elicited disdain among members of neighboring kibbutzim (particularly Lotan). Yet tikkun olam costs. Cash-strapped communities can ill afford to be charitable in the way that dividend-dispensing ones can. Compromise on the (Reform) kibbutz can thus be seen in a religious, as well as economic, light.

It can also be seen in political terms. Tikkun olam on Yahel has expanded to include participation in Arab-Israeli coexistence programs. To
spread the "message that we're a Jewish community that wants to live in a
democratic Israel," the kibbutz has hosted Arab high school students both
from the Galilee (Israel) and Aqaba (Jordan). It also provides summer
camp for "underprivileged, disadvantaged, abused" children—both Arab
and Jewish—from the city of Jaffa. In addition to arts and crafts and outings to the dolphin reef and aquarium in Eilat,

> each child is adopted by a kibbutz family. It is the first exposure
> those kids have to healthy, functioning family life. That's what they
> like more than anything when they come here.

Yahel also participates in the international Seeds of Peace program, which
brings together Israeli, Palestinian, and Jordanian youth in a variety of
camp programs.

As its own contribution to peace making in the Middle East, in the af-
termath of the Oslo Accords, Yahel took a proactive stance regarding the
transfer of its crop fields to Jordan. (Most of the kibbutz's agricultural land
was located on territory that, according to international law, actually belonged on the Jordanian side of the boundary. Re-demarcation of the border
loomed as integral to any Israeli-Jordanian peace treaty.) Lori Stark explains:

> It was much more important to us, as a community, that we have
> peace in the region than [hold on to] our piece of land. [Even if it]
> had been our livelihood for eighteen years . . .
>
> Peace is one of the highest Jewish values. [Especially] if it means
> not having to send our kids to an aggressive army [instead of] an
> army that defends. You can't give a price to the lives of our kids. You
> *can* give a price to a piece of land.

In the end, King Hussein ceded reclamation of the desert crop fields
in exchange for water rights. But Yahel had demonstrated its willingness
to make heavy economic sacrifice for a cause—peace—predicated, at least
in part, on religious principles.

A small, intentional community in which members hold to differing levels
of religiosity can easily give rise to tension. At Yahel, such conflict is occasionally aggravated by societal antagonisms between practitioners of Orthodox and Reform Judaism. "Miriam"'s bat mitzvah crystallized several
of these conflicts together . . .

An Israeli-born couple of kibbutz members has organized a dinner and luncheon for their thirteen-year-old daughter. Because this is her "bat mitzvah" the kibbutz is paying for the meals. Of course, a bat mitzvah is supposed to entail some amount of Torah study. "But if you make an issue of it," says one of the more ritually sensitive members, "they can get back at you in some other way. You can't make people do what they don't want to do. If you decide to challenge them, then they might just up and leave. And you don't want that."

Tolerance and pluralism are important concepts in Reform Judaism. Yet how tolerant can the kibbutzniks be of their deliberately nonpracticing, nonreligious fellows? There is no *sanhedrin*, no duly constituted overarching group (or even committee) to make such decisions. On Yahel, kibbutzniks need to navigate their own religious contradictions—especially when it comes to external pressures—in an ad hoc way.

Here is another bat mitzvah problem: even if the parents of the girl did want an egalitarian service worthy of Reform Judaism, they (and therefore the entire kibbutz) had to deal with the visiting grandfather. Saba, a man of traditional Iraqi background, would be offended at the sight of a girl (including his own granddaughter) being called up to the Torah. Outside family pressures are going to trump internal religious principle. Up until the last minute, it is uncertain what kind of a ceremony there will be, if at all. The prospect of this dysfunctional bat mitzvah intrigues me, becoming one of the most ironic experiences of my life: on this Saturday morning, when my own family has planned a rare beach trip to Eilat, work impels me to attend Sabbath services instead. Despite my daughter's tears ("It's a family thing!"), I have professional participant-observation obligations. Moreover, the rabbi has become an informant . . .

Kibbutz Lotan, Friday afternoon. After visiting the geodesic dome on this August, desert day, it is too hot to view the organic garden. Instead my family and I opt to spend the hour before Sabbath, as do a good number of kibbutzniks, at the swimming pool. A pre-Shabbat bongo session gets underway led by a wandering mistral, a dulcimer player of indeterminate nationality.

Eliza, the mazkira, is concerned lest I embrace outside critics' view of Lotan as being a New Wave, "touchy-feely" parody of Judaism. Yet even her husband undermines the moderate mazkira by pointing out that Lotan *is* a magnet for people with lots of "uncontrollable energy." Daniel admits danger that such kibbutzniks may not be able to confine their energy within necessary boundaries.

Alex Cicelsky provides a classical vision of Reform Judaism:

We're our own authority. We have all of the wealth of Jewish learning and text and history. We have events that we want to do differently. We don't need some rabbi to make a decision for us . . .

In their homes, Lotaniks may or may not observe traditional Jewish
dietary laws. Still, explains Alex,

The kibbutz dining hall keeps kosher. Why? We want every Jew to
be able to eat in our dining hall. Who is the authority? Not the Orthodox rabbi because we don't believe that he is more kosher than
we are. So we check ourselves—we keep ourselves kosher.

As the sun begins its final descent of the Jewish week on the desert
horizon, Eliza is concerned: The woman who is supposed to lead *kabbalat
shabbat* (opening Sabbath prayers) that evening is still nonchalantly lolling
in the cooling waters of the pool. She should get going already and prepare for services, according to the community coordinator. But this is
kibbutz—not even the mazkira will dare tell another member to get a move
on it, even if there is a religious imperative to do so.

One cannot call it a sanctuary, much less a synagogue: services on
Lotan take place in the same room used as the community hall. Whether
for prayer or play, one sits on the same plastic patio or lounge chair. What
sanctifies the room is the ark built into the wall facing Jerusalem.

"The original idea was to create one space for all of our activities,"
explains Eliza. "We reasoned that if everything we do, we do Jewishly,
there is no need for separate praying and meeting space.

"But the reality is different," she has since come to realize. "When
you spend an evening debating the budget, it's hard to see the room in the
sacred way you'd want for doing prayers the next day."

While sharing the same roof, on Yahel the beit knesset and mo'adon
(the prayer room and social hall) are two distinct spaces. In terms of architecture and furnishings, each is more elaborate than the shul-*cum*-common
room on Lotan. The mo'adon on Yahel, moreover, serves as library housing
an impressive collection of general interest books in Hebrew and English
along with heavy tomes of Judaica. On Lotan, according to the mazkira,
the so-called library consists of "some books in a bomb shelter."

Shabbat service ambience is much different on the two Reform kibbutzim. On Yahel, the faithful few arrive dressed in "Shabbat shorts" and
dress sandals. (Some even wear long pants for the occasion, a very formal

sartorial statement for desert life.) White garb is preferred. If they have not brought their own head covering, participants will pick up and don a modest white kippah (yarmulke, or skull cap) as they enter. The women may or may not wear *kippot*.

At Lotan, Shabbat dress is much more florid. Large, Yemenite style skullcaps adorn the heads of women as well as men. Tie-dyed shirts and pants and billowing trousers set the spiritual tone.

Services on Yahel, although conducted exclusively in Hebrew, are recognizable to those familiar with either Reform or Conservative services in the United States. On Lotan, in contrast, it is not immediately apparent who the *shaliach tsibur* (prayer leader) is, or even if there is one. Different people take the initiative for different passages, and not in any particular order. One young mother, who arrived a bit late, introduced the assembled the group to a new song with a quasi-Chasidic tune. "That's her trade-mark," I was told, "introducing new tunes that people can't get." (Later, I learned that it was this same woman, the one lingering at the pool, who had been designated shaliach tsibur for these welcoming Shabbat prayers. "But she often has a problem getting to places on time. Once, she was scheduled to lead services and didn't even show up at all.")

Services on Lotan are spirited, with almost a revivalist quality to them. The singing is not dutiful as it sometimes feels in Yahel, with its smaller contingent of regular daveners in its fancier beit knesset. Prayer on Lotan, moreover, encompasses a keen competition between intense spirituality and toddler control.

Post-service, pre-meal benediction (kiddush) in the communal eating hall also reflects religious differences between the two Reform kibbutzim. Yahel, in its ritualistic organization, exudes a traditional (albeit liberal) predictability. A standing microphone is set up so that all can hear the proceedings. These begin with community announcements (typically, birthdays in the upcoming week.) Then comes the blessing, chanted by another kibbutznik. After the meal, a small group of people stay behind to chant birkat hamazon. This is also done with microphone, so that grace can be heard above the din of chattering lingerers.

Kiddush on Lotan has more the feel of an animated commune* coming together to break bread (specifically, whole wheat challah in a basket). One Friday night, a member stood on a chair and used hand signals to lead the assembled in a spirited rendition of Shalom Aleichem. As with the kabbalat shabbat services, it was not immediately apparent who was actu-

---

* In 1980, I visited a French commune in the Amazonian jungle of Guyane.

ally tasked to perform the benediction: there may indeed have been a prayer "leader" seated among the kibbutznik congregants but, like an orchestra without a conductor—or an orchestra whose conductor is playing an instrument along with it—it seemed as if everyone was praying together, without leadership. Unlike at Yahel, there was no concluding grace to mark the end of the meal.

After Shabbat dinner, the community reassembled at the social hall where the wandering minstrel played her dulcimer. During one of the pieces, the young mother who had ostensibly led services before dinner handed her baby to my wife (whom she had never met before) and improvised a dance: bending, rolling, writhing on the floor, periodically raising her hands up to the heavens. It was a very moving performance, all the more so for its spontaneity. When I complemented her afterwards, she looked at me intently before declaring, "With all my soul, I am sure that I know you from before." Although such was a remote possibility—it would have to have been five years prior at the Givat Ram campus of Hebrew University in Jerusalem where I was doing an intensive Hebrew language course and she was studying theater and dance—I did not get the impression that she was referring to that kind of mundane encounter. In another life, perhaps? Not so farfetched an idea, here on Lotan.

On Lotan, says Gwen Skully, it is "a natural part of life to pray, study together, and learn more about Judaism—and about ourselves—in the process." Eliza Mayo maintains that most Lotaniks came to religion as teenagers or adults, and did not pray when they were children. As a result, "their attachment is more intellectual" and less "from the gut." But this also allows for more creative opportunities. For the upcoming Shabbat, for example, she was preparing, "a special service on the subject of the moon and the eclipse and the beginning of [the Hebrew month of] Elul." Traditional Sabbath prayer would be "minimal."

"People will be thrilled," she predicted. "It will be fun and more people will come."

As early as Hebrew school, Eliza thought about continuing on a path towards ordination. "I didn't end up becoming a rabbi," she admits, "but I may end up being married to one." Plans were afoot for husband Daniel—one of those who came to Jewish religion more as an adult than a child—to attend Hebrew Union College.

"Life cycle events are very special," according to Gwen. "Reaffirming spirituality" in "creative" ways is the essence of religion at Lotan. Ritual is inherently centered around the community in Judaism, and Lotan—albeit in a nontraditional manner—provides that strong feeling of community. Alex Cicelsky describes weddings at the kibbutz:

> We have a service with either a Reform rabbi or a representative of the kibbutz [because it is] the kibbutz that has authority in their life. But no particular person arranges it: this one is in charge of the seven blessings, that one is in charge of the wine. The ceremony may take place in an orchard or on a sand dune. . . . We write our own egalitarian *ketubot* [marriage contracts] . . .

When a child is born, Alex goes on, "we have creative services. We call it *ma'amad*, 'an event in time.'" Instead of chanting from a traditional prayer books, kibbutzniks choose selections of modern Jewish song, poetry, or writing. Friends of the parents will also make and display a wimple—a quilted Torah wrapping, for the newborn's bar or bat mitzvah thirteen years thereafter—or other works of ceremonial art.

Similar "events in time" are composed at Lotan for Israeli Independence Day, Memorial Day, or whenever a study session is deemed appropriate. This includes visits of dignitaries. When members of the Knesset (parliament) visited, for instance, they were taken out to Lotan's geodesic dome prototype and witnessed an "event in time." "Whatever particular subject is at hand," Alex explains, "we give it a moment of holiness."

Still, there are times when it is more important to provide simple community than liturgical innovation. Religious services are not held at Lotan on a daily basis. Yet after her father died, a daily minyan was easily constituted at the kibbutz so that Gwen could regularly say the *kaddish*, the traditional mourner's prayer.

Not even on Lotan, however, are the more spiritually oriented fully satisfied with the level of religious commitment among their fellow kibbutzniks. The study sessions that Gwen mentioned are not held regularly; Eliza misses having more members as religiously inclined as she and husband Daniel. (Family joke: What are Daniel's and Eliza's biggest Shabbat conflict? "Who gets stuck with the kids, and who gets to pray.") Ironically, says the religious kibbutznik, "Jewishly I could have better options in America." Even Eliza admits that she didn't really have the time to compose the special moon-sun-eclipse ceremony she was preparing. "But for my soul," she explains, "I needed it right now."

There is no full-time rabbi on Yahel. It is unclear that the kibbutz would want one, anyway: in a truly egalitarian Jewish community, why employ a

spiritual specialist? No Jew is more Jewish than any other; no Jew is closer
to God. In Reform Judaism, the community as a whole is empowered to
make the religious decisions that bind it. Deference to "holymen" is
anathema. There is an ordained rabbi on Kibbutz Lotan but she does not
officiate as clergy: she is a member who happens to be a rabbi.

Leah Ben-Ami, raised in Teaneck, New Jersey, a former pulpit rabbi
in Tuscaloosa, Alabama, is petite, short-haired, and a strong and concise
speaker. She is also quite a contradiction: an ordained rabbi for whom Judaism is all-important but who downplays her clerical expertise. Rabbi
Ben-Ami's jobs on the kibbutz include working in the baby house, land-
scaping, answering the phone and mail in the secretariat, making dental
appointments, ordering diapers, and caring for the swimming pool. But
performing as a rabbi is an outside job: "Every now and then somebody
calls me for conversion. I did a wedding back in February. Not much of
that kind of work, though." She doesn't seem to miss it a bit.

"For six years as a pulpit rabbi I had a handful of Shabbat dinners with
my family. Here I am, a person who is passionately devoted to Judaism,
and I'm the only one with kids who doesn't get to do it. No more of that.

"I want my kids to see Mom, not just up there on the pulpit, but
Mom with everybody else. Doing things together, taking shared responsibility for it. I have no problem doing it myself. But that's not what I want
my kids to want to do with other Jews. I want them to build a Jewish life
for themselves. I want it to mean as much to them as it means to me. I
don't think it's going to happen if I'm up there. You know, on a pulpit."

Is life in the desert the best environment for Rabbi Leah and her
Dutch-born husband David Schoeneveld? "I can't think of a better place
to show my children the values I really have. People should work coopera-
tively. We should learn to get along with people, despite their differences.
Kibbutz shows that. Tolerance. Democracy. All here." Yet there is one
group for which Leah, like many other Lotaniks, expresses disdain: the
Yahelniks. It came up in our discussion about religious commitment.

"They have a lot people they hire, or just pay to live there. We have
none. (Or by the end of next week we'll have none—the person who has
been paying rent is leaving.) You cannot expect those you hire or who pay
rent to believe the things you do. But I'm not paying rent. I'm paying with
my work."

Of course, Lotan has made other compromises: they'll now accept
the labor of "environmental volunteers," even if that makes the kibbutz no
longer only Hebrew-speaking. They even have hired contractors to supply
Israeli laborers for the harvesting season. ("People with professional de-

grees don't want to pick melons—and when they have kids, they're even less affective as workers.") But Leah insists that Lotan employs only Israeli laborers—that is, Arabs. Not Thai workers. Not like Yahel.

Similar sentiments about rabbinic superfluousness prevail at Yahel, but for practical reasons the kibbutz employs a part-time rabbi. Based in Jerusalem, American-born Rabbi Arik Ascherman makes the two-hour drive through the Negev desert every three weeks, principally to provide instruction for bar and bat mitzvah age children. In the intervening weeks, he helps the young kibbutzniks prepares their bar mitzvah speeches by telephone and fax.

Born in 1959 as Eric in Erie, Pennsylvania, the now lanky, bearded Arik knew from the age of seven that he had a wanted to be a rabbi. "I should do something special. Only Jews can be rabbis, so, hey, that's special." Of course, his "concept of what it meant to be a Jew and a rabbi changed many times since." Educated at Harvard, active in Interns for Peace and Rabbis for Human Rights, Ascherman admits he is not the perfect fit for being the rabbi of a small, remote kibbutz. (Indeed, not long after my stay he was replaced by a woman rabbinical student.)

"They don't need someone to lead services. In fact, I very rarely do." There is much ambivalence about the position. " 'I want a rabbi but I don't want a rabbi,' " the rabbi has heard it said. "It's also inappropriate for Yahel to have a rabbi as an authority figure in the same way that rabbis might be in other places." And yet Yahel always had and wanted to have a rabbi. Why? "In part, I think it's just to say they have a rabbi."

Arik's predecessor was Conservative—liberal for a Conservative but too judgmental. After some on-again, off-again stages, the kibbutz opted for the less sanctimonious, if less available, Ascherman.

There was an early period in which decisions about halacha— milking on Shabbat, leaving corners of fields for the poor—inspired much debate, study, and creative thinking. But this rarely occurs, anymore. "It's also part of an aging process," states the middle-aged rabbi. "When you're young and you're just on the kibbutz, you start to form your own traditions and patterns. It's not unusual. . . . But the official decisions are one thing, and the reality of living with kids is different." The rabbi speaks of the most traditionally oriented kibbutznik who now takes his son to basketball games on Friday nights.

Contradictions abound: "On the one hand, being a Reform kibbutz is a huge part of the identity" of the community. On the other hand, it's a very small group of people on the kibbutz who really participate in any way in Jewish activities, at least in the way we more traditionally think of them." There is also the tension inherent in many small communities: "You have a small group of people who run something, and complain that there are not enough people involved. Yet they send out subtle (or not so subtle) signals: 'Back off. This is our territory.'"

The Reform rabbi is aware of the pent up resentment on the kibbutz towards the Israeli Reform movement. "When the kibbutz was founded they were stars. But they have become much more secondary in this country."

Thirty minutes before the scheduled start of the bat mitzvah, the rabbi himself still does not know what is going to happen. At the sermon ("Torah talk") that he delivers before the actual bar/bat mitzvah ceremony, the congregation consists of me—alone.

It is the rabbi who most strenuously objects to what is shaping up to be a non-egalitarian service. For Reform Rabbi Arik, not having women participate is theologically wrong. Ordinarily, when faced with such circumstances, he either says prayers before or after the non-egalitarian services, so as to not endorse them. Here, however, he has been cornered into officiating. Other kibbutzniks object by boycotting—by going to the beach at Eilat, for instance.

Three minutes after 10:00 AM, the first person shows up for the scheduled services: a visitor from another kibbutz. Seven minutes after the hour, the bat mitzvah girl appears with her friends, accompanied by her father and grandfather (the one who presumably objects to women actively participating in religious services). Saba wears long, white beads and a large knitted kippah (ritual head covering). He does not pray. Perhaps it is because of the mixed seating. Perhaps it is because women may be called up to the Torah (even though they will not on this Shabbat actually read from it).

The Torah reading for this day happens to be Deuteronomy 6. It is the portion which recounts the giving of the Ten Commandments. I happen to glance at the English version just at the point where the Commandments are recited. Do not commit adultery, it says. On opposite sides of the circular prayer circle sit the couple who are divorcing, because of the wife's infidelity.

The bat mitzvah being a last minute affair, not all of the honors have been given out in advance. No one had been selected, for example, to return the Torah to the ark after it was read. The mother, whom I barely know, turns around, sees me, and on the spot asks me to perform the honor. I assent: only it is a Sephardic scroll (ironically, for a largely North

American Reform community), and I fumble to actually hold it. Such is my "participation"—nevertheless, the next day, rare thanks are given for my assistance.

According to the informal religious committee, it is a success that the girl's friends all told her that what she had just undergone was not a real bat mitzvah. One of the founders adamantly believes the kibbutz should not condone such farcical ceremonies; another insists that one take the dysfunctionality of the family into account. "We shouldn't let congregationalism get in the way of religion," he says.

There are the public foreskin problems.... "Svetlana," an immigrant mother from Russia formally converted to Judaism. Her son, however, never underwent a comparable ceremony and was never circumcised. Naturally, though, when the boy grew up the family wanted to have some kind of coming of age ritual, anyway: an "alternative" bar mitzvah that would consist not of religious ritual but a poetry reading or skit performance. Backed by one of the more traditional-minded members, the kibbutz held the line: as a condition for sponsoring the bar mitzvah, the boy would first have to undergo the "letting of blood" ritual, a pinprick of the penis that qualifies as ritual circumcision. The family (or was it the boy?) refused. Outcome? The kibbutz paid for a party but there was no actual event qualified as "bar mitzvah."

This was not the end of public discussion of Svetlana's son's foreskin: there remained concern that, once he enters the army, the boy will be teased because of his being "different."

A related foreskin flap: the newborn son of an irreligious member had a surgical circumcision in the hospital but not a ritualistic one. The parents then decided to have a ceremony in the kibbutz synagogue: not the traditional one reserved for boys but rather the naming ceremony traditionally used for girls. Still, all references to God and to the commandments were edited out. The kibbutznik who recalls the "innovation" rolls his eyes as he does so.

These are not the problems one thinks would occur in Israel. Outside of the Jewish State, especially in America, all kinds of conundra related to the contested status of individual Jews arise. But that a democratic Reform kibbutz not bound by halacha, whose overall movement does not demand circumcision for bar mitzvah, would choose to impose a halachic standard brims with irony . . .

Another emerging irony for Jewish parents on Yahel is concern about intermarriage. Even for the least religiously minded Diaspora Jew, moving to Israel is supposed to represent the greatest guarantee of Jewish continuity for one's family. How much more so in a remote desert community?

Yet now that the kibbutz accepts young (twenty-ish) volunteers of all conceivable national and religious backgrounds—from Scandinavian Lutheran to Japanese Buddhist—some parents understandably fear that one of their geographically cloistered and socially restless adolescents may eventually fall for a roving foreign Gentile.* Banning non-Jewish volunteers from their community would, however, be both antithetical to the liberal ethos of Reform Judaism and at odds with the kibbutz's economic needs. Moreover, according to Yahel's coordinator for volunteers (himself a sabra), the Jewish ones (usually from the United States and England) are actually the worst workers:

> Young Jewish people and simple, physical work don't go together . . . Many of them are lost souls looking for a place to make them feel good, warm, welcome. They are looking for a solution in their lives. If you bring your problems with you, fine—as long as you can work with them . . . [Their idea of volunteering is to do some] work, sit in the sun, and get laid . . .

The best volunteers at the kibbutz, as far as the coordinator is concerned, are the Koreans.

Rarely does one look to a rabbi for transportation. But Rabbi Arik Ascherman, who was still "servicing" Yahel every third week, was returning to Jerusalem and agreed to give me a ride up to the capital in half the time the bus takes (nearly four hours).

Driving through the Arava and the Judean Desert gave me the opportunity to probe him about some irksome trans-kibbutz and interdenominational issues. Ascherman is himself in a "mixed" marriage: he is a Reform rabbi married to a Conservative one (indeed, the first Israeli-born woman Conservative rabbi). When the issue of rabbinical officiating at gay marriages arose—he countenances it, his wife does not—he warned that it would take some time to explain his theology. Fortunately, he summarized, "we have a long drive . . .

---

* There are also organized groups of Reform youth brought to Yahel in the hope that some individuals may seek membership (this rarely happens), and to expose kibbutz children to Jewish youth and culture from abroad. They are not technically volunteers but do enjoy temporary work status.

"I believe that there was a real revelation at Sinai and that the Torah is the best approximation we have of what happened there. But it's not an exact accounting. It's like the game of telephone—the oral tradition passed down the major framework, but over the generations, until it was finally transcribed after the first dispersal, the account of the revelation got rough around the edges. There may have been Canaanite influences. Still, even if imperfect, the Torah is the best record we have of what God revealed us."

This was heavy going. It was one thing being told of revelation at Sinai by an Orthodox Jew, even a Conservative rabbi. But such literalist faith from a contemporary with whom I could identify on many levels—a Bruce Springsteen fan, not a Hebrew school teacher? That was unfamiliar terrain.

"I also believe that God wants us to argue with Him," Arik continued, eyes narrowing on the sun refracting road. "He set up Abraham to do just that, with Sodom and Gomorrah. He also did it with the sacrifice of Isaac. By the way, I consider that to be a failure on Abraham's part, that he was willing to argue with God for people he didn't even know in Sodom and Gomorrah, but he didn't argue with God over his own son."

Arik wasn't speaking in a voice laden with lofty theology. He spoke matter-of-factly, not about a legendary five thousand-year-old ancestor but as if we were discussing the character flaws of a mutual friend of ours.

"As a human being, I do feel a loyalty to a humane God, one who has greater wisdom than mere mortals. I also know I have an obligation to other human beings."

And what of injunctions to punish by death? What about stoning for gays?

"I do have a hard time with any command to harm another human being. For me, that is a red line, which pits my loyalty to God to my loyalty to other human beings. I'd have to have it proven to me—even though I know it is not logically possible—that God really meant these 'laws,' that they were not merely Canaanite or other pagan injunctions which imprinted themselves on the ancient Hebrew message. But if it were proven, then I'd conduct myself with God like a member of the loyal opposition.

"After five years in Berkeley, my wife is in disagreement with me about this. The whole experience of being exposed to a gay society has made her more cautious. She really believes gay culture is out to undermine straight culture, that part of gay society is out 'to get' the family as we know it.

"But for me, there is something holy in actual love between two persons, even of the same sex. A lack of religious sanction or approval is harming and painful when there is a truly committed couple at stake. It's a cause for big argument at home: what would I do if asked to perform a gay wedding?

"I try to be intellectually honest in working out a system of belief and faith. I'll take reason as far as it goes—but when it takes me to a point when the logic breaks down, that is okay too. Consistency is the hobbyhorse of small minds.

"One of my teachers taught that there are three paradigms, or phases, of Judaism. The first was to ask, is it permitted or forbidden? This is where many of the *haredim* [ultra-Orthodox] are stuck. But the second phase, highlighted in the haskala, in the Jewish Enlightenment, was, 'Is it true or not?' Now, the relevant question is, 'Does it help us to understand the world or not?'"

And what about us Jews being the "chosen people."

"Different peoples are chosen for different reasons. We were chosen to receive the Torah and to pass it on." Then he said, in a tone of personal shame. "We haven't done a particularly good job of it."

The Rabbi tells the parable of the elephant being touched by blind men. Each understands but one aspect of the pachyderm: the trunk, the ears, the pads. "We have our particular expression of God, on account of our own blindfold."

"There are three levels of faith" (Arik often divides questions and problems into three parts). "On the first, I am of 99.9 percent certainty that there are laws of cause and effect, of action and reaction. Whatever came into being without a prior existence must be the doing of the Supernatural. That first thing may have been chemicals, the elements of the big bang, it doesn't matter: Whatever started the world is beyond mere physics . . . I don't believe that everything is relative."

No matter how ambiguous the religious situation on the Reform kibbutz, Yahel and Lotan at least afford opportunities not available to neighboring kibbutzim which are not Jewish in a formal, institutional way. Michael Levy, the bearded farmer-turned-Arabic teacher from Detroit, typifies the sad transition of the Israelized American Jew. His kibbutz, Grofit, has no beit knesset, no synagogue, no Torah scroll, no chapel for prayer. "I come from a background comfortable with beit knesset. On the other hand, for many people like me, and certainly for me, living in Israel over the years has become an experience of being more and more alienated from religious life. Religious life in Israel is disgusting.

"You have to remember that, what's so much a part of American Jewish life—synagogue life, temple life—just isn't important on an Israeli kibbutz. Without some religious institutional activity in America, "you are probably not identified as being Jewish. We don't have that problem. The vast majority of members on Grofit are Jewish and they speak Hebrew. We celebrate all the holidays, we have Friday night dinner with another couple, and our kids, if they choose, have a class bar mitzvah." Most of the boys (but not the girls) when they turn thirteen do decide to read from the Torah (which is borrowed from down the road). "Why? To please their grandparents, to please their parents, whatever. What it means to them?" Not what it means to a boy raised in a truly religious community.

On his kibbutz, Michael adds, "people are completely secular." He estimates that on Yom Kippur, the traditional day of fasting, 30 to 40 percent of his fellow kibbutzniks eat as usual. "There are families in Grofit that keep kosher in their home but it's not a main part of the community. We do have members who aren't Jewish."

Oh?

"We have it in our bylaws that the members of the kibbutz are Jewish. On the other hand, any decision about the bylaws of the kibbutz can be turned over by a significant majority.

"I would be more comfortable living in a community that had more Jewish content in it. At least its Jewish identity is very, very honest. There is no pretense. What there is, there is. What there isn't, there isn't. It's not like one of our neighbors which for years had a thing that the kibbutz cars wouldn't travel on the Sabbath but 90 percent of its members did.

"My kids are familiar with the synagogue. Not as much as I'd like. They don't know the prayer book like I did from a young age, but it's not like they aren't exposed to it."

Our air conditioner malfunctioned at home and Danny Hayken, kibbutz electrician, came over. As he was repairing it, I was able to question him about the sermon he had delivered so fluently and passionately at the previous Shabbat. "Oh," he responded modestly, "it was nothing profound. I just spoke about the *neumot*, the speech, of Moses in Deuteronomy."

Never mind that Danny is the son of a rabbi. *He* is an electrician. Yet a wonderful speaker on Mosaic discourse. *That's* kibbutz, where on Shabbat you are inspired by the Torah talk of the weekday electrician.

9

Sibling Rivalry

(The Lotan Difference)

It is Friday morning, and the dozen or so three to five-year-olds are excited: the rabbi has arrived! Arik (even here the rabbi is called by his first name) first has the nursery school group reenact sleeping at nighttime and waking up, and then beginning the day by thanking God for life, to be awake again. Then Rabbi Arik instructs on the importance of *shalom*. "Whom should there be peace between?" he asks the reenergized Jewish tots in Hebrew. Each is eager to give the correct answer to the rabbi. "Between Kibbutz Yahel and Kibbutz Lotan!" blurts out one of them.

For all its success and specific identity today, Lotan is also a living testament to the misplaced optimism of the Reform Zionist movement of the 1970s and early 1980s. A second Reform kibbutz in the Arava would accommodate the inevitable overflow from Yahel, once the idea of desert pioneering caught on among young progressive Jews in Israel and the Diaspora. Having a thriving, like-minded community down the road would also provide synergy for the burgeoning movement. Before a name was even thought up for the second Reform kibbutz, it was thought of as Yahel II.

But the youthful throngs of idealistic Zionists with a progressive Jewish bent did not materialize at the gates of the desert kibbutzim. What arose instead was, in its most charitable characterization, a healthy competition between two similarly thinking but underpopulated communities. A more hard-nosed view is that Yahel and Lotan cannibalized each other. The most common, and diplomatic, depiction is of the "sibling rivalry" between the two.

"There are certain feelings of tensions at times towards Yahel," explains one Lotanik in a managerial position to know:

> They came to us with an offer to have full cooperation economically, about joining businesses. They were looking for a wedding, or starting to court with an eye for a future wedding. "We'll separate between the business and the community. Then the business will run for business decisions . . . and the community will make their own decisions." That's how they work. [But] Lotan is like a family business. If you own a family business, how you run your business is an expression of who you are. It's not separate from your community home life. The same ideology that we have in our home life, we want to have in our business life.

Another Lotanik takes a slightly different tack. With the creation of Lotan, he says, Yahel felt slighted. Resources that otherwise would have gone to the former went to the latter; Yahel's ability to succeed was thought to be compromised. As a result, "they decided to be less of a kibbutz." In the long run, Yahel has by far become the more materially well endowed of the two communities. "They've got the money—the seminar [a classroom complex for visiting groups], the library [a synagogue-cum-community center]." But, added this Lotanik (with perhaps a touch of youthful pride), "We've got the people."

Alex Cicelsky puts it this way: Compared to Yahel, "We're still at the stage of dreaming more. When it comes to economics, we still want to be more involved" (even though there isn't much money to go around in the first place). Whereas Yahel has a veritable fleet of vehicles, Lotan boasts only "two cars for a hundred people." Creating a nexus between desert ecology and Judaism has also given Lotan "a reason to remain ideological." Organic gardening, for Lotaniks, is as much a way of being Jewish in the desert as it is to be humanly friendly to the environment.

For a minority of Lotaniks, the deviation that Yahel represents is even more upsetting. One angry Lotanik reportedly told a group of visiting students from abroad that "Somebody ought to put a bomb to this place [Yahel]." Think of it in the way that brothers and sisters scream sentiments that they eventually regret (whether or not they meant it at the time). On Yahel, the prevailing response to such sibling resentment and rivalry is paternalism and smugness: *In a few years*, the sentiment seems to run, *they'll grow up, see the light, and do what we have done.*

These differences in sentiment and ideology are graphically apparent in the titles and substance of each kibbutz's statement of goals. Whereas Yahel's speaks of "strategic planning," Lotan's is a "vision statement."

OUR PATH TO THE FULFILLMENT OF OUR VISION

In this place, we, the members of Kibbutz Lotan, have chosen to establish our home and our future. Through our commitment to Am Yisrael, Torat Yisrael, and the State of Israel, we are working together to create a community based on Reform Zionist Jewish values:

Jewish Renewal: We work towards creating a progressive expression of Jewish religion and culture in our rituals and day-to-day life, through mitzvot in our relationships between each other and with God.

Equality: Our belief in equality is expressed through direct democracy, equality in the workplace, gender equality, and mutual responsibility.

Economic Cooperation: Together we are responsible for our livelihood and share our resources as an expression of our belief in communal action.

Ecology: We strive to fulfill the biblical ideal "to till the earth and preserve it", in our home, our region, the country and the world. We are working to create ways to live in harmony with our desert environment.

"I-Thou": We aspire to meaningful relationships with one another of openness, communication, and mutual respect.

Livelihood: We strive for economic independence, and aim to support ourselves in ways that are in keeping with our values.

Home and Community: Our commitment to our home and our community is expressed through cooperative action in work, education, culture, health, and day-to-day life.

Tikkun Olam—"Repairing the World": We work towards the betterment of ourselves, our people and the world. Our home is a community of shlichut. Our way of life constitutes a message we wish to impart to those that enter our gates and to the circles of society in which we are involved.

This declaration is a living document which requires of us ongoing involvement and action.

"It is not for you to complete the work
Neither are you free to desist from it."

FIG. 9.1. Kibbutz Lotan Vision Statement.

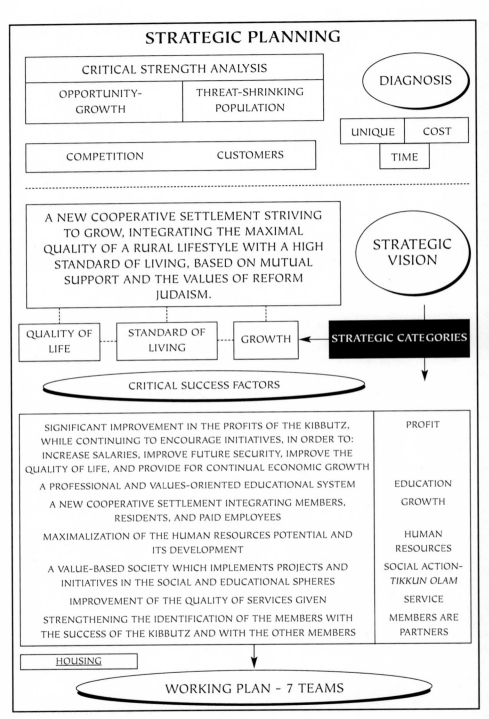

Fig. 9.2. Kibbutz Yahel Strategic Planning Diagram.

An even more living document is Lotan's membership *ketuba*, a calligraphic collection that hangs in the dining room. A ketuba, in Jewish law and custom, is a wedding contract that binds bride and groom. Often, it is an ornate piece of art. By adapting this imagery and tradition of artistic handiwork, Lotan has equated membership in the kibbutz with a commitment to the community. New members fashion for their kibbutz ketuba their favorite quotes or original sayings.

When an old culture exists in a state of retreat, reads one, *a new culture is created by the few who are not afraid to live by their ideals.* Another part of the ketuba collection has a line from what has become Lotan's unofficial theme song, written by Matti Caspi and Ehud Manar: *At the edge of the sky, and at the end of the desert, there's a distant place full of wildflowers.* Others combine ideological vision with personal philosophy: *Difficult with, difficult without: community, ideology. In everything that is said, there is a speck of wisdom.*

Perhaps Lotan needs Yahel as a relative benchmark of ideological purity. For it, too, has made compromises. They pale, for instance, in light of Yahel's much wider ranging "reforms." Still, although harshly critical of Yahel for hiring foreign laborers to work the fields, Lotan itself has broken down and hired Arab workers to do the same. At least, Lotaniks rationalize, *their* hired workers are Israeli—that is, Arabs with Israeli citizenship. Yet they are so acutely uncomfortable with appearing as "economic oppressors," as Daniel Meir puts it, that Lotan was looking to phase out those fields entirely—even though they are significant profit makers.

Lotan had also moved to accept the labor of volunteers, as well as hiring workers for specialized, professional positions. Lotaniks are uneasy with these choices, even as they rebuke Yahelniks for (more far-reaching) compromises. But there are other problems.

Adding tourism to its inventory of industries has required bending the absolute "no work on Sabbath" kibbutz policy: you can't expect paying guests to fend entirely for themselves on Saturday. With the addition of a dairy, the kibbutz also had to confront the Shabbat milking dilemma.

Institutional compromise seems to correlate with midlife transition. Lotaniks, a relatively younger group (most are still in their thirties), are more unbending in their Reform, Zionist, and socialist principles. Nor do they compromise on the centrality of religious ritualism and creativity. While increasingly conscious of the difficulty of perfectly realizing the self-sustaining, egalitarian, socialistic, and Jewishly creative community that they had originally envisioned, these American-born Reform Zionist kibbutzniks wrestle with and resist the possibility of compromised ideals.

Yahelniks, whose core membership have now already entered middle adulthood (all the American-born have already "hit forty"), reflect an economic pragmatism and flexibility that for Lotan is tantamount to "selling out."

With a single toddler one may still have the luxury, as this thirty-something mother on Lotan put it, "to flow with the now." She blithely dismisses the pretense of building "a monument to eternity." Notions of utopia still engage them in ways that most Yahelniks have long since put to bed.

"I don't know what utopia is," says Daniel Burstyn, the idealist. "But I always thought people should live in the kind of community that kibbutz is. We've chosen this particular system and are trying to make it work. We're here to make a living in the sense of *living*—not in the sense of 'We're going to make our wage and go home . . .'"

Utopia? "It felt many times at the beginning that we had created one. We realized quickly that we were so enthusiastic that people would come and at first glance fall completely head over heals in love with it. So we had to publicly fight the notion that we were a utopia. Because people would come and think this was heaven on earth and when they realized that the every day life had hardships—the heat, the food—along with the good, it would smack them in the face and they'd be quickly disillusioned."

"We're all people, for better or for worse," adds Eliza Mayo. "We all have certain shortcomings. If you're living on a daily basis in very close contact with lots of people," she laughs, "the shortcomings come up more often."

Gwen Skully also acknowledges the frustration that accompanies reform-minded idealism, of "having a minimal effect even on your immediate surroundings." Even in a small community, says Gwen, "to make any change or progress takes a lot of time and effort."

Daniel Burstyn compares Lotan with the American firm of his cousin, a "high-powered lawyer." Daniel's kibbutz, too, is an organization to which he gives "110 percent" of his energy. But, he distinguishes, "I'm doing it not to make lots of money but to be with people and create something together." But it does bother him that his standard of living is no higher than that of his parents. He realizes he needs to suppress his childhood jealousies: "the little [boy] who feels that the other kid has two more pieces of chocolate." Despite its moral and ideological clarity, Daniel, like other Lotaniks, confronts the Reform kibbutz paradox:

"It's a way of life that people don't choose. There aren't enough people here. We're stretching ourselves to our limits in order to do all the tasks that we set for ourselves. How are we going to get over this without breaking the boundaries of the game that we set for ourselves?"

Daniel's wife is mazkira, general manager, of Lotan. She describes a much looser style of management than on neighboring kibbutzim.

Part of Lotan's success as a cooperative kibbutz is that it was founded after the old frameworks, and not in this Bolshevik stance that Ketura is sometimes. . . . I trust my fellow members [with use of money] and am more free-flowing and easygoing. I'm not going to check everything and numbers and accounts. . . . Yahel couldn't see how to manage things in a business way without breaking all the old frameworks.

Unlimited possibility still undergirds the ethos of Lotan—not the financial bottom line that increasingly dominates at Yahel. Eliza Mayo provides an example:

If you have a dream, and can convince a few other crazies that it's worth it, you can do it. One guy's *mishagas* [crazy idea] was building a bird reserve in the middle of the desert south of the kibbutz. You know what? Now it's the whole kibbutz's dream. People—not just ecological freaks—volunteered hours in the afternoon planting, digging, setting down lines.

The ethos of community is similar to that expressed on Yahel; it's only the language that changes somewhat. "What is a kibbutz?" I ask. A spokeswoman replies.

On Lotan it is the feeling of extended family, of raising each others' children. A place of mutual support and assistance, which you don't find in the disconnected urban environment. Of overlapping circles of life. Interconnectedness. Trying to flow with the now—not a monument to eternity. Bringing Israeli identity closer to Jewish identity. Speaking Hebrew in public places. It is important that the kibbutz be at one with oneself.

And, perhaps as a dig at Yahel, "it is *not* privatizing. Not [entertaining] differential wage."

NU, SO WHAT'S A KIBBUTZ?

Lotaniks' idealistic view of what a kibbutz is—and is not—is best appreciated when we hear how their "cousins" at Yahel now define it. There, the notion of shared business is, if not primary, then at least intrinsic to the notion of kibbutz.

"We're a bunch of people that all own the business," explains Matt Sperber. "We own it in equal shares and pay ourselves in equal salaries. That's the bottom line." For Matt, that is what makes Yahel—as a kibbutz—among "the last of the serious cooperatives."

"It is a community and a business," confirms Ron Bernstein, and its success depends on how well the two are integrated. "If it becomes too much of a business, then individuals will be discarded and, like any big industry, the little people will be stomped on. But if it's run as a business and a community where each individual is still very important and allowed to decide where he or she works, and given a lot more job and career freedom," then it can succeed.

As economic manager, it is important for Matt that his fellow Yahelniks share in this vision of kibbutz:

> We have a very clear distinction—not legally, but on a management framework—between the community as a community and the community as a company. In the end, when we divide up the profits and ask "What did we make?", we put the two together. If the community spent more money than it was budgeted for, that comes off the profit. But before dividing up the profit, we either charge for, or benefit from, whatever has diminished it. People have integrated that into their conceptual framework.

He gives an example of which he is especially proud.

> Last night we had a meeting about spending an additional 5,000 shekels to provide electronic mailboxes for all our members. It would have come off the profits of the kibbutz. We could afford to do it, and we will do it eventually. But [for now] we decided to finish off the year at what we had budgeted.

Matt explains it in terms that the otherwise financially carefree kibbutznik must: "Members now understand that that they have two pockets but they really are connected and come together. In the end, the money is only going to come out of one pocket."

Lori Stark ventures a "three sentence definition" of her life's framework: "Today, kibbutz is a combination of business in the community where one supports the other. There's no connection between the job that someone does and the salary they receive for that job. Everyone receives an equal salary from the community."

Other women still stress the communitarian aspects of life at Yahel. Liora Cohen, general manager, puts it in terms of

> Mutual guarantee, cooperation, partnership. It comes out in three main areas—education, culture, and health. You have the opportunity to make decisions and mold the society that you are in, to voice disharmony or discontent on certain issues. And at least you know that you're going to be treated with respect.

Nancy Immerman asserts that, at Yahel, "we basically still live by the credo, 'from each according to his or her ability, to each according to his or her needs.' It's mutual responsibility, commitment to being responsible for one another. Sort of like a miniature welfare state wherein we take care of each other."

Still, Laura Sperber has "no illusions that kibbutz is going to create a new type of person." However, "it helps. It eases the way in difficult situations. Community has a function to play in people's lives, particularly when you don't have extended families anymore. More than living in an apartment in Tel Aviv where you can live for years and not even know the names of your neighbors."

Elad is eclectic in his approach: "There are as many different kinds of answers as you have types of kibbutzim. One kibbutz's answer doesn't necessarily solve the problems of another." But for most people at Yahel, Elad points out, the "red line"—the point beyond which the community ceases to be a kibbutz—is differential pay scales. Despite all the other changes, as long as the manager-member receives the "salary" as the worker-member, Yahel remains, in the eyes of its members, a kibbutz.

Not all agree, however. "I wouldn't like to see it happen," says Liora Cohen, "but I'm not worried that people get different salaries according to their position, their jobs. We could express our communal spirit in all different ways. But if there's no communal spirit, no mutual ideals, *then* we're not a community anymore."

Ever the dissident, Rosealie Sherris found flaws in Yahel's "kibbutzness" from the start:

> Right from the beginning, when I came in the early, 1980s, it became clear immediately that kibbutz wasn't what it was in the books we read. One of the great selling points of kibbutz to university students, for example, is its pure form of democracy: socialist principles. Along the way I found out that my amateurish, naïve under-

standing of democracy, as someone who grew up in the United States, was not answered in this country, in this kibbutz.

Even at Yahel, says Rosealie, over the years the idea of general assembly has been defused by centralization of the decision-making process. "Kibbutz is primarily an economic concept, not a social program."

But "if people are happy where they're living," asserts Ron Bernstein, "it will show not only in the business but in the everyday social and cultural life of the kibbutz. People will be together. Friday night dinner is a nice atmosphere. People aren't putting on an act." But it ought to show in the business.

Kibbutz, for the Yahelnik, is an evolving concept that requires flexibility of definition, and a willingness to adapt to changing times. Seen from Lotan, though, Yahel is too willing to compromise.

In my conversations with Lotaniks, poignant family details surface without equivalent among Yahelniks: a father who died of AIDS; a sibling rabbi who is lesbian; a cousin who attends a gay synagogue in New York City; a mother who had raised the future kibbutznik as Catholic.

After fifteen years of living there, one disillusioned kibbutznik encapsulates the community's ethos this way: "Lotan has become more and more 'touchy-feely'—recycling, ecological, macrobiotic, vegetarian, homeopathic. Too 'alternative' for my taste." The difference with Yahel's version of Reform Jewish kibbutz life could not be starker.

Lotan attracts people who, although Gentile according to Jewish law, "act like Jews. They haven't gone through conversion yet"—a fact complicated by the kibbutz's own rejection of Orthodox conversions. In a synagogue, this is a religious matter with implications for ritual; on a kibbutz, it's more of a bylaws issue, a matter of membership eligibility. "We have one fellow," explains Alex Cicelsky, "who comes to services and has basically made himself a Jew. Does that have authority? Do we make him do a Reform conversion? Or is it enough that he lives a Jewish life?" It is unlikely that such a person would settle at Yahel—perceived as less religiously creative than Lotan—in the first place.

Unlike Yahel, there is no tennis on Lotan. Who would have the time to play? The energy? The willingness to indulge in a public display of athletic prowess?

LOTAN'S BICULTURALS: AMERICO-ISRAELIS

Let us use "sabram" to denote the child of American parents born and raised in Israel. In a later chapter, I share my discussions with adolescent sabrams from Yahel. Sabrams there are at Lotan, but they are still too young to express the self-analytical thoughts that Yahel sabrams can and do.

Lotan does have, on the other hand, a special group of adults who were born, raised, and initially socialized in America, *then* brought to the Jewish State and "israelized." These are Lotan's biculturals. When they left America for Israel the youngest was seven, the oldest fourteen, and the others nine-years-old. Lotan was not yet even a glean in the eye of the Reform Zionist kibbutz visionaries. When I met with four of them together it was clear that, though they now ranged in age from twenty to thirty, their aliya as children in the 1970s still left deep marks on them. Between one-fifth and one-quarter of Lotan's American-born members are what I call "Americo-Israelis."

Since the age of four, claims the bearded-and-mustachioed Avi Weiss, he knew that Herzl was the founder of Zionism and that Israel was a great place. But actually moving to the Jewish State at that age? "It was a traumatic experience," he declares in uncharacteristic seriousness (for most of what Avi says comes in peals of ironic laughter). "Two plus five is sheva"—thus did Avi mix his English and Hebrew algebra when shifting schools in 1970 from Forest Hills in Queens to Jerusalem.

"It wasn't a fun place for a nine-year-old" she recalls, seventeen years later, a considerably pregnant but still timorous Shanni Reif Proforsorsky. Shanni speaks a completely unaccented English in a nevertheless tentative manner. "I was raised with the impression that Israel was a great place." But where were the electronic games? The fast food? It was tough getting used to life in the boondocks. And her first Israeli home was in Jerusalem, no less, not in any rural backwater. Indeed, "it took a long time to get over the disappointment."

For Rachel Alani, disappointment was mixed with relief. The nine-year-old from Queens, New York had a biblical image of her impending life in the land of her ancestors. "Would we live in tents?" Rachel had mused. "Were there cars?" Her first impression of her new neighborhood was ambivalent: "Just another community, with big buildings and buses." She peers into the past through her blue-tinted glasses.

Like Rachel, David Dolev—now slim and wiry, with glasses and beard—still chafes at the memory of being *told* by his parents that they were going to leave America. (Unlike Rachel, David's parents had "pre-pared" him, mostly through a summer visit before his ninth grade. But he still didn't want to come.) He also uses the word "traumatic" to describe leaving his birth land. Yet, claims the shy and quiet David, thanks to sports "within a couple of months I had friends. Soon I changed my identity." David, who was an "old" fourteen when he made aliya, knew that he had to "do it quickly," with only four years before his joining the army.

It was much less easy for Rachel. She had assumed—incorrectly—that people would like her as an American. Instead, "kids made fun of me. I didn't understand what was going on. There were years when I tried to be liked but it didn't work. . . . I was very lonely. I just waited to become eighteen so I could go back [to America]. It took a long time to feel comfortable . . ."

Why were they uprooted from urban and suburban America at such tender ages? Although each Americo-Israeli's story is somewhat different, usually, it was the father who decided.

Rachel's maiden name—Skirball—explains much by itself. Daughter of the prominent Reform Rabbi Henry F. "Hank" Skirball, Israel was al-ways in the air in their Corona, Queens household. Rachel's father was not your typical congregational cleric, but rather a youth movement rabbi. Their two-year "test period" of aliya set the stage for Rachel's eventual israelization.

David's father was *already* an Israeli. The elder Dolev had come to live in the United States at the age of seventeen. But after marrying a Massachusetts woman and beginning a family, his Zionist leanings came back to the fore. He also, according to David, wanted a more Jewish and value-oriented upbringing for his son.

Avi's parents had already divorced when his mother decided to bring him, one of his older brothers, and her mother on aliya. According to the custody agreement, his father—who had been involved in the Zionist youth movement and had even attempted aliya before the divorce—had to officially authorize any move of the children outside the United States. He signed—but only if the foreign destination was Israel. Zionism was that important to him.

Shanni Reif's father was also instrumental in the decision to move to Israel, but, in an indirect and tragic way; he died when Shani was only five-years-old. Friends of Shanni's now widowed mother, who had previously lived in Israel, convinced her to return and rebuild her family life in Jerusalem. Shanni's transition should have been smoothed by her years of attendance at a Solomon Shechter Jewish day school, and the familiarity she gained there with Hebrew.

It is not surprising that these young Americans would eventually gravitate to the kind of community that might heal their hard childhood adaptation to the rough-and-tumble Jewish state. Kibbutz life may be far from utopia, but it is much closer to the naive Zionist folk song declaration that "all Israel are brothers." Despite its harsh physical location, Lotan is a psychologically comfortable place for dual identity Americo-Israelis; not young American adults who chose to make aliya but young Israeli adults who started out as Americans before their parents, usually for ideological reasons, decided otherwise.

The road to Lotan for the Americo-Israelis passed though Nahal, post-high school national service. They were the glue who kept the fractious and oft-clashing groups of sabras and American immigrants together. Americo-Israelis were a stabilizing force on the fledgling kibbutz, says David Dolev, otherwise riven between "Israelis [who better] knew the language and culture [and the] Americans [who] were a little older and had more commitment" to Reform Zionism. "To this day," adds Avi Weiss, people at Lotan "say things that are misunderstood because of culture."

Language is a major preoccupation of Lotan's Americo-Israelis. A full three decades after moving to Israel—and though he even now writes *poetry* in Hebrew—there are still linguistic traps that "infuriate" Avi "to no end." One, says the stocky kibbutznik, is the difference between "male and female: 'Chair' is a female, 'table' is . . . there is no trick. The only way to know is by the root." And there are still a lot of roots that irk Avi. Rachel Skirball Alani echoes this frustration, vividly recalling how "unpleasant" it was as a child, grammatically confusing masculine and feminine.

But nonnative fluency is much more than a matter of mastering one's male and female plurals and adjectives. It's the very way that Hebrew is uttered that set sabras apart from sabrams and Americo-Israelis. "Hebrew sounds much rougher," says Avi. He recalls situations in which American-born kibbutzniks "felt they were being attacked because of the tone of voice" naturally employed by their Israeli-born fellow members. To their American ears, such Hebrew registered as "aggressiveness."

Israeli-born kibbutzniks, Rachel adds, are quick to "raise their voices. . . . They are *doogri*—straightforward, blunt. 'Where'd you pick up that ugly shirt,'" they'll ask, unabashedly. Often, they would "lose patience" with their slower Hebrew-speaking American-born comrades. Avi puts it diplomatically, "Manners were defined differently."

Beyond kibbutz life, coming to terms with their dual identity is an ongoing issue. For Avi, it emanates from language, but goes much beyond grammatical precision. He is sensitive about anything in his Hebrew that might give him away as a non-sabra. It is a holdover from his days as a youth, being teased in his neighborhood in Jerusalem over his American accent.

"It still gets me annoyed," interjects Rachel, "when people start talking to me in English. It drives me nuts!"

Despite his nonnative Hebrew, Avi would continually conceal his origins, denying he was an American but saying it with an American accent. "People won't ask where you were raised. They ask where you were born. Well, I was born in New York. But for a long time I would say I was born in Israel." He *still* does not volunteer the truth to fellow Israelis in their initial encounters. Indeed, for quite some time Avi did not even let on to Wendy Simon—his future wife from Bay Ridge, Brooklyn—that he could speak English. She was not amused when she discovered the anglophone truth!

Avi sees it as a defense mechanism. If potential friends or colleagues find out right away that he is not, like them, Israeli-born, Avi claims, he's "not in the loop," not completely accepted. Only after a month or so will he "come out." Interestingly, even in the United States he won't let on with fellow Jews that he is American-born and (partially) raised. Avi gives the two reasons:

"There is an assumption about my ideas and style—that I'm right-wing and gruff." This is becoming less the case, Avi says, although stereotypes about American immigrants from the 1980s on being more hardline (and Orthodox) than their predecessors do have a truthful basis. The second reason speaks to Avi's ambivalence about his identity. "Americans presume they and I have much more in common than we actually do." Concealing his American origins with his legal compatriots (for, like most sabrams and biculturals, he retains American citizenship) is Avi's "way of not having to deal" with the erroneous assumptions. His concealment of his origins as a New Yorker—among both sabras *and* Americans—stands as ironic counterpoint to the more poignant times when many Jews in America strove to "pass" as Gentiles.

"What am I?" muses Avi, echoing my query. "That is such a great question! It took me a long time to be excited about being Israeli, to accept that this is where I was, to admit I was speaking another language."

"For long," realizes David Dolev, "I had a one-track mentality—the army and kibbutz. Ten years ago I would have said, 'I am Israeli.'" Pure and simple. Everyone remembers how he struggled to make others pronounce his name Hebraically—*Da-veed*. "It has taken many years to come to terms with my having a mixed identity," he admits. "It's an issue."

Like his counterparts at Lotan, Avi can be a cultural spy. "When I'm in America, I feel it's a foreign country. People don't recognize me as a foreigner, but I do feel like one." There is an inauthenticity to his Americanness: although he has "a lot of knowledge about" his birth land, "it's all second hand." On those rare occasions on which Avi wishes to revel in his Americanness (among, say, American visitors to Lotan), Avi will resort to informational subterfuge:

> Years ago someone came to the kibbutz and I was talking to him about *Saturday Night Live*. It was big then. I talked about the actors, about whole skits. But I never saw it. To this day I haven't seen it.

If you listen carefully enough, though, there are some strange figures of speech that make their way into his otherwise fluent, American-accented English that no truly native speaker would make. "We've never had to dealt with the situation of choosing between both citizenships"; "I can talk about American things to people that come down from America"; "Those are things that I'm quite affectionate to"; "I can make a joke into American." Avi, along with the other Americo-Israelis at Lotan, is aware of mispronunciation in their maternal tongue: one struggles to say "valor"; another reminds himself that the *t* in "rapport" is silent.

For all his "secondhand knowledge," parts of American pop culture remain beyond his ken.

> When *Animal House* came out some Israelis and myself were watching this thing that had to do with—what are the houses called?—frat houses. We didn't understand what the hell these things were. We asked [my wife, who moved to Israel at a much older age than I], "Whose idea? How do they exist? Where does the money come from? What's the logic behind it?" She tried explaining but I didn't understand anything about it.

Only recently has Avi—who prides himself in his mastery of Hebrew literature—come to grips with a basic fact about himself: that it is easier for him to read English than Hebrew. The realization upset him. After all, he's someone who is "much more comfortable in a group of Israelis." (He is also someone who clings to—and has considerably expanded—the comic book collection he brought with him to Israel as a nine-year-old.) Avi dreams in both English and Hebrew "depending on the context."

It's not that Avi Weiss is ashamed of being (also) from the States: "I was always very happy and proud to be [an American]." Yet his pride is a bit askew, floating somewhere between personal genesis and ongoing self. "It's a great place to come from, you know," says the man from Forest Hills/Arava, speaking of the United States of America.

Rachel Alani (she who couldn't wait to turn eighteen and return to America) now says, "When I go to the States [now], people don't know I'm from another place. But I don't feel that America is my home. It's never an option to go live there." Still, on those trips she yearns to impart aspects of her Americanness to her Israeli-born husband and children: "I wanted my children and husband to see where I came from and things that I do [*sic*; past tense would have been more appropriate.] I introduced them to root beer and *I Love Lucy* and all of the silly things that I love . . . Tootsie Rolls. . . . They had to see these things to understand who I am." But there are cultural attributes that cannot be transferred, even between husband and wife. Humor is a major one. Rachel—but not her husband— finds "Woody Allen very funny." But Gashash—who puts her husband in stitches—leaves her indifferent.

Rachel is not alone in her unresolved nostalgia. Recounts an Americo-Israeli from Lotan:

> Last month I was in the States with my six-year-old daughter and a Good Humor truck passes by. We ask her, "Do you want some ice cream?"
>
> "Yes," she says, "but how are we going to get ice cream now?" She had no idea about Good Humor!

On both Yahel and Lotan one of my standard questions stumped some kibbutzniks even as it intrigued others: "Who would you have turned out to be if you hadn't come to Israel?" Among the Americo-Israelis, the responses were exceptionally revealing.

Shanni says "First of all, I don't think I would have made aliya. Zionism was not that much part of my upbringing. I would not have been able to pick up and leave my grandmother, my parents, and come here by myself. . . . I imagine I would have gone to college." None of these four articulate, intelligent, American-born Jews had college degrees.

Rachel has a similar answer: "I might have come to see what it was about. But I don't picture myself making aliya, leaving everything I grew up with, coming here by myself, and starting a family away from my parents. I have a lot of respect for people [who did that] but I feel sorry for them that the grandparents are far away. I grew up with my grandmother right down the hall."

Avi Weiss is convinced that he would have wound up as an adult in Israel anyway, eventually making aliya as his eldest brother did. "Israel was always a very real part of my home, even then. I'd probably wind up here, anyway."

It is striking how *more* Jewish Rachel imagines she would have been if she *hadn't* become Israeli.

> I probably would have connected more to Judaism, in a synagogue with other young people and young families. I would have sought out more Jewish connection in belonging. I would be more involved Jewishly as an adult than I was as a child. I would have looked for the Judaism, but not the Zionism.

Lotan's America-Israelis are fascinating hybrids. When I speak with them, I have to keep reminding myself that they are Israelis, too. Not just in the formal sense of having Israeli citizenship but Israeli in their primary loyalty, cultural references, and overall outlook. They are a breed apart, culturally situated between my peers who made aliya in their early twenties, and the children whom they begat as kibbutzniks. Those children—the sabrams—are also bicultural, but in a different way than the America-Israelis. Let's listen to them next.

Lotan Photos

A typical desert landscape at Kibbutz Lotan, showing fruit-bearing cactus and the Edom mountains in the background.

Showcasing Lotan's experimental geodesic dome.

Kibbutz Lotan offers visiting students and tourists an opportunity to learn sustainable development skills and acquire hand-on ecological experience through such activities as organic gardening, alternative building techniques, and creative recycling.

An example of creative recycling using old tires and decoratively painted mud to form a retaining wall.

One of many brightly painted walls constructed of recycled materials that add architectural interest and provide shade to a pathway.

A walkway lined with plants and trees and decorated with wind chimes, sculptures, and lanterns provides a pleasant approach to a Lotan residence.

The interior of a Lotan house made from mud and straw. The painted stucco walls, decorative niche, floor cushions, and patterned carpets all contribute to the Middle Eastern design scheme.

Children make bricks out of mud and straw as they learn about eco-friendly building techniques.

Children enjoy playing on this table and chairs made from recycled materials.

Warm-up for Friday night services at Lotan.

New Jersey native and *mazkira* of Lotan, Eliza Mayo.

Daniel Burstyn, originally from South Orange, N.J., husband of Eliza Mayo.

Ariela Shalev, formerly of Los Angeles.

From southern California to southern Israel: Mike Nitzan.

Gwen Skully moved to Lotan from Chicago.

Cleveland-native Richard Herman.

Leah Ben Ami, originally from Teaneck, is an ordained rabbi.

As a teenager, Daniel Meir of Cincinnati won the National Bible Contest.

Showing off the "marriage-membership" *ketuba* collection.

Commemorative quilts marking Lotan's tenth anniversary.

Lotan's biculturals: Avi Weiss, David Dolev, Shanni Reif Proforsorsky, and Rachel Skirball Alani.

Michael Livni, pioneer of Lotan and Reform kibbutz visionary. (Photographed in Jerusalem.)

10

Children of the Dream

(Kibbutz Kids)

What is the major criterion of success for an intentional community? Its longevity? The ability to provide for its members? Faithful adherence to the founding principles? Desire of the offspring to remain (or return) and rejuvenate the society?

Different kibbutzniks will answer these questions in various ways. They certainly respond differently as middle-aged parents of teenagers today than they did as unmarried or young couples building up the community in their early twenties. For now, what really counts is the question: "How have the kids come out?"

In this chapter, we listen to the children of Yahel themselves.

YAHEL'S OLDEST "CHILD"

Nineteen-year-old Shira Sperber, daughter of Long Islanders Matthew and Laura, is the eldest "child" of Yahel. (One or two children were actually born a few months before her, but their families did not remain on the kibbutz.) Except for the subtle Hebrew intonation and occasionally having to search for a word in English, you would not think while conversing with this striking, assertive, self-confident young woman that she was other than a sharp and worldly American adolescent. For Shira, however

---

The title of this chapter deliberately echoes both Bruno Bettelheim's pioneering work, *Children of the Dream*, and Melford Spiro's magisterial *Children of the Kibbutz*.

bilingual and bicultural, is first and foremost a sabra, whose first language is Hebrew and whose native land is Israel.

As "the eldest child" of Yahel, Shira is the fascinating (but no less endearing) product of a natural experiment in collective living. The overarching feature of Shira's upbringing is being the early child not of two people, but of several dozen. "Most of the members here see themselves as my parents in a certain way. Like they had a sort of custody." With hardly any other tots around, when her parents brought her into the kibbutz cafeteria "everyone wanted to hold" her. (Nowadays when she gives everyone a hug in the cafeteria, they ask her: " 'How's it going in the army?' and they care about my love life.") But being one of the only offspring of an entire community had its disadvantages as well as its advantages.

> It's fun coming to the dining room and giving everyone a hug. But they also think that they can comment on what I wear. Everyone has to see my report card, not just my parents. It's kind of a communal responsibility that they feel.

Shira, in turn, acknowledges the liberties that she has taken in return, "coming into almost any family household, sitting down, talking, putting on the TV or opening the refrigerator." She does not have just one home on the kibbutz; she has a whole slew of them.

"It's like being the oldest in a family on a larger scale. You're the first one to do everything, who has to fight all the battles, win all the wars. Being the representative of justice," for the new generation. "It's a lot of responsibility." All the younger siblings—meaning *all* the kids on the kibbutz—"then have it much easier."

Shira distinguishes two kinds of "battles": those on the formal level, such as being the representative, by default, of all children in education committee decisions; and those in the private sphere, such as the "budget agreement" she reached with her parents about purchasing items from the kibbutz store. Arrangements worked out between young Shira and Matt and Laura were inevitably adopted by other families. "A lot of what I did became the norm, would become 'this is how we do things.'" Even the way that she conducted her bat mitzvah, Shira recognized as an early teenager, "would be something looked back upon, as a reference point." Indeed, entire committees were formed to deal with all the "firsts" that the Sperbers had to decide. Helpfully, Shira "pushed" these committees to carefully deliberate on questions that they otherwise might overlook.

Younger kids, easier issues: Who chooses the youth magazine the kibbutz subscribes to—the adult head of the education committee, or the kibbutz youth themselves? How can (or should?) kibbutz children earn pocket money? What about the high school trip, that would have to be paid for?* Was acquiring a driver's license a private issue or an educational matter to be subsidized by the kibbutz? Now that Shira is in the army and lives off-kibbutz, there is a whole new range of precedents that must be established. Who finances the college education? Can she work on-kibbutz merely to save tuition? What if Yahel pays for university and she doesn't return?

As for being the first product of a Reform Jewish kibbutz, Shira has recently come to appreciate how much of her Judaism and Jewish identity she used to "take for granted."

"When I am not here on Shabbat and I'm not somewhere they have this Shabbat atmosphere," says the young woman, now working for army intelligence, "I really miss it. That's when I definitely start appreciating it more. Sometimes I succeed in creating it in other places, but not always. . . . I think I have a much richer cultural and religious life than most of my friends" who are not from Yahel. "When I come home it's something that's a part of me, a part of me that I like and understand. And believe it's something I would want for my children."

As a high school junior in the United States, it was Shira, actually a rather profound teenager, who was misculturally perceived as psychologically stunted. "Because I didn't have a boyfriend and wasn't preoccupied only with guys and romantic activity, they looked at me as being childish. That's what's is considered socially cool when you're in eleventh grade in the States. Or the whole college fraternity thing.

Attending public school in America (she was only one of about half a dozen Jews in a school of fifteen hundred) gave Shira a new perspective on

---

* Shira takes great exception to the value of her school trip, an Israeli version of "The March of the Living" that brings Jewish youth to the death camps of Poland. In an essay entitled "I'm Not Going Back," she writes:

A society that sends her children to deal with death and cruelty, and keeps reopening wounds, will never be able to recover. The trip to Poland—primarily a "synagogue and cemetery tour" that associates Judaism with death—does not have a positive impact. It may even be harmful to the participants and the society that sends them. . . . The 'Kadish' becomes the most familiar symbol of the Jewish religion and not Shabbat or the Jewish LIFE cycle. We mustn't forget, but we do not have to walk in the cold and darkness of the concentration camps in order to learn about the Holocaust.

The trip to Poland is often rationalized by the argument that it is the only way for us to understand our existence and the significance of the state of Israel. This is a fundamental mistake in developing the national identity of the next generation. I want to be a proud Israeli and live here because I'm a Zionist and love my country. Not because fifty years ago my people were murdered. Such an approach makes us all refugees instead of patriots. Basing our existence here on negative collective memories and not on a common culture and future will leave us with a history and no vision.

her Jewish identity. "It is easy to take it for granted, at home" in Israel. "Even the people who don't consider themselves Jewish at all have a Jewish lifestyle. They know exactly when the holidays are, and they celebrate them in a certain way. There's no way of avoiding it. You can't ignore it. You have Jewish sitcoms, and TV that has references to the Bible, and everybody knows what they're talking about."

And in America?

"You have to make an effort" to be Jewish. "You have to go to the synagogue, to be a member of a congregation." Living in America "made me think about it more than I did here."

It also made her aware of subtle cultural differences. Shira's hosts thought that she was "unhappy because I was so 'hostile.' This made them defensive and it caused conflict." The misunderstanding? Her Israeli habit of slamming—car doors, refrigerator doors. In Israel, "it's almost considered cool. Being free—'just slam the door!' In her Jewish-American host family, though, demonstrates Shira, almost effetely imitating their closet-shutting technique, "You close doors very gently. Click close."

Other differences were more grave. "When Rabin was assassinated, the only people I could talk to there were other Israelis. They understood what I was going through," in a way that even Jewish-Americans could not.

"When there's a terrorist attack in Tel Aviv, they don't think, 'Who would I know in the Number 5 Bus?' They don't know the route of that bus the way I do—who could have gone to visit their friends on that day and been on that bus. That's not the thought that goes through their minds."

In America, says this young woman already enlisted in the IDF, "you don't have to have your brother go to the army, and think about. . . . Right now, all my friends are in the army. If there is a war a lot of them are going to be fired at. It's a scary situation.

"If you hear in the news that a soldier died in Lebanon, or in an accident, or in some conflict in the territories, there is no chance that someone from my immediate surroundings will not know this person. Zero chance. We know everyone. It's a community. You shouldn't have to deal with this when you're nineteen."

Still, Shira rejects the easy way out—returning to the States for good, away from the military conflict, where she "would have a much easier life. It's not as complicated. I probably could make more money."

But "I don't see myself in that. I care about [Israel], want to stay here and change it, improve it."

It is intriguing to hear how this daughter of Metropolitan New York Jews confronted the issue of dating Gentiles. For the first time in her life, she wondered about the religious, as opposed to ethnic, implications of being involved with a non-Jew. For in Israel, "marrying someone who is not Jewish would be marrying someone who's an Arab"—totally out of the question, an utter refutation of national identity. But in America, Shira met non-Jews who were, at least on the surface, not so different from Israeli guys. She could even conceive of having "a small romance for fun" with someone who, in her grandparents' generation, might be pejoratively referred to as a *shaygetz*.

In the end, though, Shira concludes that it is unlikely that she would actually marry a non-Jew. Gentiles "don't have the same history and culture and language as I do. (Not only the Hebrew but physical language.) I don't think I would find real grounds for communication." As for the occasional pairings of her kibbutz peers with non-Jewish volunteers, these Shira forthrightly dismisses as being "more about sex."

But it is not easy to date as an adolescent on-kibbutz, with "someone you've grown up with since the first grade. You know them too well." Many consider it "almost like dating your brother."

Shira at first expressed incomprehension when I asked if the fact that as a child many of her friends were adults was a function of who she was "as a person or of kibbutz society." When she finally grasped the (irrelevant) distinction I was trying to make, she replied, "I can't really separate who I am as a person from the role I played growing up on the kibbutz." Shira does not feel that she is the child of Laura and Matt alone—she is the oldest daughter of the entire kibbutz. With no other children in her age group, for years she was also the kibbutz's only child.

Of all her experiences in America, that of summer camp shed the most light on the life that her parents created, in large part, for Shira's own benefit. At the end of summer the American kids began to complain, "Oh, we have to go back to the real world now." Shira didn't understand what they were talking about. "What's unreal about this?"

> Then I realized how different it was from their normal life, how extraordinary an experience it was. I came to the conclusion that that's what my parents wanted. They came to [create kibbutz in] Israel because they wanted to live at camp, like when they were little kids, forever . . .
>
> If you adopt that analogy, you can understand a lot of the problems that go on here. Camp is an extraordinary experience but it's very intense and fine for a short period. Finding people to hold it, to keep it living for years, makes it so complicated to live. You need people organizing activities—cultural activities, religious activities. When you do it for a month, that's fine. Everyone has energy for a month. But doing it for twenty years? You get tired. You have to have very special people.

As for the future, Shira is "not ruling out the possibility of coming back with a family someday." But not right after the army. She anticipates first living "in the center of the country," Jerusalem or Tel Aviv. For two reasons. First, "it's hard to change things in this country when you are so far away." Shira spent her pre-army year of service working with the youth movement of Peace Now. These kinds of efforts are difficult to maintain from a remote spot in the desert.

Second is the lack of privacy on the kibbutz: "People interfere with your life a little too much. I'd rather control my own life." Budgeting is her prime example. "There is a committee responsible for it and we reached some kind of financial agreement and understanding. [Other] people were angry that I got 'too much money' . . . Why do they know how much money I have?

"Everything is so calculated down to the last bit. Exactly what has to be. I'd rather not have a lot of money and control it than have to commit to the system."

But Shira is fully cognizant of the positive aspects of kibbutz life, and the privilege of having grown up in Yahel's unique society. It can be summarized in one word: "community."

"The whole community, the Jewish community. There's nowhere else I'd like to be on the holidays, on Shabbat. It's very pleasant, very family-like. Special, unique. Something that doesn't exist anywhere else today." For Shira, kibbutz is "the last remainder of something that's free, where you can feel secure and confident."

What if she decides not to return? "A lot of kibbutzim feel that they failed with their education if the kids don't come back." Not Yahel. "This kibbutz doesn't define having the children come back as a criteria for the success of its education. That's a very mature decision, not trying to bind you into staying here but giving you the choice and welcoming you [back] into the community if you want."

And on a personal level? "My parents say they want their kids to grow up and be good people. 'It's more important to us than if they do or don't come back. We'll be happy if they do, but we won't take it personally if they don't.' I assume they *will* take it personally," because at some level it is a rejection, by their eldest child, of the life that they chose. "But they won't feel it is something that they failed. I hope . . ."

YAHEL'S YOUNGEST MEN

His blond hair is long, his blue eyes overshadow his few pimples, and his left ear sports a ring: Shira's sixteen-year-old younger brother Noam looks like he would fit into your average American high school. But when he speaks, he uses words that few American teenagers feel comfortable mouthing: words like "responsibility" and "self-control."

Growing up on-kibbutz confers a higher level of responsibility than in "the city," says the middle Sperber child. Even as a preadult, one day a month you work for the sake of the kibbutz. He's proud of it. Noam looks forward to his year of service between finishing high school and entering the army. He would like to work on a kibbutz, "to do something physical."

This Israeli-born teenage son of Long Island Reform Jews is unusually reflective about religion. Conscious of the generalized Israeli hostility towards religion occasioned by the ultra-Orthodox, Noam admits that "many people hear 'Judaism' and think 'penguins'"—that is, the darkly dressed men in black hats whose rocking style in prayer strikes many secular Israelis as comical. But, says the adolescent defensively, "Judaism is not necessarily bad":

> A lot of Judaism is about self-control—that you're not an animal, that there is an order. Yes, for the haredim [the ultra-Orthodox] it's about following the rabbi. But for [the Reform], it provides guiding lines to help make us . . .

Like his teenage friends, Noam often feels that life on the desert kibbutz is somewhat boring. ("It's boring everywhere," comes the counter-argument. "My friends in Jerusalem are also bored, bored with computer, with TV, with going to the mall.") But he recognizes his parents' compensatory efforts: "Because we're stuck here, they give us opportunities. It's up to us how we use them."

What fascinates me most about Noam—his consummate biculturalism, or split identity, as a sabram, the offspring of Long Island Jews—turns out to be a nonissue for the teenager. "It never occurred to me to think of myself as an American," he replies to my question. Sixteen-year-old Noam Sperber, who speaks informatively about Hamas and Hezbollah, is a member of the youth wing of Peace Now.

STRESSING NORMALITY

"We're normal," insists fourteen-year-old Sarah, the desert-bred daughter of a Brooklyn mother and a Buffalo father. "People from Jerusalem think that we ride camels to school and milk cows."

Especially with Sarah, it is disconcerting to hear Yahel kids switch from native-accented Hebrew to American-style English. Sarah intersperses her commentary with colloquial idioms, such as "once in a blue moon." Her English grammar is better than that of most Americans her age: "Eytan and I," she'll say, not "me and Eytan."

Sarah is keen to let me know that there is not a Reform kibbutz kid mold. "Every person is different," she makes sure I understand. But she endorses the religious perspective of her teen peers—to promote Jewish values without being "extreme" about them. Which values? *Tzedakah*, charity. *Gemilut chasadim*, doing good deeds.

ANGLO BUT NOT AMERICAN

Although he is not the offspring of American-born kibbutzniks (his parents immigrated from South Africa), in many ways Eytan Tobias can speak for his sabram (sabra plus American) teenage counterparts. (Indeed, his English—which he speaks with only a slight hesitation—is American-accented. His little mistakes—he speaks, for example, of "illuminating" the TV and the Internet—are endearing.) At sixteen, the big, strong son of Hillel and Naomi already sports a generous growth of facial hair: mustache, beard, sideburn, the works. His long hair is tied back in a ponytail. With his hazel eyes and easy smile, it is not surprising that Eytan is known for being popular with the girls.

"It's peaceful, it's quiet," says Eytan approvingly of Yahel. "But when you get older, there's a problem—social life. You want to meet other teenagers." To protect from hostile Arab infiltration, the kibbutz is surrounded by a fence, and all entry is through a main gate. But when you're a teenager, you view this all more as a restriction than security : after dusk, you have to identify yourself whenever you go out or come back.

Eytan has begun to feel the group isolation. For sure, there are groups of similar aged youth who come through—the volunteers, American Jews of NFTY, British Jews from Netzer. And yes, he watches TV "for exposure to what's going on in the rest of the world." (He also proudly mentions his "full stereo system.")

Like Shira Sperber, Eytan Tobias feels very good about the tenets and outlooks of Reform Judaism. "My father lives Judaism, and he gave some of it to me." In the Tobias household, we "choose how to respect God. We do prayers every Friday evening. At home, we have teaching of the Torah portion." The Tobias elders have a very "interactive" style, according to Eytan, "so I know a lot about Jew Reform (*sic*) prayers by now." Since his bar mitzvah, Eytan has continued to participate in services, from Yom Kippur to Purim.

And the future: "Two more years of high school, then the army. I see myself fighting in Lebanon," defending my country." Eytan is matter-of-fact about the duties and risks of military service but emphatic about the enemy. "It is wrong to say all Arabs are alike or evil. I'll be fighting the bad ones."

After that, Eytan envisions the usual Israeli path for young Israeli veterans: travel, university, marriage. Unlike Shira, Eytan enthusiastically envisions returning to Yahel, to "make another generation." It is not a perspective one typically hears from Jewish "Anglos"—South African or North American—his age.

"In Yotvata," he says admiringly, referring to the dean of Arava valley kibbutzim, "there are three generations." "Arab villages," he continues, are even better in that respect: they will have four generations living together.

"Yahel is an amazing kibbutz," rhapsodizes the teenage boy. "I love the people here, everything about kibbutz. I hope Yahel will have a long and more prosperous future.

NEITHER ANGLO NOR AMERICAN

Although the daughter of neither Americans nor Anglophones, seventeen-year-old Na'ama speaks excellent English and reflects the maturity of Yahel teenagers about to enter the "real world" of life and army off the kibbutz. Her father, Amnon Shimoni, was from the contingent of sabras who founded Yahel. With her dark hair, deep brown yes, and beguiling smile, Na'ama takes even more closely after her sabra mother, Ofra.

Even in the span of her short life, Na'ama is conscious of changes in the spirit of the kibbutz. "Before," she claims, "there was more of a social life, more socializing." Her example? Hiking trips. Communal dancing.

Na'ama is also keenly conscious of the changing attitudes—precipitated by need—towards filthy lucre. It is a theme towards which she has conflicting attitudes. Her parents' generation, she says, built a community in "the spirit of the time. . . . They didn't come to kibbutz to make money. But for realistic reasons, they have started to chase after" it. Personally, the teenage girl claims that she "doesn't care about money. I earn it because I need to spend it." Tellingly, Na'ama didn't know exactly what her own father did—I was going to say "for a living" but this is antithetical to the kibbutz ethos—as his kibbutz job. (He is a top manager for an off-kibbutz firm.) How different from teenagers throughout the world—including Israel and America—who unabashedly crave commodities that only money can buy.

"When I see people in Tel Aviv," says the enthusiastic young Yahel-nik, she is struck by their "small houses. But here," she compares, echoing a sentiment of the proudest of adult founders as they refer to the entire kibbutz layout "all of this is mine." It is not a materialistic possessiveness. She doesn't have just two biological sisters (Ayelet, 15, and Li, 10): "I have fifteen sisters and brothers—but *really* brothers. My life," she goes on, without a hint of spin, "is more rich and [ful]filled."

In referring to the volunteers that periodically arrive at Yahel, Na'ama comments on another advantage she sees vis-à-vis her age cohorts in Tel Aviv: "I meet more people from around the world than do city" folk.

How does this antimaterialistic adolescent see her future? Na'ama cannot imagine what she will be doing ten years hence. But she says she does want to come back and live on-kibbutz ("I hope that my parents don't leave")—except for there being "no money." But then, she again contradicts herself, "it's not important."

IMMIGRANT GIRL AND FEISTY SABRAM

One week before I set off for Yahel, and three days before her eighteenth birthday, Diana Ter-Kazarian was visiting Felicia Feldman at the childhood home of my friend Lloyd/Elad on Long Island. Her guide was Chava Lending, Elad's fifteen-year-old girl. Diana had emigrated with her parents to Israel from Armenia when she was ten. But her parents never discussed the decision with her. Misha, Roseanna, Diana, and a younger brother first lived in the northern city of Ramat Gan and then the southern city of Eilat. At first, says Diana, "kibbutz was strange. Scary."

In the dining room she heard different languages. For the first four months she just read books in school. "Kids were mean. Really cruel to me." One girl threw a rock at the door she was standing next to. It took a year before she got used to the language, the school, the kibbutz.

Diana feels "sorry for people who were born on one kibbutz [or] came to Yahel and haven't gone anywhere else." Coming from Armenia and having lived in Israeli cities, the teenager finds the kibbutz to be *megubal*: confining. "Every day it's the same place, the same people. . . . It's [just] a tiny part of the world." Still, she has adapted to the more serene environment. "At first I couldn't bear the quiet of the place. Now, when I go to Tel Aviv, I get tired."

Diana recognizes the benefits of having grown up on the kibbutz from the beginning. Compared with friends and peers elsewhere, she sees how kibbutz children are "independent. They can come and go as they wish." But, on the other hand, "every step you take, people know." This is tough for the teenager. "People gossip a lot," she claims. "The kibbutz interferes too much with my personal life."

Chava, the perfectly bilingual product of my Long Island friend and his Vassar grad wife, is even more caustic about life as a teenage kibbutznik. "School is boring. You know everyone from first grade. All the boys I grew up with, I think of them as brothers. I can never think of them as . . ." She pauses, in an unusual display of shyness. "No way!"

How did this Israeli-born, communally bred, American-sounding girl come to be? "Mom came to Israel as a volunteer. Dad was looking for Zionist stuff." But the eldest child of the American Jewish idealists has no truck whatever with socialist idealism.

"I don't believe in the sharing stuff. I have a problem with sharing." Even the idea of mixing an entire community's laundry together—no longer practiced at Yahel—is more than she can bear. But that's not as bad as "working and not getting paid for it." Nor can she abide identical compensation for dissimilar work hardship. "You get the same for working in forty-two degrees outside"—the centigrade reference is a rare reminder of Chava's *not* being a cultural American—"or in the library." The air-conditioned library. And some people, she claims, don't really even work.

Both Chava and Diana are incensed at the gap between kibbutz ideology and reality. "They say we live in an equal environment and have the same thing," says one. But "some people have rich parents," says the other. "There is a difference between those who do have money and those who don't. . . . Some have villas in Tel Aviv and some don't."

The girls cannot not help noticing which of their kibbutz peers wear Nikes and receive toys and which do not. Television size is prime example of invidious comparison among a youth raised in a supposedly nonmaterialistic kibbutz culture.

For Reform Jewish Zionists, this daughter of the kibbutz constitutes a conundrum. On the one hand, Chava embodies the normalcy of living in a Jewish country. On the other hand, with that normalcy comes a tendency to relativize Judaism.

"We *have* our own country," she asserts, acknowledging the victory of the Jewish people's survival. But "religion is not the most important thing in your upbringing, in life." For sure, "you eat matzah on Pesach, light candles on Hanukkah. You *do* it"—not out of faith, but because you're "just used to it."

For as much as Diana and Chava rail against the constrictions and supposed contradictions of life at Yahel, they are still supportive of some of its religiosity. Neither minds the after-dinner prayer on Friday in the dining hall. "It's nice," says Diana. Reform is "in the middle," adds Chava. "They don't go overboard." While neither goes to synagogue on any regular basis, it is important for both that, religiously, the girls at Yahel are treated equal to the boys. But there is one aspect of Judaism—even Reform Judaism—that irks Chava.

"I don't like it when the kibbutz judges people by their religion," she rails. There is a definite stage-of-life context to her remark. "It's not their job to choose who I should be and hang out with. . . . Most of the volunteers who come [to Yahel] are not Jewish. That's a big issue . . ."—especially if a young Yahelnik decides to go out with one of them. "I should choose a person I want to marry [and] not be restricted to religion," says the pluralist sabram. "The Jews are just limiting themselves to say you should just marry a Jew." (Diana demurs: It's not just about marriage: "You have your own religion if you believe in it.")

"I don't think like them," Chava goes on, matter-of-factly, referring to Elad and Erica. "My parents are my parents." She is a maturing woman who, even as she admits to liking parties and today's music, looks forward to joining the army and then seeing the world. She easily envisions marrying a non-Jewish man and giving their children the option to choose another religion. "I know it will hurt my parents," she concedes, not without sorrow. But if her children "want to wear a cross, I'll let them."

"There's no way I'm staying on-kibbutz" afterwards, she asserts. "Only as a last resort, if I have no money." Still, she sees it as "an open door if I'm in trouble." But Chava's long-range plan is to go into business and not have to worry about money.

"I have to see the world before I decide where to live," she says at another point. "I can't imagine people who live in one place all their life. How can you do that?" It is clear why Diana the immigrant, and Chava the sabram, are close friends. One says, the other endorses, the criticism that speaks to conformity on the kibbutz: "That everyone should think the same way—I can't imagine anything worse."

There is one subject that the girls do disagree on, however. "Right after the Holocaust," Chava says, "people got married just to have more Jewish people again. We're over that. It's past." Diana, who lost family in the Shoah, is less dismissive. For her, the imperative not to forget cannot be so easily compartmentalized. She is not (yet?) as rebellious as her friend Chava: "If the parents told me not to go out with a non-Jew, I would respect them."

It is when the children of the kibbutz are speaking together that you get the most startling remarks. I found that not only listening to Diana and Chava

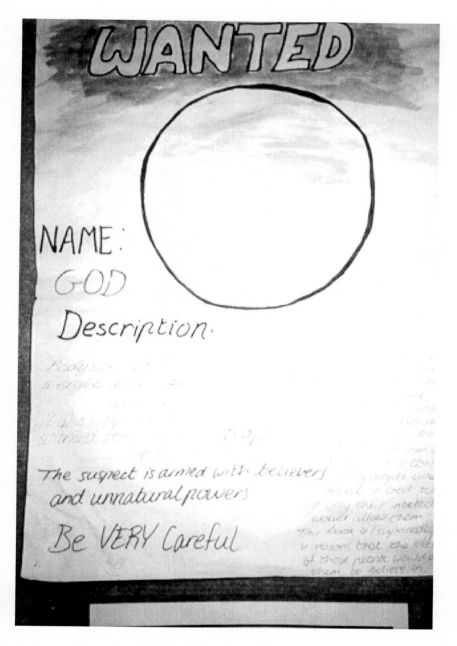

FIG. 10.1. Theological Reflections at Local High School.

visiting on Long Island, but also with other adolescents at Yahel. Debating the relative merits of city versus country life, between boredom on-kibbutz and teenage boredom off it, between desert scenery here and greenery else-where, one adolescent pipes up: "Would you like to get bombed up north?"

Being Israeli—being even a teenage Israeli—entails consciousness of constant threat to nation and friends. Still, on the remote desert kibbutz—unlike the ones near the Green Line, some of which would be targeted by terrorists during the second Intifada—there is a general feeling of safety. "It's free," says Shira. "You don't have to worry about what happens." And, adds the teenage girl-in-army-intelligence, all hush-hush and serious about the confidentiality of her military assignment, "It's the best place to raise kids."

There is another advantage to growing up on kibbutz: "You walk barefoot."

How you walk is not trivial! I have often reflected on the difference between the way Israeli adolescents (especially females) and American un-dergraduates walk. Israeli girls stride forward with confidence, purpose, determination; Americans kind of waddle ahead, meandering with reluc-tant feet, to some less defined destination. Even when they do need to get somewhere, they walk as if their feet are poor substitutes for tires.

The average age of the thirty-five children of the American-born Lotaniks is four-and-a-half while that of the twenty-two Yahel youngsters is twelve-and-a-half years. At Lotan there were no adolescent counterparts to the ones I spoke with on Yahel. Instead, I imagine how my own daughter and son—nearly twelve and ten—would have turned out had I joined Elad a decade or more before. I try to imagine Arielle and Samuel speaking fluent Hebrew in-stead of English and French. I try to imagine the inevitability of army service for this flesh and blood of mine, I who discharged a single firearm in my life (in summer camp as a kid) and didn't particularly like it. It is only then that I realize that the quest for my Zionist self—visiting the road-not-taken on a kibbutz with like-minded American Jews my age—is a secondary search. The truly compelling question is rather the unpaved path—the essence and iden-tity of my offspring had I chosen for *them* a life and childhood in the Jewish State. Becoming an Israeli kibbutznik as a young Jewish adult would have been mere commentary to a life already molded. Predetermining a Zionist upbringing for the generation behind me—*that* is the essential matter.

11

Significant Others

Nonmembers of the Community

You don't have to be a kibbutznik to have an opinion about your kibbutznik neighbors. Now that Yahel has diversified its population to include non-member residents and workers, there are a variety of perspectives that go beyond the insiders' views of themselves. In this chapter, we hear the opinions, and attitudes—many of them critical—of people who are *at* Yahel but are not fully *of* Yahel. This distinction became particularly acute to me when I approached a well thought of rent-paying sabra and expressed my desire to interview him about Yahel. "Why do you wish to talk with me?" came his genuinely baffled reply. "I just live here."

There are also individuals who do not physically inhabit Yahel space but have definite opinions about its Reform kibbutz experiment. Setting aside for now the ex-kibbutzniks (who merit their own chapter), these range from professionals involved with Yahel's creation decades before to rival Reform kibbutzniks down the road. Criticisms from these various camps abound, serving as standing testament to the difficulty of achieving Judeo-Utopia.

SHABBAT IN LITTLE THAILAND

Ambling around the kibbutz perimeter one Saturday morning, I came upon a Thai worker pounding hot peppers in a small mortar and pestle. Choklee, the gardener whom I'd photographed working on kibbutz trees, emerged from the Thai quarters and we chatted a bit. I had important news to convey—the following Thursday would bring a solar eclipse, and they were not, under any circumstances, to look directly at the sun. Choklee invited me inside for a glass of water, and I wound up sharing the entire Shabbat morning—including a Thai worker breakfast—with some of the eight Thai guest workers of Yahel.

Lotaniks and other critics had already given me unfavorable descriptions of the workers' quarters. (One temporary resident on Yahel also denounced the conditions: "They even have to pay 850 shekels a month per person for housing," she lamented. "It's just incredible.") True, the structure had originally been part of the dairy complex, and electrical boxes lined the bare cement walls. The floor, too, was bare cement. They were using an obviously leftover toaster (grimy, nonfunctioning buttons) to cook pieces of chicken. The dormitory was fitted with communal showers, shared bunk bed sleeping quarters (two to a room, in the one I saw), and a large, unadorned common area, furnished by an old sofa, a bare wooden table, and some chairs. One could indeed say that it was dingy, but dingy in the way that spartan army barracks are.

The quarters were not dirty. In the sleeping room, proper pinup posters of young Thai women, probably from magazine advertisements, provided most of the decoration. But they were not bawdy. Indeed, the Thais, most of whom were in their late twenties or early thirties, were rather quiet and reserved, not at all rambunctious. Several of them were married and already had children in the eight to fourteen-year-old range.

Choklee had both a miniature English-Thai dictionary as well as a Hebrew-Thai glossary and phrase book issued by the Royal Thai Embassy in Tel Aviv. From the former, I learned of the different kinds of rice described in the Thai language, each with its own separate word: cargo rice, soaked boiled rice, soft boiled rice, dried cooked rice, scorched rice, popped rice, roasted rice, milled rice, fermented rice, glutinous rice, glutinous rice in bamboo. Indeed, I wound up adding to Choklee's English vocabulary of maybe a hundred words the important adjective "glutinous," as in "glutinous rice." To my knowledge, there is only a single word in Hebrew for rice: *orez*. In these kibbutz quarters for foreign workers, I also picked up an all-purpose Thai word for greetings and expression of goodness: *sabadee*.

To nosh, I was offered a piece of beef which my gracious hosts had just roasted—the prime piece, the one with the greatest amount of fat. (I deftly disposed of the fat.) The rest of the meal consisted of beef prepared with assorted vegetables, each prepared in a different way, and eaten, by hand, with a scoop of (glutinous) rice.

For sure, the Thais were not in Israel as tourists or pilgrims. After an orientation outside of Tel Aviv following their flight, they were brought directly to the kibbutz. After weeks and months in the Arava, they had heard of Jerusalem but had never been there; nor was it likely they would visit the capital before leaving the country. They were obviously homesick, writing letters and, once a month, phoning home. They were integrated into the kibbutz only to the extent that they took their meals in the same dining hall and at the same hours as the rest of the community; except they were not expected at Shabbat evening meals, nor at the Jewish holiday events and feasts. Language barriers were considerable, only a handful of the Thais possessing a smattering of English and Hebrew. After lunch, they would all gather, on the ground, under a shade tree nearby the dining hall.

DISSIDENTS—AND A KILLER?—IN THEIR MIDST

In addition to hiring manual laborers from overseas, kibbutz reformers decided to take on paid specialists with professional expertise for higher end activities that kibbutz members simply did not possess. Technical specialization in desert agriculture justified one such hire. So did the desire to eat well: a professional chef is in the kibbutz direct employ. So are two women, a nurse and kindergarten teacher. A Bedouin, paid to oversee the field crops, also lives with his large family at Yahel. Some of this "hired help" are happy to partake of the advantages of kibbutz life while getting a salary to boot; they willingly accept the trade-off that deprives them of input into community decisions. Others feel like second-class citizens— Jewish and Israeli but not treated as equals by the kibbutznik "elites," even snubbed socially. And at least one of the hired help harbors a secret that none of his kibbutz hosts knows: he has killed a man with his own two hands.

Unappreciated Chef

"Ta'im" has the physique of a truck driver and the temperament of an opera singer. Of all the paid employees of Yahel, his is the work the kibbutzniks take in most directly. For Ta'im is the chef.

Ta'im assesses the inefficiencies and irrationalities of kibbutz life from the vantage of the kitchen. He is a professional who, as he sees it, strives, day in and day out to provide good tasting food for an oft unappreciative crowd of culinary boors. "I ask the members to come to a briefing on how to cook the food." Often, Ta'im will need to prepare a meal in advance and rely on kibbutzniks to fire up the oven, place the food trays inside, and remove and serve at the proper time. "But no one shows up for the briefing. Some say, 'We know what we're doing. We've been doing it for twenty years. Don't worry.'" So I prepare a good Shabbat dinner and they heat the rice in the grill mode instead of steam. They burn it." More burnt up is the sabra chef. "I can live with it, but it hurts."

Despite the general reforms in Yahel's economic structure, when it comes to the kitchen, according to the Haifa-trained chef, "things don't run like a business." Ta'im has no control or influence over who gets assigned to kitchen work. "They give me just anyone because he's a member, and they need to put him somewhere. For the sake of community, they make decisions that don't make business sense." Playing on the Hebrew word *chaver*, Ta'im teases "Not every member is a friend." (Chaver means both.)

Waste also exercises Ta'im. I am shocked at the amount of food that we threw out during my stint as Shabbat meal server and cleaner. "They just won't listen—or don't want to," bemoans Ta'im, giving me two edible examples. "Mayonnaise of today is not the same as twenty years ago. It's no longer made from eggs and oils. It doesn't go bad when you leave it outside just a little while. But it's easier for them to throw it out."

Or cheese.

"Instead of stacking the leftover cheese, they just pile it up. But then what can I do with it? A quiche, yes. But you don't need such good quality cheese to make quiche.

Ta'im is a keen observer of kibbutz life even outside the kitchen: "Not everyone comes together, anymore. Twenty percent are willing to work for the community. Eighty percent are happy to go home after work, shut the door, and not be involved. *That's* the problem.

"Have you ever seen the state of the vehicles they drive?" he challenges me.

"*Shmutz*," I reply, providing the answer he is looking for. Filth.

"Or if the red light goes on when the oil is low—they aren't going to be the first one to go have it filled."

Ta'im, inside outsider that he is, well describes the kibbutz dilemma: not all members of the society *see communally*. Without the internalization of the collective ethos by each and every one, it is left to a few to ensure the good of all. His final example brings us back to the cafeteria. Ta'im lifts a simple drinking glass.

"Some members look at this and see that it's theirs. Others don't see it as theirs, but as 'the kibbutz's.' That can create tensions. If I say, 'Hey, don't bang that, you might break it,' and the other answers, 'What's the big deal? It's only a glass'—that's the root of the problem."

There is another problem, though, of which Ta'im might not be aware. The hired chef may not control his kibbutz kitchen as much as he'd like, but he is still in charge. He is relatively well-paid and has a valued, well-respected place in the community. Whom does he supervise? Any member who is assigned to kitchen duty. Thus, situations arise in which members are actually subordinate to nonmembers, and consequently suffer from diminished status and prestige.

A Gentile's Perspective

Although one must be Jewish to be a member of the Reform kibbutz, there is no religious test for sojourning there as either resident or hired hand. "Giselle" is a jaundiced Gentile from overseas, the wife of an Israeli kibbutz employee of Orthodox background. She is bitter about the way Yahel treats nonmembers—and especially non-Jews.

"It's not a kibbutz," she declares categorically. "It's corrupt."

I tell her I don't understand; to my mind, I associate corruption with politics. "There is also corruption in a relationship," she explains, in any society. "Here, there is lots of corruption." Giselle focuses foremost on one group with low status and power.

"Look at the way they treat the volunteers. It's just not acceptable." A recent example irks her to no end.

"They put Japanese and Korean girls into cabins which can't be locked. Total absence of safety." She pronounces the last word in three separate syllables: Giselle is a very precise person. "For weeks I had been asking that they be provided with a lock and key for their quarters. Well, it finally happened—yesterday, when they returned to their cabin, they discovered that all of their valuables were gone. Cameras, tape players, everything. Gone!

"They are absolutely devastated, these poor girls. And when I brought it up [with the kibbutz], and asked for the police to be called in, I was told, 'We prefer to handle these kinds of things internally. No police.' The only reason I didn't call the police myself was on account of the Hebrew." An adolescent living on the kibbutz, with a history of some delinquency, was suspected of the theft.

For Giselle, anti-Gentile prejudice surfaces over mundane matters.

"Do you know what kind of furniture they use, the volunteers? Packing crates. So I was looking for something appropriate. And I found

that there was a whole set of decent furniture, stored away and waiting for
the Netzer group to arrive in September," a couple of months off. Netzer
is a youth wing of the Reform movement, and a major clientele for Yahel's
and Lotan's educational and tourism branches. "When I asked how that
can be"—that available furniture was being withheld from the volunteers—
"I was told, point blank, 'Netzer is a Jewish organization.' Now, you can't
help me feeling that this is discriminatory."

Giselle admits that she, too, feels she is the object of religious prejudice. "They do treat me differently because I'm not Jewish. Because I'm
Christian. They insinuate things." Although reluctant to do so, she shares
this example:

"For Holocaust Day I went to the beit knesset"—the kibbutz synagogue, where a memorial service was being observed. "I thought it fitting
to pray for all those who died in Holocaust.

"But they had put out word—which I hadn't gotten—that volunteers
were not to come, for they were not Jewish. And that included me. Oh,
the stares I got when I *did* show up. I felt that something was wrong, but
precisely because all eyes were on me, I couldn't leave."

"I say they don't act in a Christian fashion," continues the earnest
and well-intentioned woman, "and it's so misunderstood. To act in 'a
Christian way,' for me, means to act fairly, to treat others decently." Even
when angry, the delicate Giselle speaks softly. Her voice does not convey
the anger, only her words do. "And I know that they dismiss what I'm doing for the volunteers because of my miscarriage. It was five weeks ago."
Not a spontaneous abortion, either. "After they'd done the ultrasound,
they discovered the baby's heart was no longer beating."

An Inside Outsider

Another holder of a key position in the community who is not a kibbutz
member is "Mahr." For five years Mahr has attended to the needs of Yahel's schoolchildren and their parents. Despite her extensive prior experience in a city school and working with children in another institution, "it
took a long time [to] gain the respect and trust" of the Yahelniks, to get
them to appreciate Mahr's knowledge.

"I've tried to get involved, to feel part of the community," laments
Mahr, "but I will always be a 'foreigner' to them." It is good and well for
kibbutzniks to think of themselves as members of a large extended family;
but where does that leave she who is not a member? Mahr recalls with bitterness her recent exclusion from a "members only" Mother's Day fête.

The rationale? " 'Members of kibbutz are my family, and on some occasions I want to be surrounded by family only.' " The insult still stings her.

"They're never wrong," the woman characterizes kibbutzniks sarcastically. "They're always blaming other people." As an outsider, Mahr believes she can better assess the health of kibbutz interrelations. Her diagnosis: *rakoov*—rotten. "They use others without caring for them."

Mahr has a theory that likens the supposedly egalitarian kibbutz rather to a caste system. She perceives eight categories of inhabitants, ranged vertically with diminishing levels of status. At the top of the hierarchy—the Brahmins, to adapt the analogy—are the actual founders. By virtue of being there from the outset, they enjoy disproportionate influence. Then come the "newcomers"—those members who have lived on Yahel anywhere from a few years to a couple of decades. Regardless of their contributions or qualities, they can never attain Genesis generation status.

Below the actual members (who together constitute only about one-fifth of Yahel's total population) are the young Israelis performing *shnat sherut*—an optional year of work on the kibbutz that is credited to their military service. "Residents"—those who pay rent for the privilege of living on-kibbutz and enjoy the benefits of kibbutz life (but maintain their financial independence)—come next on the ladder. Because they contribute money to the kibbutz, Mahr claims that the residents are more highly regarded than her group, the hired workers. For even if those who are hired do pay for some kibbutz services (e.g., housing, food), they also *take* money from the kibbutz, as salary.

Youth groups who visit from overseas (the Reform movement's Netzer being the most prominent) come next in the pecking order. Netzer visitors stay for up to three months and are "adopted" by kibbutz families. They are valued as potential returnees—immigrants to Israel if not Reform kibbutz candidates. Volunteers constitute the next to last "caste," according to Mahr's analysis. They are the most transient of visitors, spending anywhere from two nights to six months at Yahel. Unlike Netzer youth, volunteers are not as a group invited to kibbutz holiday celebrations; after all, they are not necessarily Jewish. (Giselle's example of food waste disposal is appropriate in this quasi-caste context: "Do you know, in the dining hall, they assign a volunteer the task of throwing out the extra bread and milk? A volunteer! Yet that same volunteer, in order to purchase food—because they do not have their dinners provided—has to buy at the kibbutz store, at marked up prices. There is definitely something wrong with that, isn't there?")

Although Mahr does not use the term "untouchable" or "outcaste," the Thai laborers occupy the bottom rung of Yahel society. "If there were any Thais who were Jewish, it's not so sure anyone would know it," speculates Mahr. Indeed, there is virtually no social contact between the Thais and any other group on the kibbutz.

Although not without merit, Mahr's "caste analysis" of Yahel is incomplete. It does not establish a separate category for candidates, for instance, those potential members who, like tenure-track faculty, live with and contribute to the community for several years (3) before being voted on for lifetime membership status. Nor does it situate the status of those new immigrants from the former Soviet Union who are provided temporary homes on the kibbutz. It does not deal with the difference between Israeli- and American-born members, either, the latter of whom are sometimes envied for the private wealth they enjoy by virtue of their family of origin. Still, Mahr's caste theory reflects a profound if bitter perspective on Yahel by one who, despite her years of living among the kibbutzniks, retains her vantage as an outsider from within.

Tough Jew

When I first meet "Earl," a stocky, no-nonsense forty-eight-year-old, he is visiting the home of Abu Arar, the Bedouin worker. Earl is more tanned than most Ashkenazim in the desert, his face lined and creased from the sun. Not even the drab green clothing he is wearing detracts from his weatherbeaten color. At that first encounter, Earl attributes his coming to Israel to a truck accident that had completely broken his bones, and the subsequent entreaties of his sons, who had already made aliya, to join them in Jerusalem. L.B.J.-style, Earl proves his medical history by unexpectedly leaning over to slide down his shirt at the shoulder. Then he raises his shorts, exposing his scars there, too. "One leg is now three inches shorter than the other," he boasts. "But I don't limp—I compensate by taking longer strides with one of the legs.

"Doctors told me at first I couldn't ever walk again, even on crutches, because every single bone in my arm had been crushed and it couldn't support the weight. But three hours after I arrived in Israel, I was walking—on crutches, to be sure, but a few months later, I threw the crutches away.

"There's something about this land," affirms Earl. "If you believe, if you really believe, miraculous things can happen."

But lubricated later with liquor at a bar mitzvah party, Earl admits that the real reason he wound up in Israel has less to do with his truck ac-

cident than his legal predicament. And the source of *that* can be attributed
to the encouraging words that, in his hometown in the Diaspora, his rabbi
indirectly uttered about him at his bar mitzvah: "Is there any Jewish boy in
this town who has stood up for what he is?" For Earl already had a reputation for getting into scruffs whenever he heard, or heard of, anti-Semitic
slurs being directed against him or any other of the three dozen Jewish
students in his school.

"That cost me nearly going to the graveyard," Earl recalls the rabbi's
invocation. 'Cause after he said those words to me, I went even a little bit
further than I normally did." The frequency and intensity of those fights
did not abate with adulthood. Neither did his rage at anti-Semitism—
which Earl links to his drinking problems.

"It cost me a lot of pain and a lot of years to understand what it means
to be a Jew in an anti-Semitic environment. It took me a lot of years to
keep quiet." Then Earl urgently suggests that we go to his room to show
me a pair of overalls he was issued long ago, in his birthland. "I received it
from [where I worked]. On the back, the label read 'Jew.'

"Why did they write fucking 'Jew'? Not 'Earl.' Why didn't they write
'Earl' on the thing. I mean, Earl is my name! Is that not anti-Semitism?

"I lived and worked day in and day out for fifteen fucking years with
these bastards. I kept quiet. But every motherfucker of those knew, 'Don't
fuck with that Jew boy. You'll end up in the fucking hospital.' I have put
plenty of those fucking goys in hospital. But I'd always get away with it
in court."

"How would you get away with it?"

"I was drunk! I was intoxicated! I've been doing it all my life, mate!
I'm still doing it today," Earl insists in his slurred voice—not altogether
coherently, considering that he was now living in the Jewish State. "I will
do it until the day I die."

Earl then adopts a confessional tone. "Why did I come to Israel in
the first place? You know why?" He answers his own question by raising
his shirt and twisting.

"I've got a scar right over there. You can't see it," he's says to me on
the unlit desert kibbutz pathway, "but you can feel it. Right over there." I
oblige Earl by touching his back.

"It's a blade. Four fuckers attacked me. The chap who put the blade
in me got himself killed."

"What do you mean," I query naïvely, " 'he got himself killed'?"

Earl affects a tone of innocent sarcasm to say, "he got himself killed."
Then he turns deadly serious. "He put the knife in me with that end.

When he put the knife in me, I grabbed that hand. I did that—" at which point Earl takes my hand and pulls it behind my back. Then with his meaty hand he grabs my lower face and, saying "I put that up in there," simulates collapsing my chin into my jaw. "And I killed him."

"The [police] came to arrest me with fucking weapons. I lifted my hands up and said, 'OK, boys, you want to do what?' I put my hands up on the wall. I said to them, 'Well, just remove the blade from my back.' They weren't prepared to do that!"

"I got a five-year suspended sentence for killing. I got another two sentences for putting another two chaps in hospital. If I ever lifted my hands again, I'd absolutely do jail for another ten years. That's why I came to Israel."

With maternal encouragement.

"My Mom said to me, 'We can't keep you here anymore. You go out every night, whenever there's a disco or whatever, you go out and we never know if you're going to come back alive. Better you go to Israel. You're so involved with Israel, better you stay there.'"

Earl is an earnest Zionist. "Over here, I'm back with *my* people. Things work slowly, it's not the same as overseas. It's a lot more difficult, financially. But I'm amongst my own people. I'm happy."

With regards to working for the kibbutz, an inebriated Earl is of two minds. "It's strictly business here," he begins. "They run a tight farm. They've hired you to do a job, they give you the rules—work, don't misbehave, and they leave you alone." But then his begrudging admiration turns sour.

"The Arabs are better soldiers than any of these kibbutzniks are. This kibbutz couldn't take a hit. You know why?"

Earl assures himself I'm glued.

"Because," he says deliberately (and with what sounds like a tinge of envy), "they think they've got it all. You take the average kibbutznik over here. He thinks he's made it. He doesn't have any worries, whatsoever."

"Should he?" I ask, rising to the bait.

"Yes, he should."

Earl then turns overtly hostile, interrogating me about the book I'm writing. "What is Yahel to you? How do you sum it up?" He is convinced I am being fed propaganda. "They've changed it from being a kibbutz ideology to a financial institution.

"All Yahel is to me is a place of living," he then goes on gruffly, "a place of making my daily bread. And not even that."

"You're underpaid?" I probe. "Is that what you're saying?"

"I'm saying I'm definitely underpaid. . . . A person like me—like the rest of the guys who come here to work to make a living—gets fucked over every time. I'm not trying to cry to you or anything like that. It's a fact.

"I'm friendly with everyone," avers the hired Jewish hand, as he concludes his confession. "But I only have a few friends."

VISIONARY ADMONISHER

His hair is white but his eyebrows are still dark, and his sideburns, in relation to the top, comparatively luxurious. Wearing tortoise-style eyeglasses tied with a strap, Michael Livni (né Langer) meets me in a café in the capital. Early theoretician of Reform Zionist socialism and organizational pioneer for the movement, the Viennese-born, Canadian-bred Livni, now in his sixth decade, is by far the oldest of the Reform kibbutzniks. It was he who, while serving in the 1970s as the first Israeli emissary to the Reform movement in America, organized the earliest contingents of young Jews to Yahel.

Livni, a medical doctor by training and degree, is the author of several works on Reform Zionism, including a book by that very title. When I meet him he is on-leave from Lotan but even from the relative bustle of Jerusalem still assiduously contemplates the paths of the sister kibbutzim. He brings a similarly steely appraisal of our hummus and tahina lunch plates, each laden with one paltry pita. More, he lets the otherwise implacable waiter know, is required.

At Lotan, says Livni, there is a "radically different ambiance" than on Yahel. Much of the difference can be attributed to early relations between the American-born and sabra kibbutzniks. At Yahel, "people came without expectations of what a Reform kibbutz would be. The sabras were 'Reform' but not ideologically committed as a community." In addition, unlike those from Haifa and elsewhere in Israel, several of the Americans came to Yahel with a college education. "Because of the friction, the Americans could not provide leadership.

"But Lotan," continues he whom more than one kibbutznik regards as a gadfly, "already reflected the Israeli Reform youth movement. The Israeli [-born] were more ideologically aware about Reform. Some had been on exchange programs to the U.S. They saw the American [-born] on the same footing." Moreover, at Lotan there has been a "conscious effort" to provide higher education for the sabras.

Livni distinguishes between "pro-Israel" and "Zionist" education. Pro-Israel education is an issue of identity; Zionist education, a matter of commitment. "Pro-Israel education brings kids over to Israel to add salt-and-pepper to their Jewish identity. But the context of this education is a 'We-They' relationship, getting to know our Israeli 'cousins.' 'But we are we, they are they.'

"According to Zionist education, 'We are One.' It eliminates the Israel-Diaspora dichotomy via joint history and values. But especially, from the beginning—starting with kindergarten—it provides the option of Reform Zionism, to commit to aliya."

Livni has little faith in the long-term value of "pro-Israel education," invoking his cousin's North American grandchildren as example: "They are as proud of having a Jewish grandfather as they would have been with a Mohawk one."

Livni's own grandchildren are his ideological heirs on Lotan—he has no biological offspring. Indeed, his lifelong marriage has been with the kibbutz. Perhaps that it is why he is so demanding that the Reform kibbutz turn out right, and remain faithful to his vision.

"Will the Reform Kibbutz be able to propagate itself over a period of generations?" Michael Livni/Langer writes. "[B]y their nature the Reform kibbutzim are an inspiration to many but the life path of only a few." In his writings, Livni generously includes Yahel within "Reform Judaism's challenge to define meaningful Jewish community." But if through his choice of kibbutz membership alone, there is no doubt which of the movement's collective offspring is his favorite child.

A CONSERVATIVE CRITIQUE

Rabbi Ehud Bandel is well-known from heading the Masorti (Conservative Jewish) movement in Israel. Less well-known is that he came to Conservative Judaism via the Reform Movement, and originally envisioned life as a kibbutznik at Yahel.

Not from a traditionally observant background, as a child Ehud was nevertheless attracted to the religious life. Tensions between the secular and religious worlds were too difficult for the young Ehud to resolve, however, and he gradually left the Great Synagogue in Jerusalem for his teenage peers. An encounter at age sixteen with Jewish Americans of the Reform movement was an eye- (or soul-) opener. He was fascinated with their "synthesis between tradition and modernity, between pop music and verses from the prayer books." Not long after, he found himself within the orbit of Levine and Skirball, the two North American rabbis working to bring together Israeli and American youth to found the first Reform kibbutz. He can still easily summon the enthusiastic language of those youthful ideals:

> We take our Reform Judaism much more seriously than you adults. We are not *yehudim yom shilishi-shabbat*—Friday and Saturday Jews. We are twenty-four hour a day Jews! We live in a community immersed in Judaism, from the moment we open our eyes in the morning until the moment we go to sleep. Not only as individuals but as a community!

In 1976, as a member of Nahal, an Israeli youth program combining military service with civilian social work, Bandel volunteered to be with the first group to actually settle Yahel. It was important, he said, to be there from the very beginning "to ensure the standards of keeping kosher and religious life":

> If you start with a mess in the kitchen, turning the wheel back is impossible. I knew that if I was not there at the beginning, I wouldn't be able to trust it. It was hard to trust people who were not knowledgeable enough about how to run religious life.

It was Ehud's third year in Nahal. Half of his twenty-member team was to be assigned to kibbutz duty, the other half to uniformed army service; six months later, the two halves would switch assignments. In their infinite wisdom, the decision makers disregarded Ehud's request and assigned him to the group serving first with the army. "Perhaps," he ponders in retrospect, "I was seen as a policeman of kosher-ness, noodging all the time about observance, about services. The professional Jew, the prayer leader. 'Why can't we have a minyan today?' I became a pain. Maybe someone didn't want me there."

Ehud views the early disregard for religious standards as the seed of Yahel's supposed failure—even by Reform standards—as a religious community. In any event, it was the last straw in his drive to help found a Reform kibbutz. Rather than rejoin the *garin* (core settlers) on-kibbutz six months later, he resigned from Nahal entirely and went straight into the artillery branch of the army.

It took some years for Ehud Bandel to discover that, all along, his spiritual home had been Conservative rather than Reform Judaism, and that his insistence on halacha (Talmudic Jewish law) was misplaced among the Reform. He gives full credit to Yahel for its contribution in settling the Arava, and to the Reform movement for possessing a viable settlement "on the map" in southern Israel. (In the north, the Conservative movement has been less successful getting its own kibbutz established at Hanaton). But in terms of "correcting the faults of the founders of Zionism on the one hand and the Reform movement on the other—of creating something new, a revolution, a model for Israeli society," the Conservative rabbi brooks no illusions.

> Once you go there you ask, "Well, what really makes this kibbutz unique? Is it really a Reform kibbutz?" What about the vision of Michael Langer and the Reform Zionist perspective, the vision which was so enriching and inspiring? Of creating a synthesis [between the Reform ideology that rejected Zionism, and the Zionism that rejected Jewish tradition]? Of repairing, mending the world— tikkun olam?
>   Slowly, slowly, it became, "Well, okay, there is no need for Shabbat morning services . . ."

HOW DO YOU SAY *NUDNIK* IN ARABIC?

Aside from Abu Arar's family and the children (high school and underprivileged) hosted by the kibbutz on special programs, there are a few Arabs with whom kibbutzniks come into regular contact. During the summer, as part of its "desert experience" program for visiting adolescent groups from the United States and United Kingdom, the kibbutz contracts for a Bedouin encampment to be set up just outside the kibbutz fence. Abu Arar's extended family exhibits traditional Bedouin life.

Out by the tent I converse with Abu Arar's brother, whose regular job is teaching science in a public school near Beer Sheva. We talk shop (in Hebrew), especially about how teachers are so poorly paid—financially, his siblings make out much better than he. During visits to Yahel, he often eats at the kibbutz dining room, where my wife is working. He asks what she looks like. "A little black," I reply. He then complements me—in fine Bedouin fashion—on her physical appearance: *"Ktsat shamena, ken?* ("A little fat, yes?")

Still, through language, popular culture, and temperament (let alone citizenship), Abu Arar and his brothers are Zionistic in ways that even the most fervent Israel-loving Diaspora Jews are not. My Bedouin interlocutors' Hebrew is laced with Yiddishims: *Nu?* ("So what?"); *nudnik* (in context, a "klutz.") They refer to Israel using the same term—*Ha-Aretz* ("The Land")—that, within the Jewish context, connotes a territorial birthright.

Sami, a young tent exhibitor, imbibes Jewish history, language, and culture in Israeli public school. He, a Muslim, masters more of Judaism than do millions of assimilated Jews. Not only does Sami know what is TaNaCH,* but he has systematically studied it. What percentage of American Jews actually know what T(a)N(a)CH** stands for?

The Bedouins do not begrudge the kibbutzniks. Yahel allows them to make a few more shekels. There is certainly enough room in the desert. Even American Jews are welcome.

"Kibbutz is not for everybody." Even the most diehard kibbutznik—*especially* the most fervent Reform Zionist kibbutznik—will tell you that. Inhabiting the desert, in relative isolation, living with your coworkers, having your fortune and future tied to that of everyone else around you—yes, it takes multiple levels of commitment. Commitment to faith, commitment to people, commitment to communalism. Those nonmembers who experience the drawbacks of kibbutz life without enjoying its unique rewards are understandably going to sour on the idea. Those former members who once believed in it but discovered it is not for them are perhaps the most disillusioned. But whether their disillusionment resides more in the reality of the kibbutz, or in the depths of their soul, remains an open question.

---

* The three parts of the Hebrew Bible.
** T = Torah (Five Books of Moses); N = Nevi'im (Prophets); CH = Ketuvim (Writings)

12

Leaving the Reform Kibbutz

When I first met David Dolev during the course of my 1999 summer interviews on Lotan, he seemed like a shy thirty-six-year-old—at least by kibbutz standards. The product of a bicultural upbringing, David had been brought by his parents to Israel from America at the age of fourteen. A spiritual seeker in the style of Martin Buber, his personal identity was completely remodeled after that of Israel and the kibbutz—so much so, people joked, that they thought his name was *Milotan*. For that's how he would always identify himself on the telephone: *Daveed mi Lotan*, David from Lotan.

The next time I interviewed him, in Boston in the summer of 2003, David came across as a bit more self-assured but no less spiritually-minded. He was finishing up a leave of absence from Lotan, having worked with a synagogue in Cambridge, Massachusetts, and was preparing his return trip to Israel a week later. But David was in turmoil. For he had decided that upon his return he would inform the kibbutz—the community with which he had spent his entire adult life—that he was leaving for good. And although it was a decision he was taking together with his wife and children, he spoke about it in terms, and in a tone, associated more with painful divorce than with job resignation or home relocation.

"I would imagine that leaving kibbutz feels like betraying one's friends and community," says Nancy Immerman, who still lives at Yahel. "It's a very difficult thing for somebody who has been living here for a long time. The idea of becoming a member, making a commitment, and then breaking it."

Yet despite the pain involved, there are more members who left Yahel and Lotan than who wound up staying. This is particularly the case of the American-born. In this chapter, I give voice to those who once committed their lives to the Reform kibbutz but who, for a variety of reasons, eventually decided to strike off elsewhere. To return to my original metaphor, these are the young American Jews who did take the road of kibbutz-style Reform Zionism, but eventually veered off. What kind of lives have they lived since? How, in middle age in America, do they look back at their earlier existence as Reform kibbutzniks? Where do their Reform kibbutz experiences fit into who they are today?

The profile of the ex-kibbutzniks in America is no different from that of the American-born who have stuck it out on Yahel and Lotan. For the most part, they hailed from the same middle-class suburban communities. They had the same Reform Jewish upbringing. They came to Israel on the same high school or college programs. And they all experienced the same euphoria of building a new community of progressive Judaism in the Israeli desert.

There are multiple reasons why they decided to leave—romantic pull, material insecurity, ideological purity, personal autonomy. Each has a compelling story to tell. But whatever circumstances led them to depart, former members invariably reflect on their previous lives as kibbutzniks with a poignant dose of wistfulness and nostalgia. Often, their reflections are also tinged with regret. For there is something about kibbutz life, they all tend to feel, that sticks with you forever.

PASSING ON THE JEWISH WORK ETHIC

As with several future Yahelniks, Howie Cohen, from East Meadow, Long Island fought with his parents about finishing college: already as a teenager, active in his temple's youth group, Howie was ready and raring to make aliya. But the kibbutz he first lived on cared little for the Jewish religion— another typical experience for culturally Jewish Americans who eventually wound up choosing a Reform kibbutz.

Howie's pre-Yahel preparations—mostly *ulpan*, Hebrew-language training—took place in Arad, over an hour away. He would come visit on every possible weekend and holiday, whenever he wanted to: "being young and with no responsibilities was great," he recalls. When ulpan was over, he worked in field and factory and loved "living the dream" of the kibbutznik. Soon came the army.

Howie is a natural leader. In the army he undertook advanced training and soon rose to the status of noncommissioned officer. Back at Yahel he became work manager, director of kibbutz security, and a key member of the economic and cultural committees. But what the kibbutz really needed at the time was a mechanic and welder. So Howie enthusiastically set off to the Kfar Ruppin training school to learn agricultural mechanics—and promptly set his beard on fire as he welded the first time.

By all accounts, Howie was valued for the work ethic that he demonstrated and inspired. Upon reflection he uses the word workaholic to describe his kibbutznik self. But the negative connotation did not apply on-kibbutz—everyone was expected to join the *giyusim*, the after-hours additional work sessions (especially critical at harvesting periods).

"Most people pulled their weight," recalls Howie. But not all. And when "people were taken to task" in committee for not working hard enough, it led to "permanent bad feeling."

Howie is sensitive to the cliquish nature of kibbutz life as he recalls it: "It's a small, intense society. You eat all your meals with the same people, the people you work with. Some people felt they were left out of things. . . . For social reasons, some people didn't get voted in [for membership]—and there were surprises about people who were voted for."

Lack of privacy is a classic feature of life on-kibbutz. Returning from reserve army duty, Howie couldn't understand why everyone seemed to be smirking at him. Amy, his wife, was pregnant, and everyone on the kibbutz already knew it—everyone except for Howie, the new father-to-be.

"We'd go on kibbutz trips together. People easily got fed up with each other. Tempers flared." And for all the rhetoric about being a progressive, egalitarian society, when it came to gender roles, Yahel was hardly a trendsetter. "Women ended up in the kitchen, laundry service, child care."

The major problem of Yahel, according to H. Cohen, was insufficient forethought or planning. For the Reform and kibbutz movement emissaries, "speed of settling the land was more important than the final result." Little thought was put into what the kibbutzniks should study, both before they arrived and after. At the time, the byword was "You don't listen to your parents but you listen to your shaliach," the kibbutz movement representative. The middle-aged Cohen—now a father of teenagers—admits that the parents had it right. Better to get those accounting and engineering degrees before jumping off into uncharted waters.

Howie is also critical about the religious experiment on Yahel. "To create a Reform society is not a workable thing. There is no Reform lifestyle," similar to the Orthodox with their "real" rules and regulation. If you're Reform, he says, you just "make up rules as you go." He says this recalling the months—time that would have been better spent otherwise—devoted to rewriting the traditional birkat hamazon, the grace after meals. And for as much as "Friday night services were wonderful," obtaining a minyan, a prayer quorum, for Sabbath morning was difficult. Part of the problem was a "failure of religious integration." Frankly, when it came to creating a new communal society centered around Reform and progressive Judaism—a major objective of American-born kibbutzniks—the sabras "couldn't give a crap."

Upholding the socialist ideal also proved too difficult, according to Howie. "Rich" families in America would regularly provide gifts and clothing for their children and grandchildren living on the kibbutz: how could the Israeli-born members not be jealous? "When a woman from another kibbutz arrived with a portable washing machine," the kibbutz spent hours discussing the equity of it all. "I don't know if I could have remained in such a small society," rues Howie.

But the reasons the Cohens left had less to do with ideological or religious disillusionment, or the intensity of life without privacy, than with sheer finances: by the mid-1980s, Howie and Amy had two babies and little in the way of personal assets. "We left Israel because we had no money" says Howie, who was concerned about the children's future economic security. Back in the States, Howie took over the family printing business, then moved into imports. Today, he is a financial consultant and travels extensively. The work ethic he cultivated in the Arava desert is still with him, but in America he refuses to be defined by it: he is active in synagogue life, and particularly in promoting Israel.

Howie and Amy periodically return to Yahel but it is a bittersweet experience. "I see it as a place where I have friends [and] I thought people would be excited to see us again." But, he now knows, "there are a lot of people like us"—former members who have moved on, and who feel more connected to the kibbutz than the kibbutz can feel towards them. Howie looked at the tractor that he himself had purchased when economic manager, and realized ruefully that he no longer was welcome to drive it. And, yes, he admits a certain regret to leaving the kibbutz life behind.

"I envy their fortitude to stick it out, to believe in what they're doing." He sees that his former partners' children are now going into the army, are doing well as soldiers, and will undoubtedly succeed in college afterwards. In other words, the next generation is doing what Howie Cohen has always embodied—an ethic, as a Jew, to contribute through work.

BUT WHEN THE WORK IS NOT FULFILLING?

Howie's wife Amy admits that she is the real reason the Cohens left Yahel. Ironically, the work life that gave so much meaning to Howie on-kibbutz came to stultify Amy.

Amy and Howie were a rarity in those early days of Yahel: a married couple. She describes herself as "a nice Jewish girl from Long Island" who came from the same town as her future husband. A graduation trip from high school provided her first exposure to Israel. When Amy came home to attend college, Howie—two years older—had already decided to make aliya. They eventually did so as a couple in 1978, when she was twenty-two. "When you're at that age, you don't think of the ramifications," recalls Amy. "You make decisions, and think it's forever."

Their marital status was a major plus, according to Amy. "People looked up to us because we were married. We were accepted overwhelmingly, accepted into membership."

At first, Yahel was "idyllic," recalls the girl from East Meadow, "one big summer camp." Even though kibbutz is an especially communal endeavor, it can also be "a good lesson in independence." She recounts the various activities her husband was responsible for, including running the kitchen, ordering the entire community's food supplies, supervising the laundry operation. But for Amy herself, "there were no opportunities for me intellectually, professionally."

In September 1980, Amy gave birth to the first of their two children. At the time, it was only the third child of the kibbutz, and the arrival "started the ball rolling." With a veritable baby boomlet to follow, Yahel truly came into its own as a community—there was now a second generation to care for, not just a baby or two for all the kibbutzniks to ogle over. Paradoxically, this vital contribution to kibbutz life actually stimulated the Cohens' departure. When their son was born in 1983, a visit home to the grandparents crystallized the decision to leave.

Back in the States, Amy finally found her true calling as a teacher. It is a vocation that, for a variety of linguistic and educational reasons, just was not available to her on Yahel. Nor did the kibbutz encourage her inner pursuit. Upon reflection, she admits to having harbored a certain resentment for many years: "I always wanted to be a teacher and Israel got in the way." It is a conflict she has resolved, and in recent years she has renewed affective ties with Israelis as individuals and Israel as an idea. "Ex-Yahelniks" in particular have long constituted an important support system. Today, Amy Cohen teaches English in a middle school in New

Jersey, a job and status that bolster her sense of self-esteem that was re-pressed on Yahel.

Yet just as Amy Cohen has found peace with her work and home life, her past commitment to Zionism is catching up with her: the second Co-hen child, raised on stories of Yahel and inspired by a junior year at He-brew University, is seriously considering making his own aliya. So Amy is experiencing the same conflict between maternal instinct and ideological commitment that so many American mothers of the Reform kibbutzniks—including her own—went through in the late 1970s and 1980s. "Half of me wants his aliya to be successful," says Eema (Mom) Cohen. But only half. "We don't want to happen to him what happened to us," she says, torn between pride and protectiveness. Amy, the ex-Yahelnik, is at some level pleased that her offspring wants to live in Israel. But why does he have to live so far away?

WHEN A SPOUSE WANTS MORE RELIGION

Andy Berland, born in 1951 in Milwaukee to a Reform family, was a pio-neer: part of *shlav aleph*, the first group of American Jews specifically formed to make aliya to Kibbutz Yahel. First with a live-in orientation at nearby Kibbutz Yotvata, and then language training in Arad, Andy partic-ipated in the November 1976 dedication, with Rabbi Schindler, and actu-ally moved onto the kibbutz site in February 1977. "You can marvel at how green it is now. But then, there was nothing. Just a bunch of small, little caravans." Six months later he entered the Israeli army for an eighteen-month stint. He was the first American-born member officially inducted into membership. Andy managed a kibbutz factory, enjoyed the communal life, and was satisfied that the kibbutz was progressing eco-nomically and socially.

All in all, Andy spent five years of his adult life at Yahel. He attrib-utes his departure to the ill-advised marriage he contracted with the kib-butz nurse, a woman originally from California ("a third country"), who had converted to Judaism and "frankly found life at Yahel religiously very limiting." The intermediate step was a leave of absence to Hadassah Tech-nical College in Jerusalem, where Andy obtained a degree in computer en-gineering. But after two years, despite Andy's expectations, the couple de-cided to move back, not to Yahel but America. That was in 1983. For the first time Andy became involved in an Orthodox community, starting up and chairing the board of education for a day school. But the marriage lasted only another ten years.

Remarried to a hometown girl who coincidentally attended the Bezalel Art Academy in Jerusalem during the same period he was at Yahel, the Berlands are now affiliated with a Conservative synagogue, their daughter very active in the Conservative youth movement. A fourteen-year veteran with General Electric, Andy is now an information technology analyst in the Atlanta area for another company.

Andy last visited Yahel in 1997. He recalls that one of his best friends from Yahel, who still lives there, is "not sure who all his neighbors are." Even if this was said in an existential and not literal sense, it does betoken for Andy a fundamentally changed way of life. "It's not what it used to be. You can't go back."

Still, Andy Berland does look back on his five years on Yahel "as incredible personal growth opportunities":

It was an amazing experience that I really wouldn't have traded. The ups and downs of living a communal life in the middle of the desert certainly helps build character, to say the least."

PHILOSOPHICAL TRUCK DISPATCHER

Harold Frolkis, grandson of Jewish immigrants and son of a Southern Baptist convert to Judaism, grew up in Chicago. A precocious boy, he made aliya right out of high school, lived at Yahel for three years, and then did his military service. He then met the American woman who would be his wife. So he eventually returned to the States to marry her (they have since divorced) and started a business as a transportation broker. A fellow kibbutznik recalls Harold as the most "red-neck Jew" he had ever met, "a big ass guy who carried a 45-caliber pistol and kept us on the onion machine."

At first, Harold rationalized that he would work for a year or two in the States, make some money, and then return to the kibbutz. But then he "got caught up in the whole capitalistic thing. Money was coming too quickly. I was making too much and couldn't leave it."

A lot of times I do regret it. Because here I am at forty-seven-years-old and the question is, "Is this all there is to life?" I've got my house in the suburbs, my cars, my this and my that. There's got to be more meaning than this. While life in Yahel would have been a lot more challenging—especially financially—I still think that in a lot of respects it would have been better. I know that physically I would have been in a lot better shape than sitting at a desk all of the time. Yeah, sometimes I still regret my decision.

Harold recalls Yahel as an "exciting" place to live on a daily basis. He took on jobs that he had "never dreamed" he would do, not at any rate when he was living in Chicago: "Farming was a kick. Planning and shaping a community. Working with volunteer groups." Harold developed leadership skills he never knew he had.

Even in hindsight, he does not completely idealize the experience. Harold describes the original founders as a "power elite" who rotated leadership positions among them. He also recalls, as "upsetting," the material differences between Israeli- and American-born members of the same kibbutz: the latter "came with supplies of stereos and clothes. When married, they got fitted out." One couple's irritating extravagance came in the form of Scandinavian furniture.

As with all Israeli immigrants, being in the army was a formative experience. He enjoys recounting his assignment at the border with Lebanon.

> My job, wearing full gear and the helmet, was to get on a tourist bus and walk up and down the aisle, looking for anything suspicious. What did I know? I was a twenty-one-year-old kid from Chicago. What did I know what was suspicious?
> I'm walking down the aisle and I hear somebody yell, "Hey, Harold, is that you?" It was my Dad's next door neighbor.

Frolkus is no soft, touchy-feely Jew. In his Chicago youth, he was active in the Jewish Defense League and even became a Meir Kahane bodyguard. So there is a special poignancy to hear Harold say that what he most misses is "community. It doesn't exist here [in the States]. I'm not going to go join a synagogue to participate in the ritual just for that sense of community."

FROM DESERT GUIDE IN ISRAEL
TO PROFESSOR IN MIAMI

Ranen Omer-Sherman also was young (seventeen) when he immigrated to Israel. A Californian with a modest Jewish education ("Sunday School confirmation but no bar mitzvah"), Randy was already well-read about kibbutz life and enthusiastic about joining the Israeli army. He later became a paratrooper, seeing action in Lebanon.

The early years were the best for Ranen: establishing Yahel's agriculture (commercial flowers, citrus, date trees) and industries (desert tourism, dairy farming). The variety of worklife appealed to him (desert guide, park rangers, artificial inseminator, child educator). He was invigorated by the up-until-midnight ideological debates.

After the early years, though, altruism and self-sacrifice dissolved, and he felt the kibbutz becoming "largely an instrument of bland social conformity." Its mainstream was intolerant of its intellectual and social challengers. Most of all, though, Ranen could ill abide the reformist changes that were "hasty and ill-planned."

> Communal values were sacrificed for individualist and self-oriented goals like material possessions. . . . The community's spiritual well-being and social coherence [were abandoned]. . . . What remained besides a privileged elite?

Remaking himself as an American academic (Professor Omer-Sherman teaches at the University of Miami), he has left behind a "great deal of smugness and moral certainty as a self-satisfied kibbutznik." Ironically,

> Leaving Israel actually helped strengthen my Jewish identity [and] to appreciate the richness [and variety] of Jewish literary and cultural life in the Diaspora.

Randy retains lots of affection for many of those who did stay on. Despite lingering bitterness towards those who "so vigorously unraveled what was authentically 'kibbutz'" about it, there are many occasions when the kibbutznik-turned-professor regrets having left behind life at Yahel.

KIBBUTZNIK TO JERUSALEMITE: A LOYAL SPOUSE'S PROGRESS

The first experience Mike Madeson had living communally was at a Shaker camp in western Massachusetts. At the age of high school, the ideals of sharing and equality attracted Mike intensely. As president of his Reform temple youth group, it was perhaps natural that he would eventually gravitate to the notion of Jewish communalism, the kibbutz. But first he needed to give up on changing America for the good. An acquaintance he made at Dartmouth inadvertently aided him.

> This guy who grew up on a pig farm in Missouri was very conservative, right wing. He majored in political science and got all straight

A's. Very bright. It just didn't fit in with my picture of these types of people . . .

In my freshman year he told me that he was considered a tremendous liberal in the town where he grew up because he was the only person who had turned down a bid to join the Ku Klux Klan. I was of course shocked that it still existed or that someone would even mention it. Then he explained the reason: he felt he could contribute more to the Klan after he got a college education. And I said, "Oh, yeah, sure."

Four years later—after living on the same hall with Jews and Blacks, sharing meals, going to ball games together, being in classes studying topics that should have led him to have a different understanding of where America is and where it's heading—I asked him if he remembered our conversation. Was he still going to join the Klan? And he said, "Of course!"

If good will and multicultural education couldn't change America, a nation plagued by inequality, perhaps it was better to try in Israel, a small country where a handful of idealists could make a difference.

In the meantime, Mike had spent his sophomore year in Israel—as chance would have it, when the Yom Kippur War of 1973 broke out. Already he had posed, and answered in the affirmative, *the* Zionist question: Is this a country for which I am willing to fight and die? "If I was willing to die for it," Mike figured, "I guess I had to live here."

He was a founder, integral to the very foundation of Yahel. He would resist the dejudaizing of Israeli consciousness, something he had experienced on secular kibbutzim. "We were going to raise our children to understand what it means to be part of the Jewish world at the same time we were Israelis—to be a Jew in the modern world and still live on a kibbutz." Two children were indeed born to the Madesons while they were members.

"I love the kibbutz," Mike Madeson admits unselfconsciously, tellingly using the present tense. "It was great," he recalls, "until my wife dragged me out of it."

Avital, Mike's wife, was a sabra who "felt that she never really lived in Israel." From her parents' house she went into the army (a "very closed society of friends," she describes it, "like a family, too"); and from the army, her marriage to Mike kept her "in a very small society" in the middle of the desert, with lots of neighbors who hailed from Long Island. Not a "normal life," even by Israeli standards. What did she know of Tel Aviv or Jerusalem? Of city life in general? What did she know of the "real country" of Israel? "I wanted to try and live in the city for a year and then decide," she recalls.

Yet neither could the couple imagine totally severing connections with their close-knit community. Mike and Avital secured an arrangement that would have allowed them to live "up north" and work for the kibbutz movement while remaining members of Yahel. Mike was too principled to lay down an ultimatum. Ever the kibbutznik, he "felt that the wisdom of the community would find its expression in understanding the needs of the individual." He overrated the wisdom of his fellow kibbutzniks.

Paradoxically, it was on account of the couple's very popularity and utility that the vote did not go their way. "We were both people that everyone felt comfortable with, that everyone was talking to. We played a central role in the community and they didn't want us to leave. [Members] believed that we were so important to the social fabric of the community that they couldn't afford to let us leave. . . . Otherwise, there'd be a social crisis or something."

"But," he adds ruefully, "they ignored the fact that *we* were having a crisis."

At first they felt like "horrible traitors"—to their friends, to the Reform movement, to their own ideals. On the kibbutz, Mike had felt that he had been contributing to improving not only local society but improving educational values more broadly. In the city, "I was like a no one here, a nothing."

Nobody—including both Madesons—imagined Mike adopting a life outside of the kibbutz, so bound up had he been with Yahel. He laughs at the recollection. As "it turned out, it took me five minutes to adapt." Their most precious commodity? A door that you could close!

> It was the first time our door had been closed in ten years without people knocking on it, just coming in whenever they wanted, around the clock. The people next door [in Jerusalem] didn't come to tell me their marital problems or their children's problems or their work problems. They were just next door.

Ironically, it is Avital who has had the tougher time adjusting to life off-kibbutz. "She's still looking for the community that she's missing. She's still looking for groups of friends she can share everything with." And Mike? He who by his own accounts was "super-socially involved in the kibbutz, and was for years the person looking to solve other people's problems"—he feels great about not knowing other people's problems anymore.

Mike regained that which he never knew was important while thriving at Yahel: individuality and personal space.

> If we wanted to go out to dinner or get in the car and just drive
> around, we didn't have to get permission. It was like a vacation. But a
> vacation that lasted for years.

Born in 1954, Mike was forty-five when I met with him. As with many men in the Jewish State, it was a significant marker in the Israeli life cycle: he had now reached the official age for retirement from the military reserves. The onetime kibbutz diehard—he who had once opposed televisions in members' homes—could now devout himself unimpeded to his career as a marketing consultant. His specialty niche? "Unique items for the international Christian market." They include an electronic gizmo that beeps out wise sayings from the New Testament. Avital had just earned a masters degree in Jewish studies and was beginning to study economics.

TOO FAR FROM THE GRANDPARENTS

Lisa Schwartz from Rockland County was first "blown away" while visiting Israel with her parents at the age of seventeen. A freshman year of college in Israel clinched it: in fact, if her parents hadn't forced her, Lisa would not have returned to the States. But she did come back, earned her BA at SUNY-Albany, and then made aliya with Garin Arava, the preparatory group for the desert Reform kibbutzim.

Already there was a "big problem. Yahel was a very young and needy community," says Lisa, "and the Reform movement made the wrong decision to establish another kibbutz"—Lotan—"that was young and needy also."

Lisa sees in this poor planning the beginning of Yahel's "demise. There were just not enough idealists" being funneled through the Reform movement to the Arava. "Most of the people, who were coming from North America, who were the real ideologues—those with strong personalities, go-getters"—chose Lotan because it was brand-new. ("Yahel was five-years-old already.") Lisa includes herself among them. From 1982–84, Lisa and her future husband, Aram, made aliya together and lived on Lotan. "I always felt that we (and the movement) were not doing right by Yahel. Everybody made their own decision on where to go."

But Lotan at that time was "too new, too unorganized" for the Schwartzes, who began yearning for a more established kibbutz. Although they fully shared in the ideology and idealism, "We got tired of having to create everything everyday from scratch." Lotan was also full of "zealots." Yahelniks, in contrast, were "normal, relaxed people who were just living." As one of the only married couples at Lotan, Lisa and Aram also sought a more family environment. After an extensive search, they decided on—Yahel.

At that time, Yahel always helped Lotan out—socially, agriculturally, and so forth. Lisa recalls the dynamism—Israeli dancing, communal eating, well-attended services "We were *living* Reform Judaism." Lisa loved working with children; husband Aram thrived first as cook, then as supply manager, for the kitchen.

So why did they leave? The "reforms" were a big reason. "We didn't even want television in homes," recalls Lisa, an ardent believer in communalism. "All of a sudden kibbutzniks were encouraged to think and act and function as entrepreneurs. . . . It became less and less communal. . . . There was inequity, hired labor. Materialism became rampant. It made us angry. But majority rules."

Then came the clincher—in 1990, Lisa gave birth to her first child, and realized how important it was to be near her family back in the States. Living through the Gulf War was also "freaky." Aram reasoned that "if we were going to go back to capitalism, we might as well come back to America." In the fall of 1991, they were gone. But she found capitalism more difficult to fit into than socialism.

> It's not easy starting off with nothing. We made aliya when we were twenty-two and came back at thirty-one. We had no money. My husband had a very low-level job. We lived with my parents for several years.

Lisa, now a third grade teacher in a Jewish day school, has no regrets. "I fulfilled a dream," she recalls. But she fears a visit to Yahel today might sadden her.

MATERNAL RESISTANCE

Among the early Reform kibbutzniks, Sarah Siegal was a rarity: a first generation American, the daughter of a Holocaust survivor and a mother who had grown up as a refugee in Cuba. Going to public school in Queens, Sarah "thought everybody's parents spoke Yiddish. It wasn't until she went to college," she recalls in laughter, that she discovered that some parents spoke English! In fact, when she first went to Syracuse to study special education, the notion of being second generation was still a novelty. "I met people from Rochester. 'How could your parents be born in America?' To me they were like Pilgrims who had come on the Mayflower!"

During a summer backpacking trip with her college Sarah first "caught the bug" of Israel, but even in high school, she was enamored with the idea of kibbutz socialism. After several years of teaching, she finally signed up for a six-month Israel program on-kibbutz. She stayed on for two years, and loved it. But that kibbutz was part of a staunchly antireligious movement, and Sarah could not envision raising her future children in such an environment. Her search for an appropriate kibbutz led her to Yahel—even though she wondered, "How the heck am I ever going to lead my whole life without any green around you?" But unbeknownst to Sarah her husband-to-be—an Israeli-born agronomist—was living next door. Five years Nati and Sarah lived together on Yahel, the last half of which as parents.

It was the communal sacrifice of parenting that drove Sarah from Yahel. She recalls bringing her crying boy to the children's house for the first time. "How could anyone else understand his needs and wants?" she worried. "Why did somebody else have to be with him when he was an infant, and not me? *I* wanted to raise my children when they were young."

Maternal instinct also flew against structural change. By the early 1990s, the kibbutz was hiring people as child care providers. Children were no longer cared for by other members exclusively. "I have no idea who these people are," she told herself. "Why are they raising my child?"

Sarah still bristles at the memory of her son's fever. She was on maternity leave with her second child but still the kibbutz insisted her boy—even with 103° temperature—spend the day in the children's house, and not stay home with his mother.

"It's a very small kibbutz. After a certain number of years you don't get along with certain people." There were, particularly among the Israeli-born women, some "very strong personalities." And they are all "so involved in each other's every breathing decision."

"I had enough," recounts the otherwise compliant woman from Bayside, even though her sabra husband wanted to stay. Sarah still feels guilty about making him leave kibbutz on her account, something they did in 1992. She has other regrets. "Maybe I made a mistake, not raising my kids on-kibbutz. It is such a great environment for children, all outdoors. Everyone's together, helping each other."

The Siegels now live in Orlando, Florida, where Sarah teaches Hebrew in a Jewish day school. Even there, with an agronomic specialty in citrus fruit, Nati has had more difficulty securing employment.

LEAVING "GREAT NECK IN THE DESERT"

Raised in a Conservative synagogue in Gatsby's West Egg, as he likes to joke, Richard Kaplan found his way during high school to Great Neck's Reform temple youth lounge—initially to play pool, but eventually rising to youth group president. Unhappy with life at the University of Denver ("I was at the stage where a stale New York bagel covered in mold was better than a fresh bagel" in Colorado), Richard returned to the East Coast, attending Nassau Community College by night and working for the public works department by day. His love for machinery and heavy equipment—auto mechanics, industrial knitting (his father was in the sweater business)—would later serve him well. So would smashing walls—part of the brownstone renovation he did with a friend for his father's business friend in Brooklyn.

For his third year of studies in the late 1970s, Richard opted for the Reform movement College Academic Year on a kibbutz near Jerusalem. Subsequent trips to Yahel (especially as a guide) helped him overcome his initial resentment about going to the Reform kibbutz : at first it was "shoved down [their] throats—unnecessary indoctrination." Although he returned to the States to get a degree, Richard knew he wanted to become a kibbutznik: he had the mechanical skills and loved the lifestyle.

At first Richard was slotted to settle at Lotan, whose groundbreaking ceremony he had actually attended. But even in 1982 "there was something a little too ra-ra about it that bothered" him. The only one in the Lotan-bound group with marketable skills, Richard didn't feel the need to get his feet wet (or his "hands dirty") on a brand-new kibbutz with novices. Already, Yahel was "beginning to feel slighted" by the manpower directed to its younger sibling. Richard opted for Yahel, and went to work in the garage. Five years later, in charge of volunteers, Richard met the woman he would marry.

> I was there in the cusp years. When I first arrived it was still predominantly single, twenty-something—a cool place. Then it became a place of families. Things which give a community stability were becoming predominant. The maturity level increased. But how that plays itself out is, "God, there's nothing to do at night anymore! . . ." I'm flirting with a friend of mine. You're thirty, thirty-one—there's only so many times you can keep trying to hook up with seventeen-and eighteen-year-olds from other programs. It really doesn't work anymore.

Shmiel's accidental strangulation was traumatic. So was Yonatan Maximon's cancer death. There was a stillborn birth, a miscarriage. One couple gave birth to a child with cystic fibrosis. "The kibbutz took some hard psychological hits," says Richard Kaplan. "It made you wonder every now and then."

But what most disturbed Richard was Yahel becoming "Great Neck in the desert."

> You'd get done with work. You'd have dinner. Instead of people hanging out and socializing together, you'd now socialize in your living room with the TV.

And in middle age, you don't "want the height of your cultural exposure to be a forty-five minute trip to Eilat."

Incipient discussions about rewarding members according to performance, regardless of their objective contribution, also turned Richard off. As a mechanic at the higher end of local pay scale calculations, he would have personally benefited from such change. But that's not what Richard believed in. The snowball of departures of the late 1980s took its toll. He began looking into other Arava kibbutzim to settle on, and was even recruited by one of them, but in the end took a leave of absence and went to Boston. Part of the incentive was reuniting romantically with a volunteer he had met at Yahel—a woman whom he decided to marry. The Kaplans have not yet gone back to Israel.

Whereas Yahel was once in the vanguard of alternative or Reform Judaism—a mantle now born by Lotan—from afar, Richard Kaplan gives his former kibbutz "kudos for redefining the paradigm of what a small successful kibbutz can be." Even though he has been successful living in America, he admits that life since Yahel "has never been the same." In Israel, he reflects, "I was part of a brotherhood. Of kibbutz members. Of people living in the Arava. In a brotherhood of mechanics." Today, Richard Kaplan has a managerial position in the Carnegie Library in Pittsburgh.

A "TRAITOR" WHO DIDN'T TAKE IT PERSONALLY

Unlike most Reform kibbutzniks-to-be, Debby Gutman did not come to Israel on an organized program: she merely wrote to the same kibbutz her older sister had worked on. But like the others, Debby "got the bug." Her second time, Debby went on a program—that happened to be Reform—that would give her college credit while living and studying on a kibbutz. Debby and the other fifteen students worked in the morning, taking classes in the afternoon. She came with Garin Arava in 1979 and stayed until 1982.

Physically, "it was pretty primitive" but she had "great experiences." Debby Gutman worked with the very first children who were born to the kibbutz: "It was meaningful to me that the kibbutz wanted me to."

Raised in Skokie, Illinois, Debby laughs about the manual blunders she first committed on-kibbutz : about forgetting to unhook a water pipe attached to the tractor she was driving, thereby creating a geyser in the parched fields of the desert kibbutz; about mistakenly spraying the barn not with pesticide but with juice concentrate, creating a "biting fly zone for the Arava." Yet her fellows accepted her gaffes with good humor. "They were terrific people."

Why did she leave? A combination of personal reasons. "I had unfin-ished business. Stuff with my family." Also, "people were coupling up pretty quick and I wasn't meeting anyone. I didn't see any possibilities. I was lonely." Yet there was also a structural reason.

I was sick of the communal decision making—of hearing the same stupid people saying the same stupid things and that having an effect on *my* future.

There was a professional reason, too: she wanted to earn a masters degree in clinical social work, a course of study not then readily offered in Israel. Nor did Debby Gutman wish to be "indebted, beholden" to the kibbutz for her higher education.

It was tough to have people come up to her and say, "You're a trai-tor." But she didn't take it personally. "I understood it the way it was meant: 'We really don't want you to guys to leave.' "

There was always underlying resentment, she says, towards the American-born kibbutzniks for the greater options they had. "We could pick up and go. We had parents who could send us a ticket" home.

Yahel nevertheless "always holds a special place" in Debby's heart. Whenever she reads or hears anything about it, she still feels "That's *my* kibbutz." Back in Illinois, she has moved on from traditional social work to career counseling. She, too, has not been back to Yahel.

YOU CAN'T GO BACK

Attending a Zionistic Hebrew School whose principal was a Holocaust survivor—one who openly shared the loss of his wife and children—even as a young child Neal Frankle had the dream of going to live in Israel. A few weeks in Israel with his college youth group at San Diego State reinforced the dream. A first attempt to make aliya as a graduate student in 1980 didn't work out. Six years later he tried again, this time willing to try kibbutz. The first day he arrived at Yahel, Neal met Mimi, the sabra who would become his wife.

> When I became a father, I looked at my ability to provide for my family much differently. Also the kibbutz changed. Everyone started having kids, and everyone got TV. It became a less social thing for me, and more economic. It didn't appeal to me anymore. I didn't see the longevity of it . . .

Also, Yahel "was far away from everything, physically. Kind of isolated in terms of ideas and different people. Not the right place for me to raise kids."

Unlike most of the American-born, Neal did not have wealthy parents (again, by Israeli standards) upon whom he could fall back. Even while living on-kibbutz this made a difference. "I couldn't afford to take my wife out for our anniversary. I didn't have enough money to take her out to dinner." These were austere times for the kibbutz and Neal, who is passionate about music, couldn't afford to purchase the cassettes he so desired; nor even a pair of running shoes.

He also readily admits that he didn't have the right personality.

> The bottom line is that you need to have a certain psyche to really plug in and stay there. Number one, to leave America. Number two, to stay on a kibbutz. Then to be on a kibbutz in the middle of nowhere—to live on the moon . . .
>
> I'm not the right kind of person for kibbutz. Elad is the kind of guy who will put himself out and make things work. I want to be in a place I feel comfortable; I don't want to *make* it comfortable. So I didn't feel like investing energy trying to change something that everyone else was comfortable with. It didn't feel right. It became "This is the direction they're going in. It's not where I want to be. So, move."

Neal couldn't make a living in Jerusalem. The crazy Israeli economy being what it was, "We couldn't afford to rent an apartment—so we bought one." Neil and his wife Mimi returned to the States in 1991 to pay for it, and then tried living at Yahel again for eleven months in 1993. Even though Neil's wife was "miserable" living in America and needed to get it "out of her system,

> in retrospect [returning to the kibbutz] was a very stupid decision. I hated it. It wasn't Yahel's fault. We had changed. We had two kids

by then. We were used to living in the city. I had been pretty successful [financially], was still young, and didn't want to give up that momentum.

Neil still goes back to Yahel from time to time. "It's a beautiful, beautiful place. We didn't leave with any bad feelings." For a living, he works as a financial planner; to live, he plays music as a drummer.

"YOU PICK YOUR COMMUNITY"

Karen Shiffman of Jericho, Long Island is virtually alone among Reform kibbutnziks, current or former, to have spent a portion of her youth within an Orthodox synagogue framework. Gradually, her family gravitated towards Reform. Such a move was consistent with young Karen's esthetic bent, which eventually led to a degree in art education. Long before that, though, it eased her entry into the Long Island Federation of Temple Youth (LIFTY) and an eventual work-study experience in Israel. That was enough to convince her to make aliya, which she did as a twenty-two-year-old in 1982. Karen is therefore among the first American Jews to have settled Lotan.

"I was young and idealistic," she recounts wistfully. It was exciting, in those days, to have a whole array of work experiences: date harvesting, kitchen work, guard duty, teaching art, dining room service. When the first child of Lotan came of age (Mike and Sherri Nitzan's daughter), Karen was assigned to bring her to the day care of Yahel and to look after her, along with other children.

Karen is categorical about the benefits of kibbutz life: the "caliber of friendship formed, the camaraderie. . . . The falls are hard but the highs are great." As a "socialist at heart," she is a true believer in the ideology behind kibbutz: "You work as hard as you can and reap the benefits as a community. You have responsibility to the community, as the community has responsibility to you." In retrospect, though, she has come to realize that money worries—even in a collective way—lock even the kibbutz into a capitalist mind-set. To survive in a larger capitalist country, the kibbutz needs to adapt to capitalism. Individual kibbutzniks, too, "work the system" to get the most out of it for themselves. That is not ultimately why she departed, however.

As with most former Reform kibbutzniks, there is no single reason why Karen left Lotan. She missed her family and mistakenly thought that the longer she was away in Israel, the easier the separation would become.

("It was hard to see my parents get older.") She also found it increasingly difficult to participate in group decisions about others' lives (whether this member should receive kibbutz money to attend to a family emergency in America, for instance, or whether that member, though she already has a degree, should be sponsored for further education). "Living on-kibbutz was like always having to answer to your parents." Marrying another American-born Lotanik, who already had reservations about remaining in Israel and on-kibbutz, crystallized these other doubts. After five years at Lotan, in 1988 Karen returned with husband David to the United States. But even that move was "anxiety provoking."

First, there were the economic worries. "We had nothing," Karen recalls. At first David got a job in Chattanooga, but then was transferred to Cleveland. Their financial situation long remained a source of worry, as do their future prospects for retirement.

Second, were Karen's spiritual and communal homesickness. "I missed living Jewishly daily," she says. A community day school where Karen landed a job as a kindergarten teacher (and which her three children attend) satisfies her second worry but not her first: the Jewish day school pays her "a pittance."

Finally, life in suburban America—even in American Jewish suburbia—is rough for one who values social intercourse. Back in America, Karen says, "it took me fifteen years to make friends of the caliber I had" at Lotan. "I relish those years."

DENNIS THE MENACE

The child of a refugee from Germany the South Side of Chicago, Jay Mandelsberg attributes both his keen sense of social justice, and love of Israel, to his summer camp experiences. An older brother happened to be on a program in Israel during the Yom Kippur War of 1973, which Jay lived through vicariously. The brother stayed, making aliya.

Jay frankly admits that drugs were a major part of his high school and early college years.

> I was stoned at a Santana Concert, listening to "Let the Children Play," and tipped over my chair. There I was on the floor, still going at it. . . . The next morning I woke up scratching my head, and realized I had to get the hell out. I had to save myself. That's when I pulled out of my closet the forms I had stashed for programs to

Israel. No sooner did I get there, I immediately looked for ways
to stay . . .

I was on such a high. On another planet. I was out of the south
Chicago suburbs, this provincial little wasteland. Now, I was out of
the country. And everybody was Jewish! This juxtaposition of a foreign exotic experience and yet so oddly familiar.

As part of his program Jay visited in Yahel. It was the spring of 1978.
"They took us down to what they called 'fields'—seven rows of tomatoes,
growing in the sand. They said, 'Pick 'em.' And I picked 'em. It was love at
first tomato."

Jay's parents had already inculcated the work ethic. Here, it flour-
ished. Between Jay's superior Hebrew and willingness to labor, he fit right
in, "solidifying his love affair with the earth, working it." He settled on
Yahel in 1978, "living the dream. I felt so proud. So tall," says he who, not
that long before, hadn't even realized that he was a Zionist.

Jay's commitment to hard work and physical labor did not make him
a dour kibbutznik. To the contrary, his reputation for bringing "comic relief" to the workplace netted him the nickname Dennis the Menace.

It was during Jay's army experience—after he fudged his flat feet clas-
sification to join a battle unit—that the "first crack in [his] Zionism" set in.
In December 1980, the boy from south suburban Chicago was assigned to
Gaza. At first he wondered, "Why are they throwing rocks at me?"

We had to go patrolling in the middle of the night, knock on doors,
and burst our way in. With soldiers on either side with their machine
guns poised at you, you had to search the people. And these guys got
such a kick out of the fact that "these Arabs" were sleeping with their
identity cards! "Look how well trained we got them." This strongly
went counter to whatever sense of humanity I grew up with.

Jay volunteered to his commanding officer to take on twice as many
surveillance assignments, as long as he could join the unit patrolling the
beach as opposed to the invasive street ones. "This guy—he was religious—
he looked at me and said,

"You lefties are all the same. I don't know what you're doing here. You
could be back in America driving your Chevrolet. Let me tell you
about them. I know them! You don't know them! You'll turn around,
you'll get a knife in your back. You don't want to do this duty? You'll
do double duty!" That was the night that John Lennon was murdered.

That officer was killed at the beginning of the first Intifada. It turns out he was the son of one of the members of a Jewish underground that had conspired to plant bombs to assassinate Arab mayors of the West Bank.

With the army ordeal behind him, Jay thrived on kibbutz.

> We'd work twelve, sixteen hours a day. You're out of the army. You'd just been doing incredibly crazy and stupid things anyhow without any sleep. You had all this energy. You were invincible. You didn't need to eat—just drink coffee and smoke cigarettes. All I had to do was work. And I loved it!

But then Jay shattered his leg jumping off a tractor and was laid up with a full leg cast for six months. It was "an incredibly hard and humbling experience." He who loved working outdoors and managing the packing house was sent off-kibbutz to sort dates. By the time the cast came off, so had the "initial zeal and fire." It was not easy "to be humbled when you're twenty-two, after going at 120. It was also a time of his life when Jay was "falling in and out of love, several times a week." At the same time, Jay's army friends were getting married.

Nor did he feel comfortable with the clubbiness of membership. "You can be a member and talk about letting other people in," it was first put to him. But Jay didn't want to talk about other people: "I just wanted to work." The transience of kibbutz community began to bother him, and he too got the bug—to further his education in computer science. Yet even during his three years of coursework in Jerusalem, Jay kept returning to Yahel to offer his love—his love of labor, physical labor. Which is what he did, even after obtaining his degree. But when he finally requested to be assigned to a computer unit, a committee decided that he required yet another year of working in the fields as part of his "absorption process." That's when he felt the second wall of his kibbutz Zionism come crashing down.

> I looked at the people who were telling me this, at this committee, and I thought: "I don't have respect for you. You are not my role models. I'm not inspired, I'm not moved, I'm not motivated by you as working models." My destiny was not in my hands. Nor was it in the hands of those people who I really did look up to.

Several months later Jay Mandelsberg left Yahel for Tel Aviv. But soon, he says, "I was missing it." It was 1986. After an unhappy stint in the reserves as a prison guard, he returned to the United States in 1989. For the last decade, he has been politically active, especially in Jewish-Palestinian dialogue.

> The kibbutz definitely served its purpose. But that enterprise is no longer a healthy one today. It became a business like everything else. Maybe that's what they needed, what it's come down to. Unfortunately, some of us had that dream, and stayed in it. There is a need to let go of that [dream] and let it find its balance with the reality of today. Just accept that as it is.

SEEING BOTH SIDES: DIVER, WELDER, ORGANIZER

When he was but a mere 15–16 years old, David Borrus of New Brunswick, New Jersey knew he wished to make aliya after high school. His parents, although Reform Zionists, were "not crazy" about the idea. But for David, work in the field, with his hands, always meant more than book learning. As one of very few people to have lived at both Yahel and Lotan, David brings a rich comparative perspective to his recollections.

Of the forty youth chosen for the Eisendrath program, David was only one of eight who went to kibbutz rather than an educational program in an Israeli city. Assigned to irrigation, he loved the experience of being useful and needed. "One of the most exciting things was to be needed, accepted as part of the agricultural crew. 'We need you here. You're not going to school, tomorrow, are you?'" It was during that time that Yahel was dedicated—with David in attendance—and plans for a Yahel Bet (a second Reform kibbutz were announced).

A couple of attempts at Tufts (punctuated with a summer stint at an oil rig) went sour until David eventually graduated from where he had always wanted: a professional diver's school. It was there that he acquired another skill, greatly appreciated on-kibbutz—welding. "It made me confident in ways that other people may not have been," David recalls, referring to his peers who rather concentrated in Jewish history and Hebrew language. As a mere nineteen-year-old, he became *the* kibbutz welder. In the end, though, his welding skills were perhaps too appreciated.

There was a "tug of war" between Yahel and Lotan, which David too characterizes as an "older sibling—younger sibling rivalry." In essence, Yahel was saying to Lotan : "You're too immature." On the other hand, "Yahel was the first 'child' [of the Reform kibbutz movement]—with all the attention—and now had to share it."

During days, David worked at Yahel, returning at night to the presettlement residence of Lotan's embryonic group. They were "two different worlds."

> Yahel was already much more settled. There were parents and kids and it was becoming a family kind of place. Shizafon [Lotan's temporary quarters] was formative, free-flowing. There was no permanent settlement. People were coming in and out.

"I had tremendous doubts that Lotan would ever get its act together," says David, a stocky, bearded man of medium height and exceptional guffaw. He even announced his intention to settle at Yahel, so unsure was he about Lotan's future. Immediately after doing so, though, he boarded a bus that passed by Lotan's designated site. There was a crane! Seeing that sudden, tangible evidence made a difference. "Everyone else had faith. But the crane was commitment." David decided to stay with the Lotan group, moving there as a founder.

David, born in 1960, is one of the rare species of Ashkenazi baby boomer diasporics: a manual worker with a high IQ. His ethos has always been work; at Lotan, his religion was work. David admits getting caught in the tension between the "emotional, spiritual side of" kibbutz life and its practical, day-to-day management. His reputation, he admits, was as a "hard ass," a tough worker. The kibbutz would announce a day long seminar to discuss a particular issue about Judaism. His incredulous reaction would be: "We're going to take a day off to do *what*?" If a truck arrived late on Friday afternoon—or, God forbid, even on Saturday—for loading Lotan's ripening vegetables, he shared not the religious qualms of his fellows of whether to sell it or throw it away.

Ongoing kibbutz tensions between "spirit and work" never resolved themselves to David's satisfaction. His contrary attitude was "we're going to be spiritual *after* we get our work done." In retrospect, he admits that he "would artificially take a position that was antireligious just because it interfered with work. I didn't have a great spiritual basis," he freely acknowledges. "I made aliya not to Israel but to kibbutz. "It did not lead to "deep roots" spiritually. And even on-kibbutz, his real home was the metal workshop.

Eventually, sees David in hindsight, "I started to burn out. I didn't realize it. Any nasty job the kibbutz had I would get." Responsibility was heavy; overbearing even. He looked forward to getting away in the army, but each time he might have left for good the kibbutz convinced him that it required his skills too much.

And then his grandfather—formerly a mechanic, more a kindred soul than David's college-obsessed parents—passed away. Not only was David a continent away when Grandpa died, he couldn't get back in time for the funeral. "That really tore me up," he recalls somberly. Perhaps it was time to reconcile with his parents. He had been living on Lotan with a woman he had met in Boston, but she was now in the army, and he was unsure about their future together . . .

Leaving Lotan in 1984 was painful but David told himself it was not a permanent rupture. He would study aquaculture at the University of Rhode Island and then, he told himself, after three years return to the Arava, perhaps to work at the marine biological station in Eilat. But it didn't work out that way. He became a diver for the Environmental Protection Agency (EPA), worked on the Boston Harbor cleanup, became a salmon farm manager in Maine.

Still a kind of kibbutznik at heart, David remains a collectivist leader—as of 2004, he was an organizer for the commercial divers' parent union. "Not a day goes by that I don't think about Lotan," he told me in Boston, often "wondering 'what if': how it might have worked out."

Some time ago, an old friend from Lotan came to visit the now married father. "Lotan!" David's kids exclaimed. "That's where you grew up, Dad!"

David laughs, and admits that his children are inadvertently right. "In some ways I did grow up there."

LEAVING LOTAN

I began this chapter with David Dolev, whom I originally met on-kibbutz but who now, after twenty years at Lotan, has left. Becoming forty was a turning point for David: "I need to try a different life," he says.

"Year after year," David now sees, "I got pulled into doing things that didn't really correlate with what I wanted to do." Nobody forced him, he realizes; he took them upon himself, as a good kibbutznik.

Not only he changed. So did the ethos at Lotan. Long gone was the feeling that "we can change the world." Diminished, too, was the initial "strong feeling of community." Underlying tensions between work and spirit—he, a staunch believer in the latter—became too great. David tired of trying to convince the community to take off time for study. Rarely was it "like the '60s where you could just go pray and meditate." The belief that "we can earn the money and lead a spiritual life" was less grounded in reality than in faith.

Leaving kibbutz is never easy. Former Lotaniks and Yahelniks invoke a host of reasons: personal, economic, ideological, political, psychological. Men resent the kibbutz power elite; female kibbutzniks hardly ever mention it. Yet regardless of how long they lived there, or why they left, ex-Reform kibbutzniks all have one thing in common: an intense nostalgia for their experience as pioneers of the Arava.

13

"Today I Am a Man"

"Gadigoat," that's what we used to call Elad's agile and carefree son when, hiking together in the Arava, Gadi Lending would scamper up the desert hills like a billy goat. Now, five years later, at thirteen, he is nervously preparing for his bar mitzvah, Judaism's solemn ritual passage into manhood. With grandparents, uncles, aunts, and cousins traveling overseas all the way in from Florida, Massachusetts, and Colorado, expectations for Gadi are especially keen. Jewish kids the world over feel common pressures of performance and anticipation of partied relief. But an Israeli bar mitzvah—and especially a kibbutz one—bears little resemblance to the big bash affairs that Philip Roth launched his career by lampooning.

Elad was the first of my friends to have become a father; now, his son is paving the way for my own children. Moreover, an *Israeli* bar mitzvah, I reason in my naïvely Zionistic way, must by definition be more quintessentially Jewish than one prepared and conducted in the Diaspora. So I not only look forward to sharing the traditional *nachas*, the pleasure, of my friend's paternal pride. I anticipate witnessing the very epitome of Judaism's ancient rite of passage for adolescents. For *this* bar mitzvah would occur not only in the homeland of the Jews, but also in the historically unique expression of Jewish collectivism: kibbutz.

For sure, I have been disabused of most stereotypes and anachronisms: "the kibbutz is not what it used to be" is the most common refrain on-kibbutz today. "People come from America and are surprised we have electricity, we are living in houses, we have computers," more than one Reform kibbutznik had told me. Still, I am struck by this son's comment on his kibbutz service assignment, as his father attempted to inculcate the

219

virtue of doing "something important" for the community's land and grounds: "I would have much preferred scanning on the computer in an air-conditioned office to gardening."

Elad mentions that his daughter Chava would be spending part of the summer in a camp in the United States in a program called "kibbutz."

> It's an outdoor and community service-oriented program. But we had to explain that, although she comes from a real kibbutz, she doesn't have any experience in agriculture. And they had a hard time understanding that.

Early on, I catch hints that preparing a bar mitzvah on Kibbutz Yahel will be quite different from my own experience. In the late 1960s, in my Conservative synagogue on Long Island, I was enthralled by the latest technology to learn the chants of my *maftir* (portion from the Torah) and haftarah (passage from the Prophets): vinyl records. Haskell Rosenblum, our chain-smoking cantor (how *did* he survive the Shabbat no-smoking strictures?), had personally recorded the blessings and chants. In addition to the Tuesday, Thursday, and Sunday Hebrew school lessons, in the final months of the two-year bar mitzvah preparation, I would meet with Cantor Rosenblum once or twice a week. At home I would spin the records, aiming the needle at grooves that harbored particularly difficult tropes. My mother took me along when she met with the caterer to prepare the post-ceremony banquet. At that impressionable age, I soon learned that "bar mitzvah" was also a synonym for "big business." Whom you'd invite, what you would serve, how you would dress—these were just as integral components to the bar mitzvah experience as my tense preparatory meetings with my clean-shaven cantor and rabbi.

At Yahel, Gadi has a much more approachable mentor: the bearded but young and progressive Reform Rabbi Arik Ascherman. But Arik usually comes to the kibbutz from Jerusalem once every three Shabbatot and, although originally American himself, is rabbinically Israeli in eschewing liturgical sound recordings (by the 1990s, cassette tapes). Much of Gadi's bar mitzvah preparations—including the drafting of a *drasha*, or sermonette—are therefore conducted over telephone and by fax. The American Jew's longest melodic section—the haftarah—is not even chanted here. Still, even just reading the haftarah is, for a native Israeli boy, a considerable challenge. This is not your daily Hebrew; it is more akin to declaiming like a Shakespearian.

And the reception? The Event which, in Jewish America, can easily require a year's advance to secure a prime site and a caterer? The Event that entails options upon options for food, drinks, service, cutlery, bands, entertainment, favors? The Event that squeezes parents' wallets and defines social status?

Barely six weeks beforehand, Gadi's parents are beginning to count up how many paper plates they are going to need, and arrange to pick them up during one of the monthly shopping expeditions to Eilat.

Lotan had not yet hosted a bar mitzvah for its own, the younger kibbutz's children not yet having achieved the age. Birthdays of the entire community thus provided surrogate ceremonies of reflection. Here is what Ariela Shalev, then manager of Lotan, declared a year before Gadi's bar mitzvah, on Lotan's fifteenth anniversary.

> From where have we come, and to where have we arrived? . . . We strive to maintain cooperation, and it maintains us. Cooperation demands, and allows, openness and trust. We find ways to change and to accommodate, but not to give in to solutions which are ready-made . . .
>
> White bread has turned to whole grain. Garbage has turned to compost and buildings. Ecological awareness and a holistic approach to health have grown and entered into our Reform Zionist ideology . . .
>
> Since the euphoria of the beginning, and the "high" of the first stages of building, there has been unending challenge. . . . Like falling in love, after a while you get to the crisis of reality. From the crisis, we have settled down. . . .
>
> There is something mystical about Lotan. A certain energy . . . maybe part of it is the desert, the endless expanse in which we wandered and searched for forty years, in which we found God. . . . There is a special quality to those who have chosen to live here . . . spiritual people, looking for something beyond, open, and with a desire to share. People don't leave the same as when they came, even people who never come back. The experience of Lotan touches and changes them: the way they see the world, themselves, community . . .

We are at *havdalah*, the ritual marking the end of the Sabbath. Three weeks to go before the Event. Gadi expresses his fervent hope that he'll be able to master everything he needs to in time for the bar mitzvah. His nervousness is palpable.

What are you living for? For what purpose do you, as a modern, rational Jew, exist?

Two weeks before the bar mitzvah, invitations have been placed in members' mail boxes. Elad asks another member about borrowing plastic chairs for poolside use during the evening reception. Gadi tells me he is still concerned about his drasha. "I don't really know how to go about it. I don't know when it's finished."

"He is not an abstract thinker," Rabbi Arik confides to me. "Gadi is much more concrete, and therefore has a hard time putting the drasha together." It's not only Gadi who is worried.

Who is the better Jew, Elad or I? He the compromising kibbutznik, or I the lapsed Bible whiz kid? The ex-Long Islander who inhabits the Arava, or the one who pretends to be a New Englander? The father who rears his Hebrew-speaking kids in a gated Jewish community in Zion? Or the one whose children personify Jewishness to Gentile neighbors and friends in America?

In the end, it all comes down to the children.

That is the reason why Americans yearn, even without knowing it, for the idea of kibbutz, the ultimate community. Shootings (in schools and drive-bys), suicide (especially among teenagers), unsafe environments (or paranoia): all fuel the communitarian movement. The Reform kibbutz is all that, plus a large dollop of progressive Judaism. It is informed by the best that America can export: idealism, know-how, sensitivity and compassion.

Erev Shabbat (Friday evening), one week before the Event: A clutch of kibbutznik women is huddled in animated confusion, scrambling for an answer to a very important question. One turns around, finds me, and thinks maybe I can be the solution: "Billy, why don't you be in charge of Gadi's bar mitzvah?" One week count down, and it's uncertain who's in charge of organizing it . . .

Kibbutz may not be utopia, but it represents the highest form of organized society possible *at a given point in historical time*. What is socialistically imagined as possible is different before and after the collapse of the Soviet Union, before and after the revelations of Stalin's gulag. Sir Thomas More's *Utopia* was only possible in an era of pervasive, uncontested religious faith. A kibbutz that is not economically self-sustaining is doomed to fail. A kibbutz that is *only* bottom-line oriented is no longer a kibbutz.

At the swimming pool, a kibbutznik in charge of one part of the bar mitzvah asks me if I have Elad's cell phone number. The family guests have

arrived from America, and they are all touring the country with the bar
mitzvah family. Yet back at Yahel, with just a few days to go, there is great
uncertainty about the number of guests for which they need to prepare.
Kibbutz Bar Mitzvah.

Judaism in America is like a box. You open it up and take out of it what
you want, when you want it. For a Shabbat, a holiday or a bar mitzvah,
you unlatch the lid. Many Jews only open it up for the funerals, because
they feel that, at a loved one's life's end, they have to. Others only take
out the ethnic part, rejecting the theology while basking in the solidarity.
Some never open up the box at all, storing both Jewishness and Judaism
in their social and spiritual attics, letting it all collect dust, forgetting that
it's there at all. There is no law, after all, against becoming completely assimilated.

But in Israel, if you are Jewish, you're inside the box. In fact, you're
just a small and insignificant jack among millions. You can't escape the
box. It may be for inconsequential things, such as when the weekend begins and ends, which days you take off for holidays. But it is also for big
things, such as fights between the secular and Orthodox, rock throwing in
Jerusalem, the nature of the Jewish State, the Law of Return, coexistence
(or not) with Palestinians. An Israeli is the Jew in the box; the American
Jew, the holder of boxed Jewishness.

After weeks of looking up and wondering about the army base that looms
above Yahel, I get a chance to "infiltrate," for it is erev Shabbat, Friday
night, and we're going to bring cookies. As we drive up the outpost
mound, we pass jeeps with guns pointing out the back of the vehicle.

Elad and I are met at the gate by a fifty-ish looking soldier with au-
tomatic rifle and kippah on his head, and we march straight to the radar
room. There, three cute eighteen-year-old girls are hanging out. The
blond, with thick, black-framed glasses, wears all kinds of rings, bracelets,
and a colorful Mickey Mouse-like watch band; she's also got slight makeup
around the eyes. The brunette has a couple of rings in her left ear and a
big tear at the knee in her khaki uniform. The third girl is larger, afflicted
with the complexion of adolescence. Elad gives each of them—complete
strangers—a paternal peck on the cheek, wishes them a *Shabbat Shalom*,
and explains that the cookies are a gift of the kibbutz.

An Uzi lies carelessly on the floor. We watch the radar screen that
is picking up movement along the border region with Jordan, and look
towards the Hashemite Kingdom through giant binoculars.

We visit with the two men at the base—both are Orthodox. The older one, his rifle cradled on lap, reads what looks like a prayer book. He speaks with a Sephardi accent and a slight lisp. He's from Ashkelon. The other male soldier, in a T-shirt, is absorbed in a book about Bibi (Netanyahu). Elad and the older one speak about reserve duty, about the base—service guy talk.

It's a common theme in every interview I do at kibbutz, with men and women, adults and children: the army. When I was in the army, what I did in the army, when I got out of the army, when I will go into the army. Reserve duty. It is the common thread of Israeli life, including on the kibbutz. I consider the slight, bespectacled boy, struggling to prepare his bar mitzvah. When will my friend's son go into the army, what will he do in the army, how will he be changed by the army? . . .

Two days before the Event, Gadi and Elad are crouched together over a computer screen. Elad is stressed out. He is taking care of eighteen family guests from overseas, and the drasha is still not perfected. He apologizes to me ("Sorry I can't spend time with you, good buddy"), and, in a rare physical expression of camaraderie, stretches out his hand to touch me.

Why is the expression "growing pains" associated with the young? As we transition through different phases of life, moving on from one stage to the next, we periodically experience the discomfort of leaving one known existence for another. At Yahel, and to a lesser extent on Lotan, I have encountered aging idealists. The greatest enemy of utopia is neither fanaticism nor egotism. It is middle age.

"The tension is mounting": thus speaketh Elad, ambling to his house where his parents and stepparents are resting. Rabbi Arik is on his way from Jerusalem, a day late: he is sick. "Until yesterday," he tells me on his cell phone from near the Dead Sea, "my doctors said there was nothing to worry about, that I wasn't contagious. Today, they said that what I have might be harmful to pregnant women. So I'm going to keep a low profile."

Driven by diverse motivations but sharing basic Zionistic aspirations, young American Jews came to the Reform kibbutzim in the 1970s and 1980s. Overcoming cultural differences and personality clashes, they joined with their sabra counterparts to form more or less cohesive communities.

Two decades later, the middle-aged members who still remain do so for reasons quite different than the ones that brought them in the first place. Their dreams have changed; *they* have changed. Some American-born Reform kibbutzniks can imagine who they might have become had they stayed behind in the United States; others cannot fathom how they would have turned out living forever in Diaspora. Yet virtually all accept the material trade-offs that they have made to build, in however small a measure, and in however compromised a form, a progressive Jewish community and, by extension, a better Jewish State. In an age and world that have put Israel on the moral defensive, their conscience as Jews and (perhaps just as important to them now) as Jewish parents is clear. That they have done so by maintaining a way of life that their own compatriots view as, at best anachronistic and at worst corrupted through compromise, is all the more remarkable. The Reform kibbutz is a time capsule of idealism, tempered by middle age.

Whether or not, like my high school buddy Lloyd/Elad, they have taken new Hebrew names, these middle-class American baby boomers traded in their diasporic identities for Israeli selves. They have done what I cannot: recreate themselves as Hebrew-speaking, desert-dwelling, unambiguous Zionists. In their American-style liberalism and idealism, I can still feel traces of my own generation and peer group. But it is in the sabrams, the bicultural kibbutz kids, that I see a completely new native face of Israel. It is a good face, a hopeful face, a generous face.

My family and I are included among the overseas family guests invited to the pre-bar mitzvah dinner. We are honored, but it is an ordeal: we clamber aboard the regional bus that takes us to Eilat, and rendezvous in a somewhat seedy Sephardic restaurant. The owner, who speaks with a thick Eastern accent, wears a gold medallion around his neck. Pictures of him with minor celebrities adorn the walls. There are also framed portraits of a Yemenite bride and her wedding.

The Yemenite restaurateur of Eilat is not used to serving a multigenerational family crowd of Ashkenazim from America. And so the bar mitzvah boy's mother—petite, efficient, elegant (for the occasion, she is wearing her daintily wavy white hat with flowers from Rhodes) takes charge of the *balagan* (confusion) in the restaurant: Erica picks up a pad and pen and starts taking down the drink order herself.

Deep down, I had long believed, the Jew-in-Diaspora—or at least any self-respecting American Jew with a modicum of Zionist sympathies—is a proto-Israeli. With proper encouragement, and under the right personal circumstances, we are all hardwired into becoming potential citizens of the Jewish

State. Is not the easiest context for a new immigrant to fit into Israel the kib-butz, where community and material needs are automatically provided?

But I no longer believe that being Jewish equates with being a proto-Israeli. Not, at least, for the middle-aged Jew. Leaving your accidental birth land for an ancestral homeland is perhaps a viable choice for the young. But homeland is not necessarily soul land, the exact place in this vast world where you ought to go. Finding your own soul land can take a lifetime. For any in-dividual American Jew—the Diaspora Jew—the soul land *may* be Israel.

But there is no migratory hardwiring. Even after 1948, there are still Jews who are meant to wander.

One hour and fifteen minutes before the kaballat shabbat (the service marking the onset of the Sabbath) my childhood friend and his son saunter to their house. The bar mitzvah boy—he who ritualistically becomes a man this weekend—is barefoot. His mother, in her elegant white hat, is emptying the outdoor washing machine.

Erica is indeed busy. She herself had just been lugging chairs over from the library into the synagogue—"in case people from the region show up." (They don't.)

Kibbutz is indeed collective. But as the ceremony approaches, last minutes details turn part of it into a do-it-yourself bar mitzvah.

Supporting the Jewish State in words, prayers, and donations is all fine and good: but physically living in, building up, and contributing to the state is something else entirely. American Jews rarely consider the conun-drum that Israeli Bedouins (as well as many other Arab citizens) are better Zionists (in the sense of willingly living as Israelis in a Jewish State) than they. Jewish visitors from overseas (particularly teenagers) are led to be-lieve that this country, Israel, is "theirs"—but more so than it is for the Bedouins I have met this summer, thanks to Yahel?

SHABBAT MORNING. Prior to the service, Ed Lending, Elad's father, walks up to me. A man of conviction, a lifelong fighter, remember that Ed fought in the Spanish Civil War with the Abraham Lincoln Brigade. When he married Elad's widowed mother, taking on Elad as his stepson, it was Franco who still disturbed him. Now it is his conscience.

"I have a dilemma," he confesses. "A real one. I've been asked to read a portion from the text, for the bar mitzvah. But how can I?" A proud Jew and ex-Communist, for at least half a century he has been an un-abashed atheist.

"All my life I've been an honest man. It's always been important to me to be honest. And now I'm expected to read this mumbo jumbo that I never believed?" His stepson never presented him with this dilemma: it was only as an adult, after becoming a kibbutznik, that Elad himself had a bar mitzvah.

"The text talks about God giving us the 'true Torah,'" Ed goes on, genuinely conflicted. "The 'true Torah.' How can anyone believe anything like that? How do they know it's the 'true Torah?'

"But it's my grandson's bar mitzvah," my friend's aging father acknowledges, "and of course I don't want to mess things up for him. It's a real dilemma. So many contradictions."

Poor Gadi is more than a little distracted, and forgets to put a kippah on his head before the services for his bar mitzvah begin. But he is "dressed up," as kibbutz kids go—long pants, a buttoned-down short sleeve shirt, and a clean (if not new) pair of sneakers.

"I don't have any illusions that kibbutz is going to create a new type of person," Laura Sperber tells me. "I think it helps. It eases the way in difficult situations. Community has a function to play in people's lives, particularly when you don't have extended families anymore. More than living in an apartment in Tel Aviv where you can live for years and not even know the names of your neighbors.

"Ten years from now," she goes on, "I don't think there will be kibbutzim in the sense they exist today with economic socialism. I don't think the economic interdependency is going to continue. In the same way there are no longer any kibbutzim with children's houses." Rather, they will be "communities with elements of mutual cooperation and funds for helping each other in times of trouble." A structure for social and cultural activities, life cycle and Jewish holiday celebrations. "A community with an infrastructure of mutual cooperation without total economic interdependence.

"Whether or not it will still be called 'kibbutz' at that point," she says matter-of-factly, "is really academic. There will be those people who say that it's not and those who say that it is."

The service, conducted in English for the benefit of the American relatives, goes well: Gadi performs honorably, like the young man he is becoming. Since both of his mother's siblings are married to non-Jews, brother and sister get an *aliyah*—an honor of being called up to the Torah—together. Gadi's grandfathers and grandmothers (for this is Reform) are suitably honored, literally holding on and passing the Torah scroll to one another, and eventually to Gadi. His drasha, over which he has labored and suffered for these many months and final weeks, is worthy of any thoughtful Jew, thirteen-years-old and up:

> The most difficult dilemma for modern Israel is the fact that terrorists know that there is a good chance that they will be released in prisoner exchanges for captured Israeli soldiers or the bodies of those fallen in battle. . . . I believe that the death penalty should be eliminated all over the world—except in the case of politically motivated terrorism that leads to the murder of civilians.

In his own charge to Gadi, Rabbi Arik declares:

> By choosing to come and live in Israel, and making their home and a new Jewish community here at Kibbutz Yahel, your parents chose a Jewish path in some ways very different from that of your grandparents.
> And yet, as we know from when we passed the Torah a few minutes ago, symbolically, from generation to generation, there is a connection between all those generations of Jews, to your grandparents, to your parents, and now to you.
> Just as the Judaism of the Bible is different from the Judaism of our rabbis, and just as the Judaism of your grandparents is different from that of your parents, it may be that you, too, decide to go on your own path. Nobody knows just where that's going to take you. But by choosing to stand here in front of the community today, you have made a statement that you personally take responsibility for the next generation of our Jewish people. With all your talents, I know that it will be in the service of our people, and of tikkun olam—of making a better world.

"I wouldn't like to see it happen," says Liora Cohen, the general manager and official kibbutz booster, "but I'm not worried if people get different salaries according to their position, their jobs. We could express our communal spirit in all different ways. But if there's no communal spirit, no mutual ideals, *then* we're not a community anymore . . ."

On-kibbutz there is no congregational president, or head of the Men's Club, or Sisterhood chairlady. And so it is Liora who addresses Gadi on behalf of the community. But practically any member of Yahel could have done so. Virtually every one of them has known Gadi from birth. This ceremony is not a formal process of a religious institution: it is a heartfelt assembly of active participants in a living community. Today is not a great day just for Gadi and his family. It is a real milestone for every member of Yahel.

For Elad, as with most Yahelniks, the "red line"—the point beyond which the community ceases to be a kibbutz—is differential pay scales. Despite all the other changes, as long as the manager-member receives the same "salary" as the worker-member, Yahel remains, in the eyes of its members, a kibbutz. Still, for the bar mitzvah boy's father, "there are as many different [definitions of kibbutz] as you have types of kibbutzim. One kibbutz's answer doesn't necessarily solve the problems of another."

Rosealie, hardly a regular at services, is in attendance for the bar mitzvah. She is totally baffled to be called up to the Torah, with her daughters, for a blessing: the family is going on a year's leave back to her husband's original home in upstate New York. The blessing is for a safe journey and return. "We also hope you bring back some of that cool weather, and snow, from Buffalo."

With her trademark cynicism, Rosealie later remarks: "I certainly don't need any of this blessing crap: I worry enough without having the Master of the Universe convoked, too. I mean, really, I've got enough on my shoulders right now without them laying God on me as well."

After the bar mitzvah, who lugs the chairs out of the synagogue back to the meeting room? The bar mitzvah boy himself, Gadi's mom, and Erica's seventy-year-old father (who recently had serious heart problems).

"It is a community and a business," Ron Bernstein defines the kibbutz, "and its success depends on how well the two are integrated.

"If it becomes too much of a business," says Yahel's Man of the Orchards, "then individuals will be discarded and, like any big industry, the little people will be stomped on. But if it's run as a business and a community, where each individual is still very important and allowed to decide where he or she works, and given a lot more job and career freedom," then it can succeed.

The tall man from Long Island goes on. "If people are happy where they're living, it will show not only in the business but in the everyday social and cultural life of the kibbutz. People will be together." Ron points to Friday night dinner as an example of communal authenticity. "People aren't putting on an act."

Sad-faced Ron will not kid you. When he participates in Gadi's bar mitzvah, does he not think about his dead boy, Shai? Does he not regret that he will not have this same opportunity, as the father of a son becoming a man? When Ron speaks of the importance of community, for his life in the desert, believe him.

In the evening, Ron serves as master of ceremony for the shindig that the entire kibbutz arranges for Gadi around the swimming pool. Seating for the bar mitzvah party? Chairs borrowed from members' back porches. There are performances, children's dances, rehearsed skits, and humorous impersonations of both bar mitzvah boy and father. There is food, there is drink, there is fun. There is relief. Despite all the uncertainty in the months, weeks, and days leading up to the Event, the kibbutz pulls off a great party. It does Gadi justice, just as Gadi does the kibbutz proud. Lloyd of Long Island, once just another wandering Jewish kid from New York, is tonight one beaming kibbutznik, Elad of Yahel.

Elad confides that Chava, Gadi's restive older sister, may very well wind up moving to the States some day. She loves New York, loves the theater, loves the shops, loves the malls. Gadi, he believes, will remain in Israel. But his firstborn? . . .

From the perspective of the fun-loving teenager, Kibbutz Yahel is Chava's Long Island, a boring enclave from which she must flee to pave her own life path. Thus does the ironic cycle of Zionism and Diaspora play itself out. Half a century after the founding of the Jewish State, and a quarter of a century since Elad chose to make his life in the Israeli desert on a Reform kibbutz, my friend resignedly envisions his Israeli-born daughter "returning" to America.

Four and a half years after Gadi's bar mitzvah, Elad participates in my own son Samuel's bar mitzvah in Rhode Island. Immediately after it ends, he— the ultimate Zionist, who had traveled all the way from the Arava—pays me the supreme compliment: "*That's* the way it ought to be done."

It is good to hear, but I have already ceased wondering if Elad is a better Jew than I. Nor do I seek approval anymore from Israelis—even from my old high school friend-turned kibbutznik—of my Jewishness. For sure, of the two of us Elad is the better Zionist. But only a few American Jews can successfully renounce their Diaspora. The rest of us—not proto-Israelis, after all—shall continue "to dwell among the nations," varying starkly in our degree of misgiving.

How many others of my Jewish contemporaries have struggled to come to peace with that realization? Ironically, my acceptance that the American kibbutniks' path cannot be mine has been made easier by the admiration that I have acquired for those who took the tough road that I could not, planting inspirational visions of a modern and just Judaism, not in rich suburban America but in a soulful desert in Zion.

They may be a bit *mishuga*. But they are not mad. They're another kind of Jew.

Bibliography

Antonovksy, Aaron and David Katz. 1970. "Factors in the Adjustment to Israeli Life of American and Canadian Immigrants." *Jewish Journal of Sociology* 12:77–87.

Avruch, Kevin. 1981. *American Immigrants in Israel*. Chicago: University of Chicago Press.

Ben-Rafael, Eliezer. 1997. *Crisis and Transformation: The Kibbutz at Century's End*. Albany: The State University of New York Press.

Berry, J. J. Brian. 1992. *America's Utopian Experiments: Communal Havens from Long-Wave Crises*. Hanover, New Hampshire: University Press of New England.

Bettelheim, Bruno. 1971. *The Children of the Dream*. London: Paladin.

Blasi, Joseph. 1980. *The Communal Future: the Kibbutz and the Utopian Dilemma*. Norwood, Pennsylvania: Norwood Editions.

Bowes, Alison. 1989. *Kibbutz Goshen: An Israeli Kibbutz*. Prospect Heights, Illinois: Waveland Press.

Brandes, Stanley. 1985. *Forty: The Age and the Symbol*. Knoxville, TN: The University of Tennessee Press.

Briggs, Charles L. 1986. *Learning How to Ask. A Sociolinguistic Appraisal of the Role of the Interview in Social Science Research*. Cambridge: Cambridge University Press.

Criden, Yosef and Saadia Gelb. 1974. *The Kibbutz Experience: Dialogue in Kfar Blum*. New York: Schocken Books.

Cytron, Barry. 1993. "Midlife: From Understanding to Wisdom." In *Celebration and Renewal: Rites of Passage in Judaism*. Edited by Rela Geffen. Philadelphia: Jewish Publication Society.

Fishman, Aryei. 1983. "The Religious Kibbutz: Religion, Nationalism, and Socialism in a Communal Framework." In *The Sociology of the Kibbutz*. Edited by Ernest Krausz. New Brunswick: Transaction Books.

Frantz, Douglas and Catherine Collins. 1991. *Celebration, U.S.A. Living in Disney's Brave New Town*. New York: Henry Holt and Company.

Freedman, Samuel G. 2000. *Jew vs. Jew: The Struggle for the Soul of American Jewry*. New York: Simon & Schuster.

Gavron, Daniel. 2000. *The Kibbutz. Awakening from Utopia*. Lanham, MD: Rowman & Littlefield.

Goodwin, Barbara. 1978. *Social Sciences and Utopia: Nineteenth Century Models of Social Harmony*. Atlantic Highlands, NJ: Humanities Press.

Gordis, Daniel. 2002. *If A Place Can Make You Cry: Dispatches from an Anxious State*. New York: Crown Publishers.

Herzl, Theodor. 1960 [1902]. *Old-New Land [Altneuland]*. English translation by Lotta Levensohn: Block Publishing.

Isaacs, Harold. 1967. *American Jews in Israel*. New York: The John Day Company.

Krausz, Ernest, ed., 1983. *The Sociology of the Kibbutz*. New Brunswick: Transaction Books.

Langer, Michael. 1977. "Reform Judaism and Zionism as Responses to the Modern Age." In *A Reform Zionist Perspective. Judaism & Community in the Modern Age. An Anthology*. Edited by Michael Langer. New York: Union of American Hebrew Congregations.

Leichman, David and Idit Paz, eds. 1994. *Kibbutz. An Alternative Lifestyle*. Ramat Efal: Yad Tabenkin.

Leslau, Avraham, Avraham Polovin, and Mordechai Bar-Lev. 1993. "Subjective Well-Being on Religious Kibbutzim: The Second Generation. *Israel Social Science Research* 8, No. 1:27–46.

Leviatan, Uriel. 1994. "Leadership Functioning in Kibbutzim as Determinant of Conditions for Members' Commitment." *Journal of Rural Cooperation* 22, No. 1–2:93–111.

———.1998. "Aging—the Kibbutz Experience." In *Crisis in the Israeli Kibbutz*. Eds. Leviatan et al. New York: Praeger.

——— and Hugh Oliver, and Jack Quarter, eds. 1998. *Crisis in the Israeli Kibbutz. Meeting the Challenge of Changing Times*. Westport, CT: Praeger.

Levinson, Daniel. 1978. *The Seasons of a Man's Life*. New York, Alfred A. Knopf.

Lieblich, Amia. 1981. *Kibbutz Makom. Report from an Israeli Kibbutz*. New York: Pantheon Books.

Liebman, Charles S., and Steven M. Cohen. 1990. *Two Worlds of Judaism: The Israeli & American Experiences*. New Haven and London: Yale University Press.

Lilker, Shalom. 1982. *Kibbutz Judaism: A New Tradition in the Making*. Darby: Norwood Editions.

Livni, Michael. 1999. *Reform Zionism: Twenty Years*. Jerusalem: Geffen.

Miles, William F. S. 1997. "Twice Twenty-Three: A Bible Contest Winner Looks Back." *Israel Studies Bulletin* 12:16–20.

———. 2003. "Mid-Life Crisis, Kibbutz Style." *Shofar: An Interdisciplinary Journal of Jewish Studies* 21, No. 2:82–100.

——— and Gretchen Weismann. 2004. "Measuring Satisfaction in Jewish 'Utopia'. A Comparative Analysis of the Reform Kibbutzim." *Journal of Modern Jewish Studies* 3, No. 1:87–109.

Mittelberg, David. 1988. *Strangers in Paradise: The Israel Kibbutz Experience*. New Brunswick: Transaction Publishers.

More, Thomas. 1999 [1516]. *Utopia*. Translated by David Wootten. Indianapolis, IN: Hackett Publishing.

Near, Henry. 1986. "Paths to Utopia: The Kibbutz as a Movement for Social Change." *Jewish Social Studies* 48, No. 3–4:109–126.

———. 1992. *The Kibbutz Movement. A History: Volume I. Origins and Growth, 1909–1939*. Oxford: Oxford University Press.

———. 1997. *The Kibbutz Movement: A History. Volume II. Crisis and Achievement 1939–1995*. London: The Littman Library of Jewish Civilization.

Oved, Yaacov. 1988. *Two Hundred Years of American Communes*. New Brunswick, NJ: Transaction.

Pitzer, Donald, ed. 1997. *America's Communal Utopias*. Chapel Hill, NC: University of North Carolina Press.

Rayman, Paula. 1981. *The Kibbutz Community and Nation Building*. Princeton, NJ: Princeton University Press.

Rose Dan. 1990. *Living the Ethnographic Life*. Newbury Park, CA: Sage Publications.

Roth, Philip. 1986. *The Counterlife*. New York: Farrar, Straus, Giroux.

Sabar, Naama. 2000. *Kibbutzniks in the Diaspora*. Albany: State University of New York Press.

Saitoti, Tepilit Ole. 1986. *The Worlds of a Maasai Warrior: An Autobiography*. Los Angeles, CA: University of California Press.

Shepher, Israel. 1984. *The Kibbutz: An Anthropological Study*. Norwood, PA: Norwood Editions.

Shuman, Ellis. 2003. *The Virtual Kibbutz: Stories from a Changing Society*. New York: iUniverse.

Shuval, Judith T. 1963. *Immigrants On the Threshold*. New York: Atherton Press.

Snarey, John R., and Joseph R. Blasi. 1980. "Ego Development among Adult Kibbutzniks: A Cross-Cultural Application of Loevinger's Theory. *Genetic Psychology Monographs* 102, No. 1:117–157.

Spiro, Melford. 1956. *Kibbutz. Venture in Utopia*. Cambridge, MA: Harvard University Press.

———. 1958. *Children of the Kibbutz: A Study in Child Training and Personality*. Cambridge, MA: Harvard University Press.

Stockwell, Foster. 1998. *Encyclopedia of American Communes, 1663–1963*. Jefferson, NC: McFarland and Company.

Van Maanen, John. 1988. *Tales of the Field: On Writing Ethnography*. Chicago and London: University of Chicago Press.

Waxman, Chaim I. 1989. *American Aliyah. Portrait of an Innovative Migration Movement*. Detroit: Wayne State University Press.

———. 2001. *Jewish Baby Boomers. A Communal Perspective*. Albany: State University of New York Press.

Index